TALES

FROM THE

EDGE

TALES
FROM THE
EDGE

TRUE ADVENTURES
IN ALASKA

Edited and with an Introduction by
LARRY KANIUT

and a Preface by
DENISE LITTLE

ST. MARTIN'S GRIFFIN ✽ NEW YORK

Editor's Note

Denise Little contacted me in 2003 and asked me to co-edit this anthology. We hope to provide readers with an enticing glimpse of Alaska. I was honored to be included with the other well-known Alaskan writers. I was also humbled that Denise selected a few of my stories and asked me to write the introduction.

We hope these selections will whet your appetite for Alaskan adventures.

—LARRY KANIUT
July 19, 2004

----

www.st.martins.com

Library of Congress Cataloging-in Publication Data

Tales from the edge: true adventures in Alaska / edited by Larry Kaniut.—1st ed.
    p. cm.
  ISBN 0-312-31703-4
  EAN 978-0312-31703-4
    1. Alaska—Description and travel—Anecdotes.   2. Alaska—History, Local—Anecdotes.   3. Wilderness areas—Alaska—Anecdotes.   4. Frontier and pioneer life—Alaska—Anecdotes.   5. Outdoor life—Alaska—Anecdotes.   6. Adventure and adventurers—Alaska—Anecdotes.   7. Alaska—Biography—Anecdotes.   I Kaniut, Larry.

F904.6.T35 2005
979.8'04—dc22   2004051314

First Edition: March 2005

10   9   8   7   6   5   4   3   2   1

Contents

SECTION FOUR:
THE WILDLIFE IS *REALLY* WILD

SECTION FIVE:
CONSERVATION

SECTION SIX:
ALASKA'S DOGS

SECTION SEVEN:
NATIVE VOICES

PREFACE

Denise Little

Every day, people journey to the wilderness in Alaska to test themselves against it. Whether climbing Mount McKinley alone in the dead of winter, rowing down the Yukon River and living off the land, or kayaking along Alaska's thirty-three thousand miles of coastline, they seek to measure themselves as they pit themselves against the powers of nature and an untamed land. In a world that is becoming more urban and homogenized every day, Alaska stands as a beacon to those who need more than a mall and a McDonald's to find happiness.

Along the way, these modern adventurers have discovered unmatched scenes of natural beauty, as well as enduring hair-raising encounters with the dangers of untamed nature. From dodging bear attacks to embarking on frozen treks across glaciers, from facing stampeding moose to enjoying the triumph of standing alone on the summit of the tallest mountain in North America with the continent spread out at their feet, these hardy souls have stories to tell that command our attention and respect.

Some of the stories send chills down our spines; others allow us to look into the valley of death and feel the thrill of surviving against all odds. And in every tale the majesty of Alaska lives in our imagination as we share in the true adventures of those willing to test themselves against a vast, untamed land. A must for those who know and love Alaska, as well as a treat for arm-chair adventurers everywhere, this book is a compilation of true tales about that age-old challenge—making a journey into the unknown to test a person's soul. If a person survives (and many don't), that person will come out changed forever.

And if these travelers share what they've learned, as they do in the stories that follow, we can all share just a taste of that feeling. So here are some of the wild tales of people who were willing to take on Alaska. Enjoy the adventure. . . .

Introduction

Larry Kaniut

The silver slit across the eastern horizon enlarged as rosy fingers ushered in the day. Thick spruce forest covered the valley floor. Aspen groves polka-dotted the hillside. Alder thickets beyond shrouded the shoulders of the ridgeline. As a waterfall's whispering mist thistledowned onto the yellow-throated monkey flowers, a trio of hikers, soaking in the beauty of their sun-drenched Shangri-la, gave no thought to danger.

A short way ahead on the trail a new mother grizzly protectively watched her twin cubs frolicking near the path.

The stage of the ages was set, the players were in place, and the curtain was about to rise and the drama was about to unfold.

Neither the party of people nor the family of fauna had an inkling of the other's presence, though they were only seconds from contact.

And things were about to get interesting. . . .

Alaska.
The Last Frontier.
Literally.

The . . . Last . . . Frontier.

Few environments share Alaska's extremes—be they extremes of weather, water, terrain, or wildlife. And to these extremes her sparse population, man's mechanical conveyances, and the need for communication, and the plot thickens.

She's big enough to be her own country. Her nearly unpeopled borders, connected by just over three thousand miles of highway, house but a handful of towns numbering six hundred thousand–plus souls in an area larger than Texas . . . by a factor of two. Wilderness surrounds these outposts of civilization.

From early whalers to modern adventurers obsessed by exploration, fur, gold, adventure, oil, or escape, Alaska has lured men to her shores for over two centuries. Her Eminence, the great state of Alaska, continues to cast an aura of mystery, magic, and mystique.

As the beautiful and beguiling Sirens of Homer's *Odyssey* once tempted Odysseus and teased his shipmates to their shores, so Alaska's song of melodic magic tempts the "sailor." Just as in the ancient ballad, Alaska's beauty sings a song to those with adventure in their hearts—*seize me; squeeze me; tease me; please me.* Alaska beguiles us and beckons us to her bosom, all the while gleefully contemplating tap-dancing on our tombs.

Beneath Alaska's beckoning beauty lie forces of nature that are capable of violence beyond measure. Her furies strike without warning. Odysseus-like, we launch ourselves into the great unknown that is Alaska, plying her waters, her airways, and her landscape, entering them at our own risk. Let the "sailor" beware—when you tackle Alaska, you tiptoe along a tightrope of tragedy. A fall from that precarious perch deals you a hand stacked against you . . . in favor of the House: Alaska.

Her smiling sunrise erupts into a sinister snarl.

Her gentle weather turns vicious; her zephyr breezes turn in an instant into cold, slicing winds that cut like a knife.

She dulls the pain in your feet until frozen numbness owns your limbs.

She deceivingly mocks glacial travel, hiding yawing crevasses beneath her ice bridges.

Her snow-covered mountains roar as sheets of snow slab off and rumble toward the valley floor.

She beckons you onto her frozen rivers where fractured ice plunges you headlong into the cold, cruel current beneath the ice.

Her winking waters laughingly clutch her victims with frigid fingers of death.

The same Sirens who greeted Alaska's earliest inhabitants remain there to this day, luring men on, just like the temptresses of old. And Alaska's Sirens zealously protect their Mistress, who continues to beguile and betray all those who come to see her.

SECTION ONE

FISHING FOR ADVENTURE

FOR ANYBODY WHO thinks fishing is a relaxing way to spend a day communing with nature, it only takes one trip to Alaska to change that opinion. Commercial fishing off Alaska's coast is regularly ranked as one of the most dangerous jobs in America. Men are lost to the wild and icy seas every year, but more keep coming to take the place of those who die, because there are fortunes to be made and adventures to be had. Even pleasure fishing inland can be a terrifying experience, since bears are generally hanging around somewhere in the vicinity of every good fishing hole. When humans and bears hunt for the same prey, things can get ugly. But the bounty of Alaska's waterways, be they freshwater or salt, are unmatched in the world. As long as the salmon run, king crabs crawl, and pike rise in the waters, there will be hardy souls who want to harvest them. These are some of the spine-tingling stories of fishing in Alaska. . . .

PETER JENKINS

❧ PETER JENKINS is an intrepid adventurer and writer who has shared his adventures with readers everywhere in multiple bestselling volumes, including *A Walk Across America*, *The Walk West*, *Across China*, *Along the Edge of America*, *Close Friends*, and *Looking for Alaska*. He was born in Greenwich, Connecticut, but now lives with his wife, Rita, and their family, in Spring Hill, Tennessee. He can be reached at peter@peterjenkins.com. ❧

NO ROAD

The word *road* is so boring, so unappreciated, but so essential, even resonant. Some of my favorite songs are about hitting the road. Many of my life's most inspiring moments came from traveling down unknown roads until I found something that surprised me and I stopped for a bit. But in Alaska, so many places cannot be reached by a road. Cordova, Alaska, is one of them. Dominating barriers surround this picturesque fishing village. The Chugach Mountains and the Robinson Mountains rise up on one side, the Copper River delta on another. The ocean, which has taken so many lives, is on the other. Adding to the city's protection is glacier after glacier after glacier after glacier. They seem at first glance to be coming to crush the city, but actually they are retreating ever so slowly.

Beyond that first row of mountain, water, or glacier blockades lie even more. There are the Wrangell Mountains, which are part of the 13-million-acre Wrangell–St. Elias National Park and Preserve, the largest U.S. national park. There are also the Talkeetna Mountains, and beyond them, the Alaska Range. Seventeen of the twenty highest mountain peaks in the United States are in Alaska. Some of these, the majority of Cordovans think, help to guard Cordova. Many of the people in this fishing village are actually glad that cars, trucks, campers, and SUVs can't reach them. Of course this means they can't drive away, either. For restless people this would be awful. In Cordova you need to fulfill your need for movement in a boat, on a snowboard, in a float-plane, on a snow machine, atop a surfboard, or on foot. You could drive out their main road until it ends, over fifty miles away. A fifty-mile trip in a place like Cordova on a road is practically a cross-country journey. You would cross some of the most inspiring country in the world on a journey like that.

Being able to drive away, to listen to great long and winding road songs, is not that big of a deal to Alaskans. You cannot even drive to Juneau, the capital of Alaska. Alaskan citizens who are tough on politicians say that the governor, state senators, and representatives like being isolated and hard to reach. They claim Alaskan politicians hide behind their mountains and glaciers. In Alaska it's difficult to get mad enough at what the politicos are doing to go to the capital and protest when you can't drive there.

Roads in general are difficult to build and maintain in much of Alaska, always have been. Just as you'd imagine, the state gets massive amounts of snow in many parts. In some passes they get over seventy-five *feet* per winter. Valdez, the community closest to Cordova to the northwest, but still really hard to reach from Cordova, has so much snow they have in the past used the resulting banks as movie screens. The abundant snow around Valdez is one of the main reasons they host the extreme-snowboarding championships every winter. Then there is permafrost, ground that never thaws completely. In some places in Alaska they only have roads *after* everything freezes. They build them on the frozen foundations of snow and ice. All in all, though, there aren't many roads in Alaska, and what roads do exist are deeply appreciated and even loved for the freedom of movement they allow, just as long as they don't bring too much interference too. Alaskans are a stubborn, strong people; they must be to survive. Please, don't get in their way.

Cordova is just up the coast from Seward, but there is no easy way to get there from our Alaska home. Cordova is considered one of Alaska's larger "cities," even though it has only twelve hundred residents in the winter and twenty-five hundred in the summer. It is a city where, so far, fishermen and the people whom they support rule. The local voters have had several opportunities to vote on whether to build a road to connect them to the outside world. The road has never passed, although the last vote was the closest ever. The voters who oppose the road say the reason the vote is getting too close is because too many nonfishermen are moving into town. Even if they had a road, it would only be open in the summer, the time when most people in this fishing village are involved one way or the other in catching fish. The summer is their harvest time, when the fishermen of Cordova attempt to catch enough salmon and halibut to make the majority of their money, enough to get them through the year until the salmon and halibut return. They wouldn't get to use the road much, anyway. More important than a road is a protected place for their boats, and Cordova does have a fine natural harbor.

That the road would only be open in the summer aggravates plenty of Cordovans. Such a road would be loaded with tourists. Many Alaskans don't like driving on the same road with tourists. It would be like putting NASCAR drivers on the same racetrack with thousands of drivers like my grandfather at eighty-five. Lots of Alaskans drive like they're on the last lap of the Daytona 500 and they're one one-hundredth of a second in the lead. Tourists, on the other hand, often drive like my grandfather did right before he couldn't drive anymore because he couldn't hear and his sight was failing. They tend to speed up, then slow down to fifteen miles per hour, cross the centerline, weave onto the shoulder, and stop when there's no stop sign in sight. They drive like this not because they can't hear or can't see, but because they can. All around them their eyes and ears are filled with sights and creatures they've never seen. A bald eagle just plucked a salmon from the river running along the road. Eight tourist vehicles pull over, though there's no place for them to get completely out of the way. I once stopped right in a curve in Cooper Landing on the way to Soldotna to watch two eagles fighting over a salmon squirming on the icy bank of the river. It was not smart—there was even ice and snow on the road—but Alaska can overwhelm you until you do dumb things.

But tourists' driving habits are not the main reason certain Cordovans don't want a road. What would happen if outsiders could reach their lovely town? Cordovans aren't sure, but they have seen what's happened to the ranchers and small-town folk in Colorado, Montana, and Wyoming. Their high desert, their mountain valleys, their inspiring lands, have been discovered and much of it has been bought up. Alaskan fishermen are intelligent as well as ornery. They read national commercial-fishing magazines. They've read about their fellow fishermen in Florida. First people arrived as tourists, then they moved in and tried to take over the world that belonged to the fishermen. In Florida, some of these newly arrived used vicious tactics against the unorganized fishermen to push through a net-fishing ban in a statewide vote.

Cordovans know what has happened along all U.S. coastlines, where everybody wants waterfront property. They've read about the lobstermen of Maine, about others who harvest the sea on the West Coast, on the Gulf Coast. People with more money and more lawyers discovered these quaint, scenic fishing villages, where folks had been making a living at the world's second-oldest profession for generations. These Alaskan fishermen are worldly enough to understand what could happen to their quirky and attractive hometown if it was "discovered" by some Ted Turner type, who after making his hundreds and hundreds of millions decided to let everything go back to the bears or wolves or buffalo. One of these "know-it-all" people might try to buy up a chunk of the town as a personal retreat, have something to brag about at parties now that Aspen has been in the movie *Dumb and Dumber*.

These fishermen know these kinds of people can have inordinate power in Washington and with the media. Alaskan commercial fishermen have more political power than any other fishermen do in the United States, but mostly that influence is in Alaska. It is shrinking. Sport fishermen like me want our fish too. The commercial fishermen don't mind these kinds of people coming to visit or even getting a summer place, just as long as they respect what Cordova is and what they do. Just don't try to tell the fishermen how to make their living or where to store their boats. These fishermen and their families are ready to fight for their world, without surrender.

I imagine many people would side with the Cordovans who don't want a road. The slogan No Road sounds so cool. No Road sounds almost as good as

Save the Rain Forest. Who could be against it? It's easy to be against roads and oil drilling and the harvesting of wood when you already have as much of them as you could possibly use. How many would be against a road if they had none? Most of us have never spent a second thinking about roads, because there are so many, enough to take us in every single direction our lusty hearts might desire.

Right now the only way out of Cordova is on the Alaskan State Ferry, on your own boat, or by plane. None of the options are cheap. The way out on the sea is real slow, and you're still on foot when you get where you're going. For those who don't want a road to Cordova, such as the people I was going to visit, it's not about the romance; it's about the desire to save their way of life.

If you live in Cordova, you can drive fifty-one miles without going around and around. In Alaska, that's a bunch of road. In Angoon, on Admiralty Island, they are proud to have just three miles of road, "all paved." Some Cordova locals think their mostly Mayberry police department should not have gone so Rambo and bought the used "high-pursuit" police cars from that police department in Nevada. In Nevada it's dry and flat and people can try to outrun the police. In Cordova, all you can do to get away from the police is go out the road and past the airport before you have to come back. No one would even try to walk away from here but Wild Gene, and he would never have caused the police any trouble anyway. You could use the slowest police car in the country and just ease out the road past Lake Eyak, park, and wait. Technically, you could just wait in town until whoever you're chasing comes back. Besides, in a high-pursuit police car you could hit a nesting trumpeter swan if you ran off the road.

If Rebekah and I had been ready one day earlier, we could have taken the Alaska Marine Ferry over there from Seward. It takes eleven hours and covers 144 nautical miles, which is 164 "normal" miles for those of us road-addicted people. Many, many Alaskans gauge their travel more by nautical miles, air miles, or hours down the trail. The cost for the ferry was only $64.

HANGING BASKETS

Rebekah, my firstborn child, who is almost twenty, was sitting next to me on the milk run to Cordova. They call this Alaska Airlines flight the milk run because it stops so many times. Anchorage, Cordova, Yakutat, Juneau, Ketchikan, and finally Seattle. When the salmon are running into the Copper River delta, which is the main catch of Cordova fishermen, the jets on the milk run have large cargo sections loaded with fresh king, red, and silver salmon, high-dollar fresh fish, headed for the markets and best restaurants in Seattle and beyond. Reds and kings are worth more as cargo than any human per square foot. Rebekah was in the middle seat; a handsome, blond Scandinavian-looking guy with earrings in both ears was in the window seat next to her. She handed me her CD player and asked me if I'd heard of Dave Matthews. I wasn't sure, I said. I never thought I'd lose track of who made the best music, but I wasn't paying so much attention to popular trends anymore. She said I must have a listen, she just knew I'd like it. I was a Dave Matthews fan after hearing her two favorite songs. Responding so intently this quickly to new music was rare for me. I closed my eyes, laid my head back, and listened.

When I opened my eyes to tell Rebekah how awesome I thought her music was, she was lost in conversation with the strong blond. Turned out he was headed to Petersburg, Alaska, the fishing village they call "little Norway," to crew on his dad's long-line halibut boat. He was a sophomore at the University of Alaska at Fairbanks. Being with Rebekah was an almost constant replay of my younger life. I watched her relate to people; I remembered what it was like. I listened to her music, some of which was mine first—Van Morrison, the Allman Brothers. I was honored she would even go to Cordova with me, but I got the feeling sitting on the plane she would have liked to change her plans and head to Petersburg. There was no way I could have hung around with my mother when I was Rebekah's age.

Landing the 737 at Cordova, if that's what we were doing now, was at once frightening and otherworldly. As we made our approach, if that's what it was, I couldn't even see a runway or any airport buildings, just the many fingers of the Copper River delta. It looked almost like the Mississippi River delta, except it was surrounded by plane-humbling mountain ranges and glaciers. It was raining one second, sunny the next, foggy here and there, over this chunk of Alaska. The jet engines seemed to be making a noise I hadn't heard before, but then I've learned that flying experiences in other places have little to do with Alaska.

We landed. There was no fence around this runway, which appeared to be hacked out of the wilderness by renegade bulldozers; what if a moose or a bear had been standing in our way? We could see one small building. Everybody got off and walked down some stairs into the real world. Inside the building were plaques celebrating that 2 million pounds of wild salmon and halibut had passed out of Cordova's airport on their way to the outside world. Some mounted salmon were on one wall alongside a diagram of the Copper River delta, which is one of the world's most alive, productive, and clean wetland areas. How did they ever get bulldozers out here, not to mention gravel and asphalt to make a runway? All over the state, Alaskans land planes on surfaces you have to see to believe.

We had arranged to meet up with Per Nolan, a local salmon fisherman. His wife, Neva, had invited us to come stay with them after she had heard me interviewed by the guru of Spenard, Alaska, Steve Heimel of Alaska Public Radio. She said she had known me from my earlier writings, and they wanted to show us their slice of Alaska. Alaska is one big pizza. Neva said it would be good if I could go out with a gillnetter while I was here, but her husband was a big guy and there was only one small bunk on his boat. We'd have to see about that. I asked Neva if it would be all right if I brought my daughter Rebekah with me. Neva said, great, bring the whole family. That was a typical Alaskan response. They always seem ready to take you in, feed you, provide you with shelter. It's been that way forever up here. Imagine Per as a cross between John Candy and an offensive lineman for the University of Idaho. He is funny; large-framed, not cut like a bodybuilder, he is surprisingly spry on his feet when he needs to be. Until you experience Per in a bar, you wouldn't know he is also a pool shark and the life of the party. Per is an observer. He was in college in Hawaii when John Travolta and disco hit, and he told us he had had the "disco fever" shiny suit, the open-at-the-chest shirt, the gold chain, and the platform shoes. After being in Cordova only a half hour, I could not imagine him wearing anything like that. Cordova is a flannel-shirt, blue-jeans, and work-boots kind of place.

Driving in from the airport, the wind was either chilled blowing off the glaciers or warmer coming out of the wetlands. To the south was the Gulf of Alaska. Compared to Cordova, Seward was wide-open. Per told us that if we could walk to the nearest town, Valdez, which was west along the tide line, it would be 140 to 150 miles. By boat, it's only 55 to 60 miles. This illustrates why Alaska has more coastline than the whole lower forty-eight states combined, thanks to thousands and thousands of bays and countless islands. And Cordova has the fishing industry that goes along with this vast area. Some Cordova fishermen became "spill-ionaires," renting themselves and their fishing boats to Exxon during the cleanup.

Per pulled up in town next to a ladder set up by a hanging basket spilling over with vividly colored flowers halfway to the ground. Neva, who grew up in Wrangell, took care of all the many hanging baskets of growing flowers on Main Street in Cordova. She stood atop the ladder, watering the basket carefully. She'd attached a greenhouse to the side of their trailer that was more than half the size of their home. It was instantly obvious, the way she lifted up the flowers to water them, the way she finished her job before turning to us, that she found much inspiration in the beauty, rich color, and delicate petals of her charges. Neva had an exotic look, almost Mediterranean. She said she took care of thirty hanging baskets in Cordova.

Cordova was not what I expected. Alaskan communities are competitive with each other. Don't ask a person from Seward what he thinks of Cordova. If you are in Soldotna and you want to know what Seward's like, don't ask a longtime Soldotna resident. They'll tell you all it does is rain in Seward, that moss grows on everything. And so it goes all over Alaska. I'd ask some people I knew in Seward what they thought of Cordova. "It's badly in need of a paint job." "There are too many old hippies and eccentrics."

The four of us stood on Main Street by Laura's Liquors, next to a flower box. Neva explained that here on the Alaskan coast she had to plant flowers that could survive wind and lots of rain. Daisies, pansies, petunias, lobelias, grew nicely until the end of October. The town was also adorned with brightly colored banners with sea otters, red salmon, waves, and wildflowers on them, which were hung from the streetlights. Imprinted in the concrete sidewalks were drawings of octopuses, starfish, and salmon. The sun shone down on Cordova and made all things bright.

Neva told us, "One day of sunshine is worth a week of rain." I'd heard that at least ten times since I'd arrived in Alaska. People truly appreciate sunny weather in the summer. It's like a wonderful meal someone else cooked and left as a surprise at your house. The people who live here year-round earn their portions.

Around us, people were walking everywhere, living their lives here. Cordova was impressively set up for so small a town; after all, all this art and these banners and Neva's flowers were provided by the city and her neighbors just to inspire the locals. Visitors like us, newcomers, were welcome, but life in Cordova was not designed for them. The town's biggest yearly festival was the Iceworm Festival, held the first week of February, put on for the benefit of just the year-round folk. Cordova even held their Fourth of July fireworks in February because it didn't get dark enough in July until too late for the little ones.

Neva drove an eighties Nissan Sentra. It had few miles on it; how could anyone put many miles on any vehicle here? Rebekah was going to help Neva with the rest of her watering while Per and I walked down the street; the boat docks and Orca Inlet were on the block below us. Per said it was common to see two hundred or more sea otters just off the docks by St. Elias Ocean Products and North Pacific Processors in the winter. We headed to Orca Book and Sound and the Killer Whale Café. Inside, we could have been in Seattle in the late eighties. Kelly, the owner, was once a kayak guide; he used to be mayor, but he had lost the most recent election to Margie by one vote. Margie owns the restaurant and motel one block below called the Reluctant Fisherman and is a passionate supporter of the road and the tourism industry.

We got a couple of mochas from Scott and wandered out to the sidewalk. I began asking Per questions about passersby. Who is that coming out of that store, who's parking that truck? Who is that leaning against the front of the smaller grocery store in town—why does that lady seem too dressed up for an Alaskan fishing town? (Turns out it was Phyllis Blake, secretary of the Prince William Sound Aquaculture Association. She always dresses nice, Per told me.)

Per knew every single person who walked, bicycled, or rode by in a car, truck, motorcycle, or van. As I pressed him for information on each person, he could and did speak detail after detail about everyone we saw. He knew more about people in this town than a normal person would at their own family reunion. Then as a joke and I thought something of a challenge, I asked him to name everyone we saw from behind, without seeing faces. He did it. Mary, who ran Muscle Mary's, a workout place, was an easy ID. She had about 2 percent body fat. Few people I saw in Cordova looked like her, from any angle. Per said that if we hadn't spotted her from the rear, I would have noticed that she always smiled, was always happy. Mary always took part in Cordova's biggest adult-female event of the year held in late February or early March. The local women decided on a theme every year. One recent theme was Dressed to Thrill. Per served as a bartender for that one, and he remembered Mary's outfit because it consisted of paint. She painted on her Dress to Thrill costume. They'd had a disco theme, one with evening gowns, one to "dress as slutty as you could." Per remembered one woman went wrapped in Saran Wrap for that one. Because everyone in Cordova knows almost everything about everyone else, having these parties is more like playing dress-up with your sisters.

Per acted surprised when he saw one fisherman with a woman he thought was involved with someone else. It reminded him of the often-repeated Alaskan mantra: "In Alaska you don't lose your girlfriend, you lose your turn." If you're the type who can't live around someone you went out with or were married to, don't move to Alaska.

A red Ford F250 pickup pulled up in front of the bookstore, which was next to the office of the Cordova District Fishermen United. CDFU lobbied, followed political winds of change, and fought for the rights of local commercial fishermen. The guy who parked the truck was Mark King; in his mid-to-late forties, he was a second-generation Cordova gillnetter and seiner, like Per. Gillnet fishermen like Per and Mark are the cowboys of the Alaskan fleet, the fast runners. They are after the big-dollar fish, the kings and the reds.

Floatplanes often flew over downtown. All gillnetting for king and red salmon, which was the current season, is tightly controlled by Alaska Fish and Game and usually done in "openings" of twenty-four hours, sometimes only twelve hours. The Alaska Fish and Game office in Cordova is responsible for deciding when and for how long salmon fishing will take place. The openings were scheduled based on a sonar salmon counter fifty miles up the Copper River. A certain number of salmon had to be passing by to allow fishing in the ocean. When they're ready, they announce the time and duration of the opening, usually a day or so before the appointed hour.

All the Cordova fishermen, including Per and Mark, were trying to decide where to go next time Alaska Fish and Game announced an opening. The word was flying around town like a bag of money ripped open in a west wind that there would be an opening in the next few days. It took the fish nine days to get from the ocean to the Copper River sonar counter. Some of the Copper River fish went over two hundred miles upriver to spawn, and it's having to travel so far that makes these salmon so full of oils and good fat. Once salmon enter freshwater, they stop feeding and must survive from their own energy stores. The longer, more difficult, and swifter a river they must swim up, the more body oil and fat they need. Some Alaskan salmon don't swim over five miles. Don't ask an Alaskan fisherman about the pen-raised salmon of Norway, the salmon most Americans eat. Pen-raised fish do not have to struggle to survive and to catch their prey; their meat is not as firm and rich. They do not spawn, they don't have the fat and oil that give Alaskan salmon such flavor. It is illegal in Alaska to pen-raise salmon, only the wild will do.

"Only the wild will do," my theme for Alaska salmon, should be the theme for the state, exempting some federal government employees. "Only the wild will do" could be added to the state flag as a motto. Only the wild salmon will do. Only the wild bears will do. Only the wild eagles will do. Only the wild rivers will do. Only the wild whales will do. Only the wild Alaskans will do. There would have to be a committee appointed with Native and non-Native representation. Members of this committee could be named based on percentages of how the people voted in the last presidential election. Then these Alaskans, along with a couple state lawyers, would write up the definition of what makes a "wild Alaskan human," what makes "a wild salmon," and so on.

WILD GENE

Down our side of the sidewalk came a man that Per explained had been in a terrible motorcycle accident. He is partially blind and moved slowly. My first reaction was to try to help him, but that would have been the wrong impulse toward such a determined person. Per said he was headed to shoot pool at the Alaskan Hotel and Bar, a block or two down toward where we'd first seen Neva.

Several people walked or drove by, but Per didn't say anything about who they were. When he noticed I was waiting, he quickly rattled off their identities: a teacher, one of his fishing partners from the state of Washington, one of the stars of the high school basketball team, one of his neighbors from the trailer park. Then he told me about someone we hadn't seen, a Cordova resident who had died several years ago.

"Watching the people with you reminded me that I hadn't thought about Wild Gene in a while. Seems like most towns in Alaska had someone like Wild Gene in the seventies and eighties, but you don't see people like him much anymore," Per said.

Neva and Rebekah were getting closer to us as they watered the hanging baskets.

Per explained that Gene just showed up in Cordova one day; Per didn't know why or how Gene had chosen their town. Some people just materialize in Alaska. When they choose a town like Cordova where most everyone knows each other, they are not really paid much attention at first. They could be a tourist who got off the ferry and stayed. They will usually leave in a day or a week or after the summer. If they make it through a winter, some people will begin to notice them and open up to them, perhaps not fully accept them as one of their own, but open the door.

Gene didn't look too different at first, especially since he got here sometime in the seventies. Per graduated as salutatorian from Cordova High School, class of 1979, one of nineteen in his class. He remembers Gene being around during his later high school years, even during the time Per drove off the dock with his girlfriend in the car. (That's another story.) After Gene had been around awhile, people began to find out things about him. He was from the Seattle area; his family members were important people in that state, wealthy people, and it turns out caring people too. People found out that Gene had been raised by nannies. He had grown up wearing blue blazers; he had graduated from an Ivy League–type college. People noticed that members of Gene's family would come to town and visit him; he didn't have a phone, so surely they got in touch with him through the mail. Per knew Gene got mail because Per's mother, a high school English and drama teacher, belonged to the Fruit of the Month club and so did Gene. Per's mother and Gene started having tea together, partly because they shared a Fruit of the Month club membership, and because, although he was odd, Gene and Per's mother were both very intelligent.

Gene would often disappear into the wilderness for long periods and live off the land. Around Cordova even the locals don't venture into its extremities very often. Mountain-goat hunters, some of the most extreme outdoorsmen in Alaska as they have to hike up to the frigid mountain peaks, traveled as far out as just about any human ventured in Alaska. Gene would often surface more than seventy-five miles from Cordova. One time he just appeared, as if he could astral project, right after a couple hunters had shot a mountain goat. He cut the balls off and popped them in his mouth, unfried, fresh Alaskan mountain oysters. His appearances and his appearance shocked some, and Alaskans are the hardest people to shock that I've ever met.

People would see Gene out on the road, past the airport, thirty miles out of town, pulling a 150-pound log by some rope. He told people if they asked that he was training to walk across Russia. He would load his pack with rocks, shoulder it, and hike the mountains, cross the glaciers, and even wade the surging rivers filled with small icebergs.

Some locals thought Gene had told them that he was here to write his master's thesis, on what they were not sure. When his family would arrive to visit—Gene never left Cordova except to explore the surrounding wilderness—they would eat at the Reluctant Fisherman. They realized, surely, as many Cordovans did, that Gene had entered a place that most of us cannot or will not go. Although I'm sure they hoped to be able to find him there and help him return, they never did. Gene stayed the rest of his life in Cordova, and it became almost impossible near the end to find him, even when he sat right next to you on Main Street.

Per said he looked like someone from the movie *Quest for Fire*. He lived in a primitive shack in Hippie Cove, Cordova's tent city. Almost every place in Alaska that has a cannery, where young college students, adventurers, drifters, and escapers work, has a place in the deep woods at the edge of town where people squat. Some like Gene squat in these camps for years. Per said Gene had a small woodstove but no pipe for the smoke to flow properly out of his shelter. His body was saturated by wood smoke because he didn't have a way to bathe regularly. Some said he didn't believe in washing off the skin's oils. Per, always a good swimmer and basketball player, swam laps to stay in shape; he said he always knew when Gene came to Cordova's public pool to swim. Per would be swimming laps, his head down, and suddenly he'd taste something odd in the water. It seemed to be the distinctive taste/smell of wood smoke. The first time he noticed it he dismissed it, but then the second and third and fourth times he'd stop swimming laps and look to see who was in the pool. There was Wild Gene. Per would just keep swimming; he's a fisherman—fish slime is money to him—and a little smoke is not going to bother him.

"People who came to visit Cordova would see him and ask me, *who is that?*" Per remembered. Even I knew that to stand out in Alaska enough that people asked about you suggests you are extraordinary.

Although Gene looked as if he could break you in half, he never hurt anyone. For the first few years Per said Gene was exceedingly dark and handsome and well built. You don't pull 150-pound logs down an Alaskan logging road for days without getting fantastically in shape. He also rarely said much of anything to anyone. In his journeys into the Alaskan wilds alone he certainly saw more of this rare wilderness world than almost everyone, maybe more than anyone else.

"He actually lived the life of a Neanderthal. He put himself through such tough conditions his body just wore down after several years of it," Per said.

We saw Neva and Rebekah lingering at one of the hanging baskets down the block; Neva was talking to someone she knew.

People around town began to notice Gene was getting thinner. His muscles were disappearing; he was not training anymore, not to walk across Russia nor for whatever reason he used when he'd first come to Cordova. By now, he was part of the town. People cared about him, wondered why he was the way he was, wondered why he wouldn't eat well. Wild Gene had earned the townspeople's respect; he could survive Alaska, in all its severity. Some said all he ate toward the end was Crisco, some bread, and crackers. Surely he had support from his family if he needed it, or a ticket out at any time. But he didn't use it.

One day, someone who knew his habits noticed he hadn't been around. Worried about him, the friend finally checked and found him in his shelter with a knife in his stomach, dead. Many people had come to respect Gene's wild ways, the ability that almost none of them had to survive in the wilderness and live amid its extremity and brilliance. He was not buried at the local graveyard past Nirvana Park; he was taken back to finally be among his family in Washington, who had missed him.

Rebekah had joined us on the sidewalk in the moss-drying sunlight. Across the street from Orca Book and Sound where we stood was Davis Super Foods. It was a smallish grocery store; amazingly, Cordova had two and the other one was quite large. A dark-haired, athletic-looking young man standing out front was wearing *X Games*–style sunglasses; he wasn't looking right at us, but beyond.

"That's Andy Johnson," Per said, continuing to ID every person we saw. "He's a third-generation fisherman. He's in his early twenties, and he's a snowboarder."

Per gestured high into the air above downtown Cordova, toward the east to one of several large mountains that surround Cordova in a semicircle completed by ocean.

"That mountain, that's Mount Eccles, it looks over the town. Andy's best friend, Teal, another top snowboarder, was the first to snowboard it." Per pointed out that this time of year, because of snowmelt, the side of this mountain was shaped like a lady in a flowing dress.

I couldn't imagine anyone flying down that mountain's face. It looked almost vertical from here, and mountains always appear less steep than they are when you're looking at them from below and far away.

"When Teal died in a car wreck, Andy snowboarded down it as a tribute to him," Per said.

Andy was crossing the street toward us. Either he could tell we were talking about him, recognized (like just about everyone else) we were new in town, or had noticed Rebekah.

A cab went by. Per said Cordova was the kind of town where if a cabdriver saw your dog running loose, he'd give your puppy a ride home if he could get it to obey him.

Andy had short hair and the calm assurance of a daredevil who has never been seriously injured. He could have been one of those models in an Armani ad, one of those fit Italians. He walked slowly, like someone used to doing things at speeds faster than just about anyone else can. Per introduced us; Andy shook my hand politely and lingered just a fraction saying hello to Rebekah. Per explained to Andy what we were doing. When he heard we were writers, he told us he was planning to take a screenwriting class in L.A. in the off-season.

"Hey, man, you want to talk about writing sometime while you're here, get in touch with me," Andy said. He looked down the road and strode away before I could answer, his step light and long.

I called out to him, "Yeah, if I have some time, sure."

"I always know Andy's boat—he has an older bow-picker he bought from his grandfather—because he almost always has a surfboard strapped to the roof," Per said. "Around here, Andy and I, in the beginning of the season, we fish with gill nets. You make a set and sit awhile, let the fish swim into the net. Well, Andy will put on his wet suit and fish the beach side. He'll catch a wave or two before pulling up and picking the fish out of the nets." Per remembered Andy had been on the Junior Olympic ski team in the sixth grade.

An exotic-looking and quick-stepping woman walked by. Per said she was Hanna, one of the bartenders at the Alaskan Hotel and Bar. She's been here since the mideighties. She'd come from Africa, came here with a fisherman she'd met, but it didn't work out. Per thought Hanna was from northern Africa, and he said she worked out at Muscle Mary's.

When these fishermen have big earning years, when the salmon are thick and the price is good, some travel to far-off, hot, dry, sunny places to have some fun. Given the dangers of the way they make a living, exotic and dangerous travel locations don't faze them at all. Some return with almost no money left and accompanied by a different woman from the one they had when they left.

THE ANNOUNCEMENT

Neva had finished watering her hanging baskets. Per asked if we were hungry, and everyone was. We went to the café frequented by the fishermen and locals, in a back room of the Cordova Hotel and Bar. Next door, the Alaskan Hotel and

Bar sign outside was purposefully hung upside down, had been for some time. These bars looked as if they had been floated here from the Wild West, though Alaska *is* the Wild West. You could either walk through the bar or through a dark hallway. The hallway back to the Cordova Café was barely lit; the carpet was old and worn and a popular style from a decade or two ago. It was obviously a local's place. It felt as if we were entering a speakeasy or some other place where illegal acts were perpetrated. Almost every table was full. There were pictures on the walls taken by local commercial fishermen, photos of the fantastic situations all fishermen dream about.

"One time I know of, I think it was the largest single set ever, this gillnetter had thirty-eight thousand pounds of reds. That was in Bristol Bay," Per said, reminding himself, getting himself psyched up. These fishermen try to forget the sets with zero fish or three fish or twelve fish.

I looked at the decorations on the walls. There were pictures of old gillnet boats, the slow boats before they began using fiberglass hulls and fast $40,000 diesel engines. There was a mounted king crab and a picture of a seine boat with its net so full of pink salmon the boat leaned over into the water. Most exciting to these cowboys of the gulf was the picture of a gill net in the water, white foam all across the top of the net. This happens, Per explained, when hundreds of red salmon hit the net at once. Even better is when it's a smashing hit of salmon. Then the whole top of the net foams and splashes, corks even disappear. The picture represents every fisherman's dream; it is why they take all the risks. It is why when there are only five fish in their net after an hour, they still hope for the set when they will fill their icebox. The picture, that dream come true, is why they spend so much time grunting it out, rushing here and there in the ocean.

As we finished at the Cordova Café, Per introduced us to a couple of his fishing partners, Pip and Butch. Many of these fishermen belong to small groups. During an opening they fan out and fish in different places that have been hot in the past and might be again. Per had been debating with himself for hours. "Should I go around Ester Island and pick chum salmon? I'd be about guaranteed there would be lots of them at forty cents a pound. Or should I gamble and risk an opening going for the much higher priced kings and reds?" They're called reds because of their bright, bright red flesh.

The buyers don't like to announce the price until an opening has begun; it's always highest in the beginning of the season, and if numbers caught are high, it can drop. The fishermen-talk at the tables underneath the pictures of full nets at the Cordova Café was that kings might be $2.50 a pound, and they were hoping $1.60 to $1.80 for reds. Kings are not plentiful, but a couple twenty-pound kings in the net is 100 dollars' worth of salmon. Reds weighing five, six pounds are more abundant. If reds average five pounds each, and the buyers are paying $1.75 a pound or $8.75 a fish, 15 reds are $131.25, 150 reds are $1,312.50. If there are 1,500 fish, the net is quaking and shaking and half-sunk, and your dream is alive in the daytime, that's $13,125 in one full net. Per told me as we hit the street and headed back to their trailer park that he's made sets without one salmon, and sets when the Steller's sea lions had a chance to pick them out before he did.

On the Cordova sidewalk, standing on a piece imprinted with a sea otter, Neva started talking to an older gentleman named Guy Beedle. He is her flower-growing buddy, a retiree who has created the latest excitement in the Cordova flower-growing community. He'd begun growing native Alaskan iris from seed. Guy wore his ever-present brown Carhartts. All over Alaska they have Carhartt fashion shows, or would that be antifashion shows? Whichever, it would be the only fashion show I would ever have a chance to star in. Neva was asking Guy about planting flowers near her church. She's active in St. George's Episcopal Church, an enchanted sanctuary with a peaked roof surrounded by old spruce trees that do not let in much sunlight. About 75 percent of the time one of the few parishioners led the service because there was no permanent clergy, just a priest who served them as well as several other isolated congregations. Guy's inspiration, Neva thought, came more from flowers, their care and growing, than organized religion. But Guy said he'd help her plant his vibrant flowers, several of which he'd grown from seed, around her church.

We walked down to Council Street, then to Railroad Avenue. We were headed to the Alaska Department of Fish and Game office. They are the permission givers—they schedule the openings. Daniel Sharp, the area management biologist, was a powerful man around here. His decisions were debated, directly questioned, but generally respected in town, Per said. What a job: to have to live in the town, a town with no road in or out, with no way to avoid the fishermen whose lives you affect in so many ways. And if the fishermen didn't have enough money, they couldn't hire crews, boat cleaners, engine mechanics. They couldn't belong to Muscle Mary's, buy books at Orca Book and Sound. Per and Neva couldn't eat out too often at the Cordova Café. Boats had to be used for several more years, engines pampered, propellers repaired one more time. Houses went unpainted, church offering plates showed more bottom, school fund-raisers brought in less, sports trips that required hundreds of miles of air travel were curtailed. This city depends on the exquisite salmon: kings, reds, chum, pinks, and halibut. Daniel Sharp was like a god here, but he could also be like a strict parent, making you come home early or not allowing you to go out at all.

"It's for your own good," they'd say. And it is. Fishermen like Per Nolan and Andy Johnson, second- and third-generation fishermen, want their way of life to continue. It's why they don't want the road and why they respect the inexact yet demanding job their management biologist must do. They know that the creatures they catch in their nets are wild. Every year the salmon must be able to get upriver in numbers large enough to lay their eggs so that there will be a next generation. The fingerlings must grow strong and return to the ocean. They must be fast and sleek and magnificent. Per hopes at least one of his sons will be a fisherman; Seth, the oldest, is already a full share hand on the family's seine boat.

We walked into the AF&G office. There was a Fish and Game handout there; it appeared there would be an opening. The announcement said:

Commercial Fisheries Announcement, Alaska Dept. of Fish and Game. Prince William Sound Salmon, Announcement #15, 2:00 P.M., Wednesday, June 23, 1999. Copper/Bering River Districts. The closure on Monday, June 21, in the Copper and Bering River Districts is anticipated to have improved sockeye salmon escapement in the Copper River delta systems. [Escapement means fish not getting caught in nets and making it up the river to spawn.] An aerial survey is scheduled for Friday, June 25, the results of which will be used to help determine the management strategy for the coming week. Survey results will be provided in Saturday's announcement. With early timed upriver stocks past their peak run timing, wild stock sockeye salmon escapement into the Copper River delta becomes the primary management consideration in determining fishing time in the Copper and Bering River Districts. Through June 22, the actual cumulative escapement past the Miles Lake sonar counter is 284,928 fish versus an anticipated cumulative count of 296,311 fish. The Copper and Bering River Districts will open for a 24-hour period beginning 7:00 P.M. Thursday, June 24, and ending at 7:00 P.M. on Friday, June 25.

Even though lately fishing time had been cut back, any chance to fish was cause for a big energy boost, a shot of hope. There would be an immediate and palpable increase in energy around Cordova. Per read it; it was shorthand to him. He first shook his head slightly in disappointment. Twenty-four hours is not much time to chase down the elusive reds and kings. It's an immense ocean, who knows where they are and when they will be there. You could catch stragglers for the twenty-four hours, and an hour after you roll up your net the big school comes through. It's the gamble they all take, no fish, no money, no living. And then a glow came to his face. In the end, he lives to be on the water to fish, fishing is his life.

Several fishermen leave Cordova when the season is closed and work as carpenters in Washington State. Pip was a commercial painter in Arizona and with a few partners owned a smoked-and-processed-fish company called Copper River Fine Seafoods. Several also fish out in Bristol Bay. Per made Cordova his home year-round; gillnetting for reds and kings and seining are his living. It used to be he could support Neva and their two young sons, Seth and Keith, but the past few years the openings have been short and Neva's had to take a full-time job.

ON THE *TERMINAL HARVESTER*

"You want to come fishing with me for this opening?" Per asked me as we stood in the office. Every phone was busy, every person was answering questions about the opening.

"Of course I would," I answered. I had no idea how big his boat was or how rough the ocean might get or where we'd eat or sleep, but for the excitement of twenty-four hours of fishing, it couldn't matter too much.

"There's only one bunk in my boat, the cabin's not very large, and we're not small men, but it'll be fine. You don't think I'm beautiful, do you?" Per said. He started walking toward their trailer park, past the school off Whiteshed Road.

"No, you're ugly," I answered.

"Good. We'll be leaving tomorrow afternoon. I don't cook either," Per added, enjoying himself. "If I can't buy it at the grocery store, we can't eat it."

Their trailer was fourteen feet wide by sixty-two feet long, with an added-on room housing their TV and woodstove. Neva's greenhouse was built on the side. Inside their arctic entry were two bright red survival suits, hanging on hooks. If a fisherman's boat sinks and he can get into one of these, fasten all the buttons and zippers, and pull on the hood, he might live to be rescued. When disaster strikes these gillnet boats, they normally either flip over in the surf or catch on fire. Either event leaves little or no time to get the suit on.

Per mentioned that if they lived in any of the towns west of here on Prince William Sound, such as Valdez or Whittier, Neva's adjoining greenhouse would be crushed by the snow. Cordova gets "only" about 106 inches of snow per year, about nine feet, but Cordova's not between the mountains and the glaciers. It's set in front of them, in the open, so storms can blow through town rather than getting trapped. Hurricane- and gale-force winds are common here.

Inside, Neva was making her famous BBQ salmon for dinner. Rebekah said we'd been given their boys' room. On the bunk was a dinosaur quilt made by his grandmother. Legos were everywhere. I noticed again how adaptable Rebekah was to strange situations and how people seemed to like her immediately. She already had her stuff stored away and told me she'd take the top bunk.

"I don't like top bunks, Dad, but then I'm not sure if it is strong enough to hold you," she said. The bunk bed was so short I could not straighten out. Rebekah told me in the morning that I'd talked in my sleep loud enough to wake her up.

The inside of the trailer was popping and crackling with anticipation.

When you count all the days in a year, there is little actual fishing going on. There are all the days and nights spent waiting for these openings, when Per and the other permit holders are allowed to fish. No wonder Neva fixed a special meal and Per brought home bags full of expensive groceries. Soon, for twenty-four hours, Per would be able to make money. His new thirty-thousand-dollar diesel engine could be put to use again. The nets could catch again. All Per's decades of fishing savvy could come alive. It was still possible that he could come back without enough fish to cover his expenses. Or, hopefully, he could spend hours and hours picking kings and reds from his net, returning triumphant from the sea, his face red from the weather and wind. More than likely the results would be somewhere in between.

"Man, this summer's going by fast," Per said from out of nowhere. It was the early evening of June 23, one of the longest days of the year. When the last of the fishermen emerged from the Alaskan Hotel and Bar at 2:00 A.M., it would not be dark yet. Soon these cowboys would be cut loose to ride and chase down their prey, the highest-priced salmon in Alaska. Their fast-riding, big-motored gill nets are their sleek horses, nine hundred feet of net their ropes to lasso the fish. The big difference between them and cowboys that ride horses, other than the killer ocean they ride, is they can't see what they're after.

Per's fishing began at exactly 7:00 P.M., June 24, and would end at exactly 7:00 P.M., June 25. The whole family came down to the docks to see off Per and me. There are planes and observation boats with the best binoculars watching for lawbreakers. Gillnetters almost always fish alone out of Cordova. Per said his high-strung side comes out at these times. A couple of the boats had already started their engines. All of us, including Per's two small sons, carried something to the boat, the *Terminal Harvester*, which had been built in 1991 in the state of Washington. As we loaded our supplies, a fisherman named Gerald Kompkoff was on the dock mending his net. Per said he was part Aleut and part Russian. He worked on the boat the *Inseine*.

We loaded up the groceries and idled out to a cannery, Ocean Beauty, to load up the boat's built-in fish box with crushed ice. Boats were coming from every direction, like people on horseback and in wagons easing up to the starting line

of the Oklahoma land rush. Neva, Rebekah, Keith, and Seth waved, as did wives
and partners and lovers and children and grandparents and parents all over
Cordova's docks. Bankers and merchants and mechanics and fiberglass repair-
ers and boatbuilders and electronics suppliers had their fingers crossed.

The prime area targeted by Per and his fishing partners is in the Prince
William Sound management area. "It includes all coastal waters and inland
drainages entering the north central Gulf of Alaska between Cape Suckling
and Cape Fairfield. The area includes the Bering River, the Copper River, and
all of Prince William Sound with a total adjacent land area of approximately
38,000 square miles." A report from one of the first explorations of the Copper River area by the United States, headed by Lieutenant Henry T. Allen of
the Second U.S. Cavalry, in 1885 had nothing to do with salmon stocks. "In
view of the fact that so little is known of the interior of the Territory of Alaska,
and that the conflicting interests between the white people and the Indians of
that Territory may in the near future result in serious disturbances between
the two races, the department commander authorizes you to proceed to that
Territory for the purpose of obtaining all information which will be valuable
and important, especially to the military branch of the Government."

From atop a mountain between twenty-five hundred and three thousand
feet high, there was a clear vision of the formidable obstacles that lay before
them: "We had gained a sufficient altitude to see, far to the northeast, a high
wall of ice, visible as far back as the eye (aided with a field glass) could see. To
the north and almost joining the glacier on the northeast, we saw another
monster moving off to the northeast. In our front, or east, lay a collection of
thousands of small islands, varying from one-sixteenth of an acre to fifty
acres in size, surrounded by light gray liquid, varying in breadth from a mile
to a small stream, and in depth being about three feet here and about eighteen
inches further down. This was the Copper River, that we thought might be ascended in a steamer for 50 to 100 miles!"

Lieutenant Allen, in his report upon return from their remarkable "recon-
naissance in Alaska" concluded, "Should the natives of the Tanana or Copper
River commit outrages upon the whites who may be making their way into the
interior, of such a nature to justify the intervention of the military, many diffi-
culties would be encountered before redress could be obtained. To stop the sale

of ammunition and arms would be a sad blow to them, but a decidedly negative retaliation. . . . Once on the Copper River, food in the form of salmon
would be abundant, and a severe retaliation could be inflicted by patrolling the
river, thus preventing, if possible, the natives from taking fish during the summer. By this means a large number of them would perish the following winter."

A hundred and fifteen years later, some Cordova fishermen believe that
there are many organizations, not just the U.S. government, trying to prevent
them from fishing. Some believe these organizations would like to shut them
down completely, by posting patrols to control them until eventually their
lifestyle would perish. The fishermen will fight this vigorously, hoping too
that it does not happen so subtly and incrementally that they do not fight until it's too late.

Once we were out of the "no wake" zone and into Orca Inlet, Per and all
the other bow-pickers of the Gulf of Alaska let their motors roar. Some had
larger boats than Per, made of aluminum, powered by twin diesels, and worth
close to $150,000. But no boat seemed to be gaining on us. Inside the cabin,
Per told me a few fishermen, like "that macrobiotic eating" Sully, still had the
wooden, slow boats. Sully sometimes left a day before the rest, and still, if they
had to run to Controller Bay, where the Bering River empties, or near Strawberry Point, the fast boats beat him there. Sully and his artist wife, Rocky, are
originally from the Northeast. Sully, who sometimes wore his white hair in a
ponytail, was a beatnik, before *hippie* was a word. He is sixty-two or so; when
he was younger, he had a huge beard, and he had always been lean, Per said.
Sully was an extreme skier before there was even a word for these snow mani-
acs. Sully has a run named after him in Telluride, Sully's Gully. Pip, an excellent skier and one of Per's fishing partners, skied Telluride once, saw the run,
and decided to pass on it for another lifetime. Per's boat ran twenty to twenty-
five knots; Sully's little white boat does six to eight knots. Sully began as a
fisherman as a crewman on Per's stepdad's seine boat. Per says Sully survives
on beans and rice. Per would feel much more at home at the dinner table with
ex–football coaches John Madden and Mike Ditka.

The sky was slate gray and peppered with slow-moving puffs of light gray
clouds. It was about fifty degrees. The ocean was smooth and lime green; the
spray splashing up on both sides of our boat was silver. I could see something

in the water, which was so shallow with sandbars and even isolated rocks that Per had to keep the boat up on plane, at full speed, so it could run without hitting anything. At first I thought it was some old kelp washing in from the ocean, but I kept seeing it. Per directed me out onto the deck. The cabin was at the back of this boat, the working area on the front two-thirds. Floating on their backs everywhere in the water, so many I could not count them all, were sea otters. Here they were protected by Egg Island. Most had their babies on their bellies, where they nursed and napped, nursed and napped. The wakes the gillnetting boats left gave the otters a modest ride. Per said he'd seen "rafts" of over a hundred sea otters before.

We'd passed Mummy Island and squeezed through the dangerous Whiteshed Point. Some barrier islands—Cooper Sands, Grass Island Bar, Kokinhenik Bar, and Strawberry Reef—shield the Copper River delta. We were headed there to claim our spot to be able to begin fishing at 7:00 P.M. exactly. Per said there would be about three hundred boats in this district. Some would fish inside the islands, some up the river a bit—wherever they thought the salmon were. Where were the "high-liners" going? everyone wondered. High-liners are those fishermen seeking salmon who consistently seem to find the fish and catch more than the other professionals.

We were now in the Gulf of Alaska. On the beach of the barrier island to our left, three bald eagles fed on some dead flesh. What I wondered was, how do these fishermen keep from being completely overwhelmed? Water surrounded us, its surface giving no hint to what lay below. Per had said that they look for jumpers, salmon that occasionally leapt from the sea. But that worked more for seiners, when the fish were in larger schools. How intimidating it seemed that there are so many spots to let your net out into the water.

Per chose a spot and let his net out. We watched the net for top water splashes, for signs that reds or, even better, kings were hitting the net. The top would move and buoys would pop down in the water when they hit at first. Our hopes would soar—we hoped it would happen again. Per let some sets last an hour, or even less; a few were for three hours, when he would just leave the net fishing without pulling it up. The net jutted straight out from the boat's bow, stretching nine hundred feet and sinking twenty-three or twenty-four feet down. There was time for storytelling and for chats with Per's fishing partners on the radio. Pip called and said that the opening price was set by Norquest at $1.80 per pound for reds and $2.50 for kings. Per felt that the price would go up because the take would be small. He was having second thoughts; maybe we should have gone to another place to catch netfuls of cheap pink salmon. The situation made him thoughtful.

"This life on the water runs in our family. My father, he was studying the information obtained by Gary Powers's U-2 spy plane. He is a university-trained physicist, but he didn't want to work for the industrial war complex. So we moved to Alaska," Per said.

He kept the motor running and his thirty-foot-long bow-picker in gear to keep the net straight. Without the power of the engine, the current or the net could suck us toward the breakers, where several boats have been flipped and fishermen killed.

Per explained how his father, an adventurer on many levels, had taken a huge spruce log from the Northwest and put two axles underneath it. He then towed it from Washington to Monterey, California. There he hollowed it out and sailed it, as a trimaran, from California to the Marquesas and then to the Big Island of Hawaii. He took a sextant and a book on celestial navigation and learned how to guide himself on the way there. Per's dad, also an inventor, fishes Bristol Bay and winters in Fiji. Bristol Bay is believed to have the most abundant run of red salmon in the world.

A Steller's sea lion popped up right along the net. Per had already told me to look for them; he said they knew the sound of the gillnet boats; to them it was the sound of an all-you-can-eat buffet. It certainly was easier for them to just rip the fish from the net instead of speeding through the ocean, darting and cutting, to catch these quick, sleek silver-sided salmon. Occasionally, a seven-foot-long salmon shark would about tear the nets in half, leaving gaping, expensive holes. Dolphin and killer whales, normally, were too intelligent to mess with the nets. Even the salmon could sometimes see the net and avoid it.

Per noticed a fisherman whose boat he did not know making a set close to the beach. Fishermen are tempted to head inland because salmon often run close to the beach. How do the fish find their way for possibly several thousand miles back to the exact place they were born? There are no landmarks underwater to follow; surely they don't "smell" their home freshwaters diluted beyond recognition in ocean waters. The return of the salmon is one of the unknown miracles of nature.

"Last year we lost a fisherman who got too close to the breakers," Per remembered, his voice tinged with a sadness for the young family in Oregon and a knowledge that most serious accidents are a result of a seemingly small, inconsequential decision. He explained how the fisherman's boat got turned sideways in the breakers. Then the full power of the ocean hits the boat broadside, wanting to turn it over. It flipped this boat; it was upside down, the engine might still have been running. The cabin probably filled with fumes and it was totally black. The man struggled frantically to find air to breathe and became disoriented, knowing he must get out.

Fish and Game happened to be around. They responded and went into the shallow breakers after him in their inflatable. The breakers flipped them, also, into waist-deep water. They spotted gas leaking from the fisherman's flipped gas tanks. The Fish and Game guys got a chain saw and cut a hole in the upside-down hull. One spark could have caused the whole thing to blow up. The fisherman had probably broken bones from being slammed inside the dark cabin by the waves breaking on his capsized boat. And after his boat had rolled, his net had broken loose. Fish and Game could never get to him; he died, Per told me, with no indication that the story was part of the norm for an Alaskan fisherman's life. People died every year and many more came close.

"My sister's boat, a seiner, rolled and sank in deep water three years ago," Per said. She and her crew were rescued.

Often the gillnetters are hustling around, walking on decks and bows and side rails smeared with salmon slime and ocean water. There's even the simple risk of slipping and falling off your boat, hitting your head on the way into the ocean. Your boat's running, you're knocked out or dazed. The gillnetters often fish all night. I saw no one wearing a life preserver, much less a survival suit. The water is never warm enough so someone would be able to swim to safety unless he's right outside the breakers, like where Andy Johnson the surfer likes to catch a wave. I'd been looking for a gillnet boat with a surfboard strapped to the top but had not seen one.

THE ABUSED SECRET CODE

The brotherhood of Per, Pip, Art, and Marc didn't talk to each other much at first. Was it because the excitement and anticipation of netfuls of salmon, what keeps all fishermen coming back, turned to disappointment? Per checked in with Pip and he was doing worse than we were and that was bad. Neither Marc nor Art was catching much either, or so Per discerned from the code-speak over the marine radio. Marc, who was from Washington and a rabid Washington State football fan, found out I was from Tennessee. The big debate this year in college football was over who would be the better pro quarterback, his Ryan Leaf of WSU or Peyton Manning of the University of Tennessee. I offered up all my reasons why Peyton would smoke Ryan. Marc knew it would go the other way—Ryan was the man. The argument over the radio went Peyton, Ryan, Peyton, Ryan, *Peyton, Ryan,* until Per had to step in and referee.

Per had made several sets, laying out the net, letting it set, reeling it in, and picking out the salmon. The faster the net came in, the less picking, the smaller the amount of salmon, the less money to survive. And the twenty-four hours were ticking, ticking away. Who knew when the sonar god and biologist god would let them fish again?

Excerpt from *Coming Back Alive*

SPIKE WALKER

⬧ SPIKE WALKER has worked as a deckhand on commercial fishing boats for more than two decades. He's all too familiar with the perils and joys of the treacherous seas off Alaska's coastline. He's now a full-time writer, with multiple classic books to his name, including *Coming Back Alive, Working on the Edge, Alaska: Tales of Adventure from the Last Frontier,* and *Nights of Ice.* He divides his time between Castle Rock, Washington; Kodiak, Alaska; and Catskanie, Oregon. His titles are available from St. Martin's Press as well as online and at fine bookstores everywhere. ⬧

As he steered his speeding twenty-six-foot gillnet boat *Marlene* out across the Copper River delta in Alaska's Prince William Sound on a gray, windblown afternoon in 1981, Skip Holden could not have known that within hours he would be engaged in a hellish struggle just to survive, nor could he have imagined how many lives would be so profoundly affected by the outcome.

Bold and enterprising, but never reckless, "Holden," as his friends like to call him, was looking forward to doing what he did best, and that was to net salmon.

Eight years earlier, Skip Holden and his wife, Marlene, had set out from San Leandro, California, to hitchhike to Alaska. They headed north, holding a sign that read ALASKA OR BUST! They arrived in Cordova nearly broke, found work together in a local cannery, and, in a month, managed to save twelve hundred dollars. They bought a twenty-foot boat for exactly that amount. They lived on it, fished off of it, and used a bucket for a toilet.

It was a romantic, albeit bare-bones, beginning in the rugged little fishing village located in a wild, sprawling land bursting with boomtown opportunity and colorful characters. There was a local stripper named Tequilla, whose writhing style of dancing naked was known to cause almost a riot as lonely, affection-starved fishermen trampled one another for a closer look.

Then there was Machine Gun Betty. She was a large Indian woman who worked as a bartender at a local watering hole. Her way of dealing with a rowdy crowd of drunken fishermen (who refused to leave at quitting time) was to pull out a Thompson submachine gun, level it on her rambunctious patrons, and order them off the premises. "It's closing time! Get the hell out!" she'd say as the bar emptied.

During those eight years of hard work as a commercial fisherman, Skip Holden had seen some sights—such as the time the Fish and Game Department opened the season up in the fjord near Coghill Point, and he and his, fishing pals had netted 1 million sockeye salmon in a single week of red-hot fishing.

Named after Skip's wife, the F/V *Marlene* was known in fishing circles as a Snowball bow-picker. She had a six-foot-high reel mounted in the center of her foredeck. This spool-like contraption was designed to feed the one-thousand-foot-long gillnet off her bow and reel it back aboard via the same route.

Along the way, Skip had learned a few things about the nature of successful fishermen, too. Foremost, he had learned not to try to be like anybody else: The best fishermen fished according to the dictates of their own personalities.

As a rule, Holden worked alone. More of a hunter-type person himself, he liked to motor past the main sandbars (where most of his more conservative fellow gillnetters chose to make their "drifts") and out through the surf. He enjoyed fishing the deep waters of the open ocean. When possible, he liked to intercept the fish well before they reached the main branch of the river, something at which he was quite adept, now having the self-assurance of a seasoned fisherman, one who had paid his dues and acquired a fair amount of fishing savvy along the way.

Armed with little more than a compass and a Fathometer, he roamed as far as ten miles out from the wild and ever-changing sixty-mile-wide delta of sandbars and tidelands known as the Copper River Flats, fishing the salmon-rich waters as far out as Cape Hinchinbrook.

Some fishermen didn't like the stress of making "sets," laying out their gill-nets and fishing out in the open ocean. They generally fished the inside waters. They didn't seem to mind fighting the crowds, or having to pull their gillnets back aboard every few minutes, then run back up the line, lay them out again, and start from scratch. By contrast, Skip Holden liked to fish the deep, outside waters. He liked the sight of free, open spaces and uncluttered horizons. He'd been raised that way. When he was a boy, sailing off the California coast, his father had taught him the art of navigation, as well as how to keep a ship in good repair and how to tie the rope knots that were essential to life at sea. Most important, his father instilled in his son the belief that shallow water is a fisherman's worst enemy.

It was the going out and coming back in over the sandbars at entrance channels, especially those at Softuk, and Strawberry, and Egg Island, that local fishermen feared most. Let an out-rushing tide confront a strong flow of on-shore wind, and the waves can really stack up.

Even for Skip Holden, getting trapped out on the open sea in a sudden blow was something to be avoided if at all possible. Let him receive a warning over the local CB fishing channel announcing that the sandbar was closing, and Holden would rush his net aboard and make a mad scramble in over the building breakers before they closed him out. Once inside the punishing surf line, he would wait out the storm in the shelter of one of the tideland coves carved out of tens of miles of sandbars by the thirteen-foot tides that flooded in over the area several times each day.

Miss the closing, get cut off by a sudden storm, and a fisherman would have few options, all of them dangerous. Left unprotected by island or berm, caught tens of miles from Cordova, a fisherman could either jog into the storm and weather (which might last for several days and nights) or make the near-impossible journey around the thirty-mile length of Hinchinbrook Island, running broadside to the storm winds and waves crashing ashore the entire way. Lose an engine, throw a prop, and you would be history.

Regardless, Holden was always hanging it out there, working on the edge. Unlike some wanna-be fishermen, however, Holden had the touch. And during the season, it wasn't unusual for him to intercept as much as four thousand dollars' worth of the migrating fish in a single week.

On that gray day in 1981, Holden had already gone for two days and nights without sleep, standing anchor watch, waiting out the past few days of blustery weather in a featureless, godforsaken reach inside Softuk Bar. It was no big deal, really. Gillnetting the flats had always been a young man's sport. And Holden could go for days without sleep. But when the winds finally did calm down, he thought, That's it. Time to go fishing, and, pulling anchor, he fled out across the bar.

Once at sea, however, Holden soon found himself idling up the high, sloping faces of the unusually large swells lumbering in toward shore. Enormous as they were, the swells weren't breaking, and he drifted over them one by one, the bulging waters passing smoothly underneath him. It was the air around him, however, that spooked him. The enveloping air had turned "eerie calm, like out of breath," as he put it. It was a little like entering into the eye of a hurricane. Skip Holden had never experienced anything quite like it.

Shortly, the sky grew dark, and as the unexpected storm intensified, strong winds burst up the scene. Blowing directly in against the outrushing tide, the winds soon whipped the sea into a cresting frenzy. In only minutes, thunderous breakers began collapsing across the entire width of the bar, effectively closing off any possible retreat.

Still, Holden was determined to give it a try, and so he maneuvered into the roiling waters of the bar. He had managed to weave his way past several rows of breakers, when, in the gray-black of the dim evening light, he spotted a single white lightbulb mounted atop the mast of another salmon boat. Having learned of Holden's plight, a fellow fisherman had apparently left the safety of his snug anchorage and was now motoring back and forth just inside the breakers, trying to guide Holden into the deeper waters of the main channel, through at least five thousand feet of breaking waves and lathering foam.

Maybe I can make it through this, thought Holden, focusing on the challenge at hand. *Now, should I go around this breaker and through that one?* he asked himself as he pushed ahead. *Is it deeper there? What's my Fathometer reading? Uh-oh—too shallow. I'll try this way.*

Finally conceding defeat, Holden fought his way back out through the marching rows of breakers, then began motoring down the sixty-mile delta of sandbars and bordering channels.

When he arrived at the channel leading past Egg Island, he found stiff seventy-mile-per-hour winds driving heavy seas ashore, and the bar closed. Without one of the powerful VHF radios on board with which to call out, he was forced to rely on the comparatively feeble power of his CB radio.

"Hey, Phil, what's happening?" he radioed his good friend Phil Thum. "Is there a way in? Do you see any way in there?"

"No, I don't think you can get in, Holden. It's breaking all the way across the bar here."

The entire time he talked, Holden was jogging along the outside edge of the sandbar at the Egg Island entrance, quickly looking for an opening in the surf. *Either I find my way in past Egg Island here,* he thought, *or I'll be out here all night. It's now or never.* He cruised up and down the bar, but was unable to find anything like an opening.

"I really don't see any way in there," Holden radioed Thum finally.

"There is no way in," cut in the anonymous voice of another fisherman.

And suddenly, all cross-chatter on his CB radio ceased, followed by a dead silence. Holden caught the full measure of what this meant. Everyone listening knew that there was no way back, and that in the building seas, the trip out and around Hinchinbrook Island would be pure suicide. His only hope would be to try to jog into the storm, however long it might last, however severe it might be.

Well, this will be good for a laugh with my buddies back at the Reluctant Fisherman saloon in Cordova, he thought. *Old Holden thought he could beat Mother Nature, and he got his butt kicked.*

"Boy, I'm sure glad I'm safe and sound and anchored up in here," bragged another fisherman over the CB, laying it on thick.

"I sure wouldn't want to be out there in this kind of weather," remarked another in a tone of sincere empathy.

Sometimes, Holden knew, a fisherman could find a place where he could kind of surf in where the waves weren't actually breaking. But the winds were gusting past eighty miles an hour now, and as the dark, peculiar cloud cover pressed down on him, Holden continued to motor back and forth along the outside edge of the breaking surf, praying all the while for a freak opening through which he and his boat might pass.

It was then that the steering on his boat went out.

"Damn!" he said aloud.

Suddenly caught dead in the water, Holden knew that he was in serious trouble. The winds seemed determined to blow him broadside into the Hawaiian-sized breakers now folding over and exploding with boat-crushing furor all along the mouth of the bar.

He refused to let the instinct to panic have its way. Somehow, in the breaking seas and wild, punishing winds, Holden searched for a way to stabilize his boat. Like any seasoned fisherman, he knew the score: Lose the boat, lose your life.

Then, cleverly, he hit upon the solution. He would play out three-quarters of his one-thousand-foot-long gillnet and, if the tide was right, catch a ride on the tidal currents as they flowed offshore and away from the breakers, all the while using the net (with the departing waters pushing against it) as a kind of sea anchor.

He fed the 750-foot trail of webbing and buoys off his bow roller and watched as the offshore flow caught it. He was in luck. The tide was going out. The net, buoys, and ship were being swept out to sea and away from the pounding surf. The vessel's bow swung to point into the accelerating storm winds, exactly as he had hoped.

Holden tied the net off on the ship's bow cleats to prevent the six-foot-high, four-foot-wide aluminum reel from being torn from its steel deck mounts and jerked overboard.

As the darkness closed in, Holden found it difficult to see anything clearly. His eyes strained toward something in the distance. He stood squinting in the dim light, peering through the haze of rain and blowing spray. He couldn't be certain. The misty vision was either one of breakers demolishing themselves on nearby rocks or the flash of the buoy marker over on Wessels Reef.

"Holden, how are you doing out there?" radioed Phil Thum, who was anchored off in a wind-raked channel amid the barren sands of Egg Island. "Do you want me to call the Coast Guard?"

"Well, Phil, I'm still alive here," replied Holden. "If a Coast Guard rescue basket were to somehow land on my deck, I'd climb right in. But there's just no way a helicopter could make it out here. It's too damned windy."

As the night progressed, the storm intensified and the wind pushed the waves higher. In the gathering darkness, the winds were soon hissing across the water at ninety miles per hour, with stronger gusts ranging out of wave valleys large enough to hold a football field, complete with goalposts.

Getting trapped on the outside in such a blow in a relatively tiny boat (26 feet compared to one of the weather-busting king-crab boats, some of which are 150 feet long and 40 feet wide) was one of the worst experiences a Prince William Sound salmon fisherman could have.

Holden was hoping that the driving wind and torrential rains would soon blow themselves out. What he could not have known was that one of the most formidable storms in the history of storm-ravaged Prince William Sound had pushed into the area, catching him flat-footed and leaving him cut off, with nowhere to run. In addition to the wicked winds, more rain would fall on the area of the Copper River Flats over the next three days in the shortest amount of time ever recorded, some fourteen inches in all.

Skip Holden opened the door leading into the tiny space of his wheelhouse and quickly stepped inside. He was still dripping wet when the F/V *Marlene*'s main engine coughed heavily. Holden bent over, removed one section of the floorboard, and peered down into the small engine compartment. It was not an encouraging sight. The bilge area was full of water, which was now lapping at the sides of the gas engine.

Then Holden recalled how he'd been running along with his back door left open slightly to flush out all engine fumes from inside his cabin. Seawater, he surmised, had silently and surreptitiously been seeping in through the opening since the storm had first kicked up. The engine's carburetor and wiring were getting drenched. *I need to get busy now and bail some water out of here,* he told himself. *I've got to shut down this engine and very methodically remove the seawater from the bilge. One thing at a time.*

Holden slammed the back door and tied it shut, securing the handle with a length of rope. With the engine turned off, he knew that the bilge would soon run the battery down to the point where it could no longer turn the engine over. Then all hope of somehow getting the carburetor dried out and the engine started would be lost. Holden tore away the remaining floorboards, leapt down into the chest-deep engine compartment, and immediately went to work bailing out the water. When, more than a hour later, he looked up again from his sweaty efforts, the compartment was relatively free of seawater, while outside, the dull gray evening had given way to a coal black void of blasting winds and pummeling rain.

Normally, when he was fishing and drifting along on a given set, Holden could feel the currents gently tugging at his net. On this night, however, the gillnet playing off his bow roller (and now stretching several hundred yards beyond it) remained as tight as a bowstring as the offshore currents tugging at his net and buoys came into direct conflict with the force created by fierce onshore winds driving hard against every exposed inch of the *Marlene*'s superstructure. The wind shrieked constantly over the wheelhouse, and the torrential rains and surf thrumming against the fiberglass hull of the *Marlene* echoed inside with the irregular thump of beating drums.

Well, what do you think we should do here, Skip?" radioed Phil Thum finally. "Do you want me to call out a Mayday and get the Coast Guard people on their way?"

Thum knew that such a decision was not to be taken lightly. A commercial fisherman could not justify sending out a Mayday unless someone's life was in imminent peril.

"I don't know what to do," replied Holden finally.

The pocket in which Skip Holden was cornered, in between the sandbars and channel entrances at Softuk and Strawberry, was famous, Thum knew, for turning boats into kindling. Under the current conditions, the place had become a kind of death trap, a small-boat killing field. Thum was certain that his friend was about to lose his life there.

Undeterred by fear or the gravity of the decision, Phil Thum lifted the handheld mike from his powerful VHF radio set. "Mayday! Mayday!" he called out for the entire fleet to hear. "This is the fishing vessel. *Keeper*! The fishing vessel *Keeper*! We have a fisherman in trouble, and we are in need of assistance."

"This is United States Coast Guard, Comsat Kodiak! Comsat Kodiak!" came the quick reply. "We receive your message. Please give us the name of the skipper and boat in trouble and its exact position. Over."

Thum identified himself and gave Holden's current position. "I am relaying this message from a CB radio broadcasting for a man named Skip Holden," Thum explained. "He is on board the F/V *Marlene,* and he's been caught outside near the Egg Island entrance. He doesn't have a VHF, so I'll be talking to him and relaying that information on to you, and I'll relay what you say to me back to him."

Not until every question had been asked and answered did the Coast Guard finally render their decision.

"Please relay to Skip Holden that we're on our way," radioed the petty officer.

"Roger. I'll be standing by on channel twenty-three," Thum confirmed.

"Holden, the Coast Guard is on their way," Thum announced, excitedly passing on the message.

"Good," acknowledged Holden.

As soon as Holden heard the news, he turned and began donning his survival suit. *I've got to keep my eyes peeled,* he told himself. *If those chopper boys are really going to come out here in this crap, I want to be ready and help all I can.*

Holden knew it was easily the most impossible predicament that he'd ever faced. Inside the rocking, battering space of the ship's cabin, Holden tried to prepare himself for the end. In the scheme of things, he knew, he was just an ant-sized creature caught in an exceptionally tough spot. Yet he refused to allow himself to slip into the emotional quicksand fear produced. Even as the storm outside seemed about to tear his boat to pieces and bury him on the spot, Holden made a conscious choice to stay focused, concentrating on performing each individual task he faced as quickly and efficiently as he could.

If the gillnet jumped out of the bow rollers and slid amidships along the pivoting boat, however, Holden was certain that the *Marlene* would instantly flip over and all would be lost. He made repeated trips out the wheelhouse door to see if the net, reel, and cleats securing it were in need of repair. Each time, as he worked his way forward, thigh-deep water came crashing in over the sides. The rampaging sea threatened to knock his legs from under him and sweep him down the open deck and over the side.

It would be several hours before a four-engined U.S. Coast Guard C-130 search and rescue (SAR) airplane reached the scene.

H ow are you doing down there?" radioed Lt. Jim Hatfield, the copilot and officer in charge of the C-130 now circling at some eighteen thousand feet overhead.

Although Holden had been unable (other than relaying his messages through Phil Thum) to even come close, with his tiny CB radio, to reaching Air Station Kodiak some three hundred miles away, he could now hear Lieutenant Hatfield's voice clearly.

"The boat's hanging on," said Holden, "but I don't think there's any way you're going to be able to hoist me off of her. It'd be like trying to thread a needle from up there."

"Let us worry about that," replied Hatfield. Then he informed Holden that an H-3 "Pelican" Sikorsky helicopter had landed in Cordova (following the terrific beating of a three-hour flight over from Kodiak Island) and was preparing for the rescue attempt.

"Don't be surprised if you get a static electric shock when the basket first gets to you," Hatfield said. "But don't worry about it; it won't hurt you. He'll be shooting a cradle [a body strap] down that line to you."

Hatfield's plan was to guide the H-3 chopper close enough to pluck Holden off the *Marlene*'s front deck, air-lifting him into the stormy heavens like a sack of potatoes.

"Right now, I need you to take your antenna down, because we don't want it to get tangled up in the rescue basket."

"Roger," said Holden coolly.

Up until that time, Holden felt sure that he'd kept a tight rein on his emotions. But he was soon forced to acknowledge that he had felt a bit more shaken than he'd been letting on, because when he hurried outside and grabbed hold of the two-inch-thick base of the twenty-foot-high CB antenna, it broke off in his hand, snapping in two, as if it were no more substantial than a bone-dry strand of uncooked spaghetti. Suddenly, all communications with the outside world came to a close, as far as he could tell. He would continue to send out messages on the CB radio, but he would have no way of knowing if anyone could actually hear them.

It was approximately 1:00 A.M. when Holden spied the blinking navigation light of a helicopter far off his stern. He rushed to illuminate his cabin and make sure that his small mast light was turned on and shining brightly. *Lit up like I am,* thought Holden, *I must look like a little torch out here on the water.*

Then he set off a flare, launching it out the side window of his wheelhouse. He was sure the helicopter pilot had spotted him. *Okay,* thought Holden. *Now I've got to get ready here for what's going to happen.*

Leaving the security of his radio and the protection of his bathroom-sized wheelhouse, he crouched down like a wrestler against the wind and currents, waded out onto the front deck, and stood there waiting for the helicopter to arrive.

When Holden caught sight of them again, they were gunning their engines and coming straight for him, closing along an invisible line stretching directly downwind of the boat. Holden could see that the pilot was making an attempt to pull up even with him. What worried Holden, however, was the straining sound of the helicopter's engines and gears. They were producing an unbelievably loud whining, a kind of metallic screaming.

Just then, Holden looked to his left and spied a large sea otter floating alongside his boat. The otter was lying on its back and wore what appeared to be a broad grin across its face. *Isn't that weird,* thought Holden. The sea otter seemed to be saying, *Look, the next step will probably be to come in and join me, and when you do, it's not going to be a big deal.* Holden was beginning to understand that it might just come to that. *If I somehow wind up in the water in my suit,* he calculated, *I'm going to act just like that sea otter. I'm just going to dig it and have a nice big smile and a good time.*

Holden was also aware that he was caught in a steady drift that was carrying him ever farther out into the vast wind-raked reaches of the Gulf of Alaska. Each time his small boat teetered up and over the top of one of the long, sweeping faces of the storm waves, he thought he could make out, through the demolishing forces of wind and spray, the indistinct speck of a buoy marker's light blinking off in the distance.

The downpour and the blowing spray tumbling across the face of the sea had joined forces and were now creating near whiteout conditions. Out of the vacuum of sea spray, rain, and wind engulfing him came ungainly waves twenty-five feet high. Now and then, in the reflective glow coming from his wheelhouse, Holden could make out the mountains of seawater approaching. He could feel each wave lifting him, sweeping him up and up and up, and then the free fall as the wave discarded him and moved on. And he thought, *I've fished Kayak Island and Cape St. Elias in a big swell, but this is something that I've never seen before.* At times, the winds blew so hard that the sea itself seemed to contort under the pressure.

Abruptly, the chopper pilot turned on his floodlights, and for a few seconds, it looked like broad daylight. Several times, as the helicopter maneuvered overhead in the intensifying storm, Holden found that he could no longer determine for sure whether he was hearing the roar of the jet engines or the sound of the wind shrieking past. He was certain that if someone were standing right next to him and he yelled into that person's ear, the sound of his voice would never be heard.

Holden felt a tremendous surge, and the *Marlene* was swept to the top of a wave. From its crest, he could see the helicopter clearly in the wave valley stretching out before him. Just 150 feet away, Holden took in the startling vision of the chopper's main rotor blades spinning at eye level with him. And yet the chopper's fifteen-foot-tall body hung down into the trough below. *Man, he's way too close to the ocean,* thought Holden. *His blades are going to hit that wave!* Seconds later, however, the chopper's volatile course carried it past directly overhead.

Though Holden felt relieved, something was still bothering him. Then, as he watched the chopper maneuver, it struck him. The pilot was flying as though he couldn't actually *see* the waves; it was as if somebody else were describing the water below to him. One second, the waves would be practically licking at the bottom of the helicopter, and in the next, the helo would be one hundred feet above them. The helicopter staggered along like a drunken sailor—inebriated but still on his feet. And as it drew nearer, Holden noticed the sharp, clipped flash of a tiny blue-white strobe light mounted on the aircraft's underbelly.

The F/V *Marlene* was yawing back and forth when a sneaker wave struck her from the starboard side, flooding her main deck and knocking her sideways through the frenzied surf. She was still pitching violently, pivoting from one side to the other, when the helicopter swung in overhead again.

Holden was more than a little taken aback when a shot bag with a line attached to it plopped down next to him, smack in the middle of his deck. The valiant Coast Guard crewmen aboard the wind-tossed helicopter overhead had managed to zero in on a space just eight feet wide, hitting the mark as if it were the most common, everyday thing to do. Holden was amazed. *These guys are phenomenal!* he thought. *They're out here risking their lives for me. I've just got to do the best I can for them.*

Yet, with no way of communicating, Holden couldn't have known that the line trailing the shot bag was a tending line. In less extreme weather conditions, Coast Guard helicopter crews ordinarily used it as a way of feeding the basket down to the party awaiting rescue on the deck below. Holden grabbed the line trailing down out of the sky, thinking, *If they can't get the rescue basket down to me, maybe they can just reel me up. If I feel something solid on the end of this line,* he reasoned further, *I'm just going to wrap it around my hand, swing from the end of the line, and just go for it. I'll pull on this line until I feel some tension, and when I feel something really secure on the other end, I'll hook it around my body and they'll just winch me up.* What worried Holden most was the quality of the cord line that he held. It was made of loosely woven polyester fiber. Just three-eighths of an inch thick, it looked little more substantial than a dog leash.

At that moment, an overpowering gust of wind swept the helicopter away, carrying it tail-first, well downwind of Holden. The line in Skip Holden's hand went slack. *What do they want me to do with this now?* he wondered. *Oh, they had to let go of the line,* he then realized as he coiled it aboard.

When the helo drew near to Holden once again, he spotted the rescue basket.

It was swinging violently about in the wind, below the open side door, underneath the aircraft's white belly. The helicopter managed to pull almost even with his bow, when, once again, he heard the high-pitched, almost supersonic whine of the aircraft's engines. With it came the grinding sound of metal crunching, like a washing machine falling apart. It didn't sound right. Holden was certain that they were in serious trouble.

Then it appeared as though some powerful hand had reached out and grabbed the helicopter and catapulted it back into space. One second, it was holding its own, the next, it went shooting back off the *Marlene*'s stern as if shot out of a cannon. It appeared to be traveling backward at about the same speed as the wind, as helpless in the one-hundred-mile-per-hour blasts as an errant mosquito. Holden hung on to the gillnet reel with both hands, his legs spread-eagle, as thigh-deep water crashed aboard and drained out the boat's side scuppers.

Then, well downwind of the *Marlene*'s stern, the rescue helicopter staggered several hundred feet into the air and paused there—a minuscule dot of tentative light hovering against a vast backdrop of all-enveloping darkness. All Holden could see was the tiny pulse of her navigation lights blinking and the hazy swath of a spotlight shining down on the ocean. *They must be having some kind of trouble,* he reasoned. *Or perhaps they're having a powwow of some kind.*

He was still studying the lights of the chopper, now suspended in the air more than half a mile away, when, as if in a slow motion, the helicopter dipped sharply to one side and toppled from the sky. With its nose down and its tail trailing up and behind, the helo plunged toward the water. A moment later, the rotor blades on one side plowed into the ocean's surface. "Oh no! No! No! No!" screamed Holden as the aircraft crashed into the sea. "Oh my God, I can't believe this!"

Time seemed to stand still. For one long moment, he could see the glow of the navigation lights blinking beneath the water. Then the night just seemed to swallow them. Holden's mind raced. *What if there are survivors inside that helicopter?* he asked himself. *They must still be alive back there. And now they're waiting for me to rescue them. But how can I pull this off? I don't have a searchlight. I don't have a radio. My steering is bonkers. Maybe I can get my engine warmed up and see if I can't somehow back down on them and pick up whoever* has survived. *But if I get too near the helicopter in these winds and seas, it'll put a hole in my boat and I'll go down, too. Then we'll all be lost!*

Still, I've got to try, reasoned Holden finally. *I'll just fire up my engine and see what I've got here. Then I'll untie my gillnet from the cleats and reel and play out some more net. If I can play it out far enough and drift in close enough, perhaps some of them can swim over to it and grab ahold.*

First things first, Holden, he told himself. *Let's start the engine.* He turned the key and was pleased to find that his battery was still strong. But although his engine cranked over and over, it ultimately refused to start. *The wiring on my engine is soaked,* he was forced to acknowledge. *Just totally soaked.*

Each time he'd gone out the back door to await a rescue basket, more of the torrential rains and sea spray had washed down onto his motor. He deeply regretted now not having bought the diesel engine that he'd contemplated installing the winter before.

Holden was certain that the crewmen were back there in the water, freezing their tails off, if they were alive at all. Frantically, again and again, he cranked over his sea-soaked engine, but with no luck. Finding himself entirely without power now, Holden asked himself, *Is there any way in the world I can still rescue those guys?*

"Mayday! Mayday!" called Skip Holden over his silent radio. "This is the fishing vessel *Marlene*! The fishing vessel *Marlene*! Does anybody hear me?" Though he heard no response, he continued to send out the call. "The Coast Guard helicopter that came out here to get me has crashed! The helicopter's there, but I can't get my engine started!"

With his antenna gone, his battery power running down, and the regenerating powers of the F/V *Marlene*'s main engine flooded out, Skip Holden's radio transmissions had been reduced almost to nothing.

Though Jim Hatfield could no longer hear anything, at that very moment Phil Thum was hanging on every syllable of the bitter news spilling out of his static-filled CB radio. His friend's voice was racked with emotion.

"Oh God, the helicopter crashed!" added Holden. "It got too low and it crashed! The chopper's down! I've got to try and get over to them!"

Thum wasted no time in relaying the message to Lt. Jim Hatfield and his crew in the C-130 circling above.

"Sir, I just received a CB radio transmission from Skip Holden, the skipper aboard the F/V *Marlene*. And he reports that your chopper has just crashed into the water."

The C-130 pilot wept over the radio.

When Skip Holden came back over the radio once again, he, too, was crying. "Don't send anybody else! No more! No more!" Then all radio transmissions from Holden went dead. It was the last anyone heard from him that night.

With the helicopter down, the long nightmarish hours that followed were filled with incessant waves of guilt. Without his engine, Holden knew, he had no hope of saving the crew of the downed Coast Guard helicopter. They would have to make do for themselves, or be lost. For Skip Holden, it was the sickest feeling in the world to know that there was nothing more he could do.

Perhaps the chopper has sunk to the bottom of the ocean with the Coast Guard crew trapped inside, he thought. *Or maybe they were able to deploy their life raft and save themselves.* He prayed that the latter had happened.

Battered and fatigued, but still in the battle, Skip Holden stood out on deck in the first gray light of day and took stock of the prodigious combers that continued to sweep through the area. The wind still howled across the deck and around his wheelhouse, but it was gusting to around fifty miles per hour, rather than the primitive forces of the previous night, which clearly had exceeded one hundred miles per hour.

At last, he felt like he had a chance to do something about his predicament. He finished bailing the latest influx of seawater from his bilge, hauled the remaining bucketfuls of water up out of the hold, and flung them out the door. Then he attempted to repair the CB antenna, but again without luck. Finally, he grabbed a can of starter fluid, sprayed it into the carburetor, and turned the engine over. This time, it rumbled to life.

Throughout the night, Holden's gillnet had been his lifeline. Now, with the engine started and a lonely gray light marking the dawn, he decided to pull in his gillnet and go search for the crew of the Coast Guard helicopter. When he began reeling the net in, however, he found it choked with silver salmon.

If the crewmen were still somehow clinging to life, he needed to move quickly. Tossing several hundred pounds of the fish into the bottom of his hold for ballast, he took a deck hatchet and chopped at the net. The thousand-foot line parted with a sudden explosion, freeing up the boat and releasing the net, buoys, and mother lode of salmon back to the currents.

Holden raced back to the wheelhouse and immediately pointed the *Marlene* toward Cordova. Though he tried to take it slowly, idling carefully along, he found himself from time to time literally surfing down the faces of the towering spires of gray-green ocean passing by underneath him. Any slower and the wheelhouse of the tiny *Marlene* could have been decapitated by the storm waves; any faster and the vessel would have ended up pitchpoling end over end, and he'd have been lost.

Holden had been inching his way along toward the Softuk Bar for close to an hour, keeping his eyes focused on his compass, when, entirely by accident, he stumbled upon the Coast Guard helicopter floating upside down. Except for a set of tires jutting skyward from her amphibious white underbelly, the hull of the inverted H-3 helicopter might have been mistaken for an overturned boat. The two black tires sticking up on a single strut, he would learn later, were part of the nose landing gear, which extended automatically when the aircraft's electrical power was lost.

In the light of day, with his bilge emptied and his engine finally running, Holden had chanced to run upon them. He was ecstatic. *Now I can rescue these guys,* he thought. *Even if I just get one, it'll be worth it.* Holden could hardly believe it. Had he varied so much as a single degree on his course either way, he'd have missed them completely.

A greasy island of fuel and oil lingered around the inverted wreckage, and it somehow appeared to be keeping the foamy portion of the waves from breaking quite so forcefully in the immediate area. He made a large loop out and around the helicopter, "surfing" much of the time, working his way downwind and slowly back again. It was then, as he drew close, that he spotted one of the crew members. He appeared to be tethered by a single hand to the wheel well of the chopper. He was lying facedown in the water in a dead man's float.

"You better be alive!" screamed Holden over and over as he approached. "You better be alive!"

He knew how he was going to rescue the man, too. He was going to motor upwind and toss out a buoy ball with a line attached to it. He'd feed it out and float it back downwind to the waiting crewman. But when he pulled to within twenty feet of the body, he could see that the man was dead. His body was motionless, his arms and legs both outstretched.

Every time a swell went by, the big white hull of the overturned helicopter would sink, disappearing into the depths, a hundred feet or more below, dragging the man's body along with it. To Holden, the helo seemed to remain submerged "forever" before floating back to the surface once again. Realizing finally that there was nothing more he could do, Holden began motoring in around Cape Hinchinbrook. Three hours of running time later, he ran into fellow fisherman Andy Halverson. Halverson thought he was seeing a ghost. "He thought that I was dead," recalls Holden. "He'd heard it on the radio. He'd heard that the F/V *Marlene* was lost and that the four USCG guys were lost, as well."

U.S. Coast Guard helicopter pilot Lt. Pat Rivas (pronounced ree-vas) and copilot Lt. Joe Spoja, as well as flight mechanic Scott Frinfrock and navigator John Snyder, had been out on an ordinary training exercise over on Kodiak Island when Phil Thum's Mayday call first came in.

Several hard-won hours of flight later, they found themselves caught in an unending torrent of record-breaking rainfall, battling fierce ninety-mile-per-hour winds in Prince William Sound. They were flying blind in near whiteout conditions when their Loran C navigational computer shut down, their radar quit, and the onboard HF radio went out. With so much critical equipment malfunctioning, and without the light of day to aid them, it would be tough going.

"Do you know where you are?" asked the C-130 pilot, Lt. Dale Harrington. "Could you give us a position?"

"Okay," replied Pat Rivas. "I think that I'm on a two-hundred-and-twenty-degree bearing from Cordova, about twenty-two miles out. That's the best I can do for you."

A little later, copilot Lt. Jim Hatfield checked back with them. "Hey, boys," he radioed. "Are you all right?"

"We're all right," answered Lt. Joe Spoja. "But we're busy. Please stand by."

Lt. Jim Hatfield remembers it this way: "They made several attempts to get the basket down, with little or no luck because it's such a small boat, a small target, and the seas were terrific and they could not see what they were doing and the boat was swinging around. Pat Rivas was obviously getting concerned that his fatigue would become a factor in this. He mentioned that he was going to be going to Cordova to land . . . that they were getting tired and kicked around quite a bit."

Lt. Dale Harrington recalls that "there was some discussion going on, concerns about fatigue, and Pat felt that he had given it his best shot, obviously, and his comment that I recall was, 'I have tried everything that I know how to do, and under these conditions, the seas, the smallness of the boat, it bobbing around in the wind, and with no hoist reference, I've done everything that I can. Maybe somebody else can come out here and perform this hoist, but I can't. It's beyond my capability. I just can't do it."

It was the last transmission anyone received from the pilot of the doomed chopper.

Faced with dismal weather conditions and massive instrument failure, the crew of helo 1471 had been attempting the rescue under very demanding conditions for an extraordinarily long time; hoists under favorable conditions are often completed in as little as ten minutes. Proceeding with the mission under highly stressful conditions, with no water references except for the occasional glimpses of the fishing vessel *Marlene,* they spent their final hour battling on-scene, trying to remain over the boat and out of the water. And this came directly on the heels of an exhausting three-hour flight from their base on Kodiak Island, which was preceded by another hour or more of flying assigned maneuvers before even being called out on what would be their final mission.

Ultimately, Rivas was forced to acknowledge that he would not be able to complete the hoist. But the decision was made that, before recovering to Cordova for fuel, food, and rest, and to await daylight, they would try and deliver a handheld radio down to Skip Holden. It was then, as they were preparing to do so, a Coast Guard Accident Analysis Board would later surmise, that "they probably relaxed a little. And a slight relaxing was all that was necessary to invite disaster."

The helicopter, the board found, had probably backed down, tail-first, into a passing wave crest. Spinning within precise tolerances at blinding speeds, the tall rotor blades exploded upon impact with the seawater, instantly shearing the four-inch-thick, fifteen-foot-long steel tail-rudder shaft.

The initial impact with the water bent the tail section up. A microsecond later, the chopper's main rotor blades severed it from its own body. This catastrophic mechanical failure sent the H-3 helicopter into a ragged teeter. Staggering through the air like a gyroscope in its last energetic throes, the helo struggled to right itself. Ultimately, however, the unbridled torque toppled the helicopter from the sky as if it had been shoved over a cliff.

When the main rotor blades plowed into the sea itself, they disintegrated upon impact, shattering like icicles fragmenting. Amid the scattering of G-forces and flying plane parts, the twenty-five-foot-long blades were instantly reduced to jagged stubs just twenty-eight inches long. With the weight of her main engines and gearbox both mounted atop the aircraft's back, the straying helicopter immediately flipped over.

The crash and the struggle to survive it must have been nothing short of a nightmare. In the panic of the moment, as the jolting black ice water roared into the inverted space of the helicopter's cabin, the four gasping Coast Guardsmen fought to free themselves and get out.

Those who gained the surface faced what must have been a kind of elemental madness. The spray stung their faces, and as they struggled to see in the wet, suffocating darkness, and to be heard over the roar of the wind filling their ears, twenty-five-foot storm waves began crashing in over them.

Though his body was never found, copilot Lt. Joseph Spoja, thirty-one, exited the plane without a survival suit. The exact specifics of most of his experience will forever remain a mystery, but left to tread the wild, flesh-numbing, forty-four-degree waters of the Gulf of Alaska that night, he could not have survived for long without the thermal protection of either a survival suit or a wet suit, and none were found to be missing.

It was Lieutenant Spoja's first night on duty at the base in Kodiak. The father of three young children, his wife pregnant with the fourth, Spoja hadn't even finished unloading his furniture and belongings back in Kodiak when he was called out on the mission.

Only recently married, twenty-one-year-old radio man John Snyder probably succumbed soon after the crash as a result of partial incapacitation from head injuries and because his flotation collar had not been inflated. Clad in a wet suit as he was, Snyder might have lived for several hours, eventually expiring due to his injuries and his inability to keep his head out of the water.

Although no one was killed outright by the impact of the crash itself, the helicopter's pilot, the ever-popular and athletic Lt. Earnie "Pat" Rivas, age thirty-three, was tossed forward so violently that he struck the instrument panel with his head, shattering the sixth cervical vertebra in his neck. Still, he did manage to exit the inverted aircraft.

With his neck fractured and blood draining from a cut on his forehead, Rivas was no doubt certain in the knowledge that since he was without a survival suit, hypothermia would soon disable and kill him. Yet somehow he maintained enough clarity of mind in his injured state to unlace and remove both of his heavy, steel-toed flight boots, probably in an effort to facilitate swimming.

Somebody had to go back inside the inverted helicopter to locate and retrieve the life raft strapped inside. Perhaps Scotty Frinfrock had also helped. Dragged to the surface, the powerful CO_2 canisters inflated the raft with a burst, and the pressing storm winds immediately launched it across the water. But when the sea-painter line (which serves as both the canister activator and the line tethering the raft to the individual holding it) came tight, unbelievably, the knot on the raft-end parted, and the windblown raft began to streak away. The speed of its departure was checked only by the fact that the raft was ballasted with pockets of cloth that fill up with water, built into the bottom of the raft.

After all the equipment failure, and the surreal experience of the crash itself, and with two small children and his lovely wife Linnea at home awaiting his safe return back in Kodiak, the vision of the departing life raft must have broken Pat Rivas' heart. Shattered vertebra or not, he was in exceptional physical condition and, as those close to him will tell you, bulldog-determined to wrestle the best that could be had from any given situation. Having already disposed of his flight boots, and dressed in little more than his standard pilot's thin blue cotton jumpsuit, with his water-wings inflated (two sets of air bags connected by straps slung under both armpits), Pat Rivas probably decided to give chase. He must have known that the life raft was their only real chance.

Seated by the helicopter's side door, twenty-five-year-old hoist operator (flight mechanic) Scott Frinfrock was, in all likelihood, the first to escape, and the last to die. While his crewmates swam off, were washed away, or were fast dying of a combination of hypothermia and injuries, he carried out a furious campaign to remain with the aircraft and to survive the ordeal. Despite the icy sweep of angry wave-water twenty feet deep pounding over him, Frinfrock not only refused to give up; he waged open war.

Wearing a one-piece wet suit, booties, and a survival vest, Frinfrock battled the impossible. When the F/V *Daryl J* came upon the inverted helo several days later near Naked Island up in Prince William Sound, divers flown to the scene soon discovered that someone had removed the strobe light and the ancient AR/URT-33A Emergency Locator Transmitter (ELT) from inside the overturned helicopter and had tied them to a fitting near the aircraft's side door. The MK13 flares had also been removed and were missing, as was a signaling mirror.

Five of seven cartridges in Frinfrock's own pen-gun flare kit were either spent or missing. Scotty might have made it, too, had his ELT worked properly, but its off/on switch had somehow been broken off, leaving him no way to activate it.

When they found his body washed up on the rocky shore the next day, he was wearing an orange wet suit, an uninflated neck pillow, and no headgear or gloves. Coast Guard searchers also found a thirty-foot-long section of yellow trail line attached to him. In one final, last-ditch effort, Scotty Frinfrock had apparently tried to tether himself to the hulk of the overturned helicopter. He may have continued the struggle for as long as six hours before the force of the pummeling seas finally broke the line that held him, sweeping him away.

And so, with the life raft gone, the relentless onslaught of storm waves thundering down upon them, and no electronic means of signaling others of the location of their downed helicopter, the fate of the heroic crew of helo 1471 was sealed. Lost and adrift at night, scattered across the vast wilderness waters of the Gulf of Alaska, these men stood no chance of being rescued.

At first light, a massive manhunt was launched. Search and rescue airplanes, boats, and helicopters from the Coast Guard and air force bases in Anchorage, Juneau, Kodiak, and Sitka relentlessly combed the area for any signs of life.

Searchers soon found the life raft, fully inflated and in perfect repair (without the tethering line), washed up on rugged Montague Island. Nearby, they came upon the body of one of the crewmen lying facedown, partially buried in the surf and sand. The man was wearing little more than a pilot's thin blue cotton jumpsuit and a set of water-wings under each arm. Then the shaken Coast Guard searchers noticed something odd; both of the man's flight boots were missing.

Excerpt from *Journeys Through the Inside Passage*

JOE UPTON

JOE UPTON is a writer and fisherman with more than twenty years' experience exploring the waters of Alaska and British Columbia. He currently lives on Bainbridge Island, Washington, with his wife and two children. This title can be found at fine bookstores everywhere and at www.gacpc.com.

How could I forget that night Stormy was born? We were beach logging that winter, that whole stretch from Ratz Harbor down to Thorne Bay, and living in a tent on the shore. Each day we'd be out there from first light until dusk, trying to get those big ones off the beach. Sometimes we'd work a whole day just getting the one log off. You'd have to cut smaller logs to skid them with, and then use the big screw jacks, just a couple of inches at a time until finally you got them down where the tide could reach them. George, he had a big saw, with a forty-eight-inch bar on it, and he could barely get through some of those logs, going both ways, that's how big they were. But what wood—beautiful, straight-grained stuff, the kind they call piano spruce. If [the logging company] had known the kind of wood along there, they would never have sold us the rights so cheap. Or maybe they just figured it was so exposed along there that no one could ever get them logs off.

Four months we worked to get the raft together. It was going to be a good paycheck, and we were talking about buying some land or a new boat.

I went into labor the day before the tug came to tow the raft over to the sawmill. George called for a plane with the CB we had in the tent. I don't think the pilot would have even tried to get in, the wind was blowing so bad by then, if he didn't know that my baby was coming. He finally set her down on about the fifth try, and came alongside the log raft and I got in. George had to stay with the logs and wait for the tug. We wouldn't get paid until we delivered those logs to the mill, so we couldn't take chances . . . we had a whole winter's work into those logs. When we took off, I could look down and see George working on the lines that kept the log raft tied in the cove, keeping 'em from chafing. He said he'd hitch a ride in with the tug and see me in town.

It blew like hell that whole night I was in the hospital, and all I could think about was them logs and George and that raft in that cove. I had a little boy, right in the middle of the worst of it.

George came in the next morning, and right off when I saw his face I knew something had happened.

"The raft's gone," he said. "I thought we could make it. We got about halfway across, then the chains busted . . . those logs are scattered up and down the strait now."

That whole winter's work, gone just like that. The nurse gave him the little boy then, and he asked me what I thought up for a name.

"Stormy," I said. I knew right off without thinking . . . we'd name him for the night he came into the world and when all them logs was lost.

—A friend

The woods and the sea—in no other place in North America are the two as intertwined in the lives of the inhabitants as they are along the coast of Southeast Alaska.

Stormy's mom and dad lived in a home built on a raft of floating logs in a cove away from town. In the winter they would trap in the woods for beaver, living for long periods in tiny shacks dotted along the watersheds of Prince of Wales Island. Sometimes, after Stormy came along, his mom would hunt with him in a backpack. Once, she tracked a wounded deer for most of a day, deeper and deeper into the forest. When she had found and skinned it, she shifted the child around to her front, put the meat on her back, and walked through the night to their home. In the summer the couple would take their small gill-net boat up a remote slough near the British Columbia border. They would haul a log-float and cabin off the beach, tie it between two islands, and live out of it during the salmon season.

Living in a home on a log raft was rarely dull. When it was rainy she might send the kids to fish through the seat in the outhouse into the clear salt water below. Problems could develop that a land person would never encounter.

We kept smelling propane around our float home, and finally George tracked it down to the propane tank: you know, one of those hundred-pound cylinders. Well, he tried to tighten it, but it just started leaking worse, and we had a wood stove inside and all, plus the smoker going, and we were just afraid that the whole thing was going to catch on fire. So he just unhooked it and rolled it into the bay, let it start drifting out with the tide. George just figured he'd let 'er float out a ways and then sink it with a shot from his rifle.

This was something different to watch, course, so I was out there with the kids, watching. But then his first shot, it knocked the valve off that sucker, and with all that gas shooting out of it, it started heading right back at us, just like a goddamned torpedo! If it had ever hit the raft at the speed it was going, it would probably have blown up and we all would have been goners! We got a porthole set into our door, and he got up there and rested his rifle in it to get a better shot. But that darned propane bottle, it wasn't making it very easy for him. Every time he got a good bead on it, it'd take a dive and plow under water for ten or twenty yards before surfacing, still headed right for us. When he finally got it, on the third shot, he blew a hole right in its side, sent it spinning before it finally sank, but for a while there, I was sure we were goners.

—A friend

Today the infant she carried works in a log-sorting yard forty miles away on the other side of the island. His mother works as a flagger on the logging roads that crisscross the land. She has no phone for direct communication with her son and new granddaughter, but occasionally a driver of one of the huge log trucks will toot his horn, slow, and point to a message spray-painted on the rough sides of the logs: "Hi Mom, Annie got her first tooth, hope you're O.K. Love, Stormy."

When Vancouver explored this area of Clarence Strait, which is the wide channel north from Ketchikan, it was late in his second season of exploration. He had traveled almost a thousand miles with his two ships and many more in the small boats since entering the Juan de Fuca Strait the previous June. If he was discouraged, he didn't say so.

Here and in most of Southeast Alaska, the peaks that define the boundary with Canada form a dramatic snowy wall in the east. In the mornings, the mountains, shining and cold, loom above the land along the coast. It would be hard for an explorer to see these and think there might be a path through. Yet Vancouver continued north, drafting his chart with remarkable accuracy. He must have been an unusually talented seaman, or unusually lucky, for his journey became a series of close calls with stormy weather, poor visibility, and rocky shores.

Vancouver's crews' relations with the natives seemed to be deteriorating. On August 12, in a place he named Traitors Cove, twenty-five miles north of what is now Ketchikan, Vancouver and his party were attacked. Only Lieutenant Swaine's timely arrival in the launch and his firing a volley of pistol shot into the natives saved the situation. The natives fled, but the incident was a reason for alarm. Vancouver speculated that white traders had begun to show up on the coast, and that they were giving inferior goods for the highly valued sea otter pelts.

And I am extremely concerned to be compelled to state here, that many of the traders from the civilised world have not only pursued a line of conduct, diametrically opposite to the true principles of justice in their commercial dealings, but have fomented discords, and stirred up contentions, between the different tribes, in order to increase the demand for these destructive engines. They have been likewise eager to instruct the natives in the use of European arms of all descriptions, and have shewn by their own example, that they consider gain as the only object of pursuit; and whether this be acquired by fair and honorable means, or otherwise, so long as the advantage is secured, the manner how it is obtained seems to have been, with too many of them, but a very secondary consideration.

—Vancouver, *A Voyage of Discovery*

CLARENCE STRAIT

In February 1971, I traveled up Clarence Strait in a new, 108-foot, steel king-crab boat. The vast clear-cuts in the Tongass National Forest that would so change the face of the land within a decade or so were still for the most part hidden behind the hills. We traveled the entire strait without seeing another boat, and so I suppose what we saw, except for the snow, was little different from what Vancouver had seen.

The morning was still. We'd passed Ketchikan in the night, and first light came to us in lower Clarence Strait. A thin, cold, low, winter light shafted across the cold and snow-covered land from the border peaks. All day we steamed north between forested and snow-covered shores. If there was any life on the land we passed, we couldn't see it.

In the early northern dusk we came to Wrangell Narrows. There the channel winds for twenty miles between two islands, in places barely a stone's throw wide. Partway through, we passed a log cabin, its windows lit both from within and from the pastel sky above. Smoke from the chimney rose into still air. Snow lay deep around it, a graceful little wooden vessel at a mooring before it.

The rest of our trip north was terrible. We were bound for the ice pack, the winter fishery in the desolate reaches of the Bering Sea, far to the west and north on the edge of Siberia. The bitter cold froze the spray instantly to our hull, making us dangerously top-heavy with ice. What should have taken a week stretched into a month.

The Bering Sea was a windy wasteland, on whose shores there were few trees, settlements, or shelter for boats. The wind blew the cups off the anemometer; the ice chewed the paint off our hull.

But in 1971, the Bering Sea king crab fishery was the equivalent of the gold rush. Deep beneath the stormy surface, a vast herd of king crab, spidery creatures with leg spans of perhaps six feet, roamed. We fished with pots the size of a small room, seven by seven by three feet. In some places we had our pots as close together as we could place them without tangling the buoy lines. Fishing around the clock and pulling each trap every day and a half, we would bring up pots so full the meshes were bulging, some containing a ton of legal-size crab. It was apparent that the herd of crab on the bottom was several feet thick. Fishing was simply a contest of how long the crew could stay awake.

We began our season on the edge of the ice pack, fishing two or three weeks at a time without seeing another boat. We ended it crowded in with the rest of the fleet, off the turbulent mouths of the passes between the North Pacific Ocean and the Bering Sea.

All that time, fishing off that treeless, bleak, and windy shore, the memory of the log cabin seen in Clarence Strait in winter dusk stayed with me. When the season was over and the opportunity presented itself, I bought a thirty-two-foot salmon gill-net boat and made plans to return to the forested island wilderness of Southeast Alaska.

I came by chance to the roadless settlement of Port Protection on the northern tip of Prince of Wales Island in June of 1972. "Port P," the locals call the place. This is the anchorage Vancouver found when he desperately needed it on Sunday evening, September 8, 1793. His two ships had been exploring the north side of Sumner Strait, making sure they missed no navigable channel. A storm had been threatening from the south all day long, and the ships crossed to the southern shore to try to anchor. But the water was deep right up to the beach, and the ships couldn't anchor; with the light failing, they faced the prospect of a difficult night. At dusk, Lieutenant Broughton in the *Chatham* passed Point Baker, where the shore turns sharply from west to southwest, and he signaled Vancouver that he had found what appeared to be an anchorage.

We had scarcely furled the sails, when the wind shifting to the southeast, the threatened storm from that quarter, began to blow, and continued with increasing violence during the whole night; we had, however, very providentially reached an anchorage that completely sheltered us from its fury, and most probably from imminent danger, if not from total destruction. Grateful for such an asylum, I named it Port Protection.

—Vancouver, *A Voyage of Discovery*

Near Port Protection, Susanna and I built a cabin looking out on Sumner Strait. The tide runs hard there, filling any still night with its distant roar. When the wind blew and the trees swayed and creaked around the cabin, I'd look out our window at the churning strait and the wild and unpeopled land beyond. I would imagine Vancouver and his men sailing those cumbersome ships on that evening 180 years before, passing just off our cabin site anxiously seeking shelter.

Or I would think of all the ships that had carried the herd of humanity to the Klondike: the *Valencia* and the *Cottage City*, the *Clara Nevada* and the *Al-Ki*, the *Islander*, the *Yucatan*, the *City of Seattle*, and dozens of others.

In the black distance, winking as it bobbed up and down in the swell pushing up the strait from the ocean, was the buoy that marked Mariposa Reef. Here, on a November night in 1917, Captain Johnny O'Brien napped in his cabin, his vessel steered by a pilot. Sumner Strait runs like a river, and the swift currents carried the fast and beautifully appointed liner, *Mariposa*, onto the rocks, where she remained.

Ghosts passed before me. The three-master, *Star of Bengal*, was towed past Point Baker in September 1920 behind two tugs. Before they reached the open sea where they would free her for the trip to San Francisco, a storm drove in from the gulf. The tugs cut the big bark loose and ran for shelter. At Helm Point, a thousand-foot sheer cliff on the south side of Coronation Island, the sea became the grave for 111 out of the 132 aboard.

When we had come there, the settlements at Port Protection and Point Baker, two miles apart, formed a community of perhaps sixty people. They created an Alaska very different from the towns where the sawmills and the canneries were. Settlements like these were reached only by boat and floatplane. They were communities unto themselves, isolated from the bustle of the larger towns. There was no telephone, no central power or water, no school.

In 1972 these two places had something few other spots in Southeast Alaska had: a piece of land a person could buy. Almost all the land was part of the Tongass National Forest; little was available for settlers. Before the discovery of oil in Prudhoe Bay, when Alaska was a slower-paced place, the forest service, which administers the Tongass National Forest, had a more casual approach to squatters on government land. But the oil rush and the seventies brought people seeking their own little piece of the wilderness, and the forest service, faced with an increasing number of illegal squatters, had little choice but to enforce the law.

Fortunately, the forest service had established a policy of opening for further settlement places around existing communities. In a few sheltered coves, of which Port Protection was one, a person could lease a building lot for a nominal fee.

One of the new families was a young couple from Chicago. They came because they heard land was available; they leased a piece and began to clear it. They were city folk, their woods skills little developed, and they became the butt of jokes for doing things like leaving their chain saw on the beach and wondering where it was when the tide came up. The locals had built their homes on the beach or close enough to it for good access. They thought the newcomers foolish for trying to build on a site so high they'd had to construct a cable tramway from the beach to haul up supplies.

One October day, when our fishing season was done, I visited their home site. The lot was a stubby peninsula, dividing the outer bay from the sheltered cove. It was thickly wooded and rose to a ridge perhaps sixty feet up from the water. They had chosen the top of the ridge to build on, a crest, falling away to the water on both sides. They had completed the platform, the plywood base on which their house would be erected. Enough of the great spruces and hemlocks had been felled to frame dramatic views of the water. It was cool the day we visited, and our breath hung in the air before us. The first frost of the fall lay on the yellowish plywood and the fallen trees that surrounded us.

It was a magic place. The broad plywood floor seemed the size of a dance hall, and it commanded a dramatic view of Sumner Strait to the north and west and of Wooden Wheel Cove, the cabins, the boats, and the community to the south and east. Our new friends described how they were going to build, where the windows and the door would be. I barely listened, wandering back and forth across the plywood in awe of what they were doing. No matter what others thought for building up there, it was a hauntingly beautiful place for a home.

The following spring, the house was up. At first they had tried to build a stockade-style log home from the dozens of huge trees that lay felled like pickup sticks all around the house site. The logs, so heavy they had to be jacked and winched in place, kept falling over. Finally they ordered a load of timbers to be sent out on the mail boat from the sawmill in Wrangell, forty-two miles east. The mail boat lowered the timbers into the water. They floated them to the beach and hauled them up a few at a time on the pulleys of the gasoline-powered tramway.

Then they built the house, as if with Lincoln Logs, stacking and spiking the timbers together on their sides and cutting out the door and window openings later with a chain saw.

It wasn't perfect. The green timbers, spiked together with little or no caulking, dried and shrank from the heat of the woodstove inside, allowing snow and wind to blow through the cracks. The crudely cut and split cedar shakes that covered the exterior walls ran in drooping lines. The bottom of the stairs ended in a wall, without room for a landing. The woodstove leaked; the inside of the house smelled of creosote and stale food.

The house was something settlers a hundred years before might have put together. But for those new Alaskans, it was a remarkable achievement, although it hadn't been without a price. As temporary quarters they had constructed a tiny, perhaps eight-by-ten, windowless cabin in the thick woods. The winter there had been dark, gloomy, and extremely long. In the fall, my friend's wife had been cheery, outgoing. In the spring, she seemed almost catatonically depressed; it took her years to recover.

My own cabin was a simple twelve-by-sixteen frame affair with a covered back porch and a sleeping loft. It came down to what was the least expensive structure that we would live in. We got our windows and doors at Seattle garage sales and prefabricated the kitchen counter, sink, and drawers. Friends hauled the pieces of our new life north on their fish packers. We took the rest aboard our own boat and headed north, towing a skiff laden with all the odds and ends needed to build a cabin. It was May 1973.

Early every morning we'd take our little outboard from the dock at Point Baker and motor through the twisting back channel between the cabins of our neighbors. We'd come around the corner into our cove and look with awe at the little home we were creating.

When it was done, we walked around it in wonder. Sumner Strait was out the front, Mount Calder and the channel to Port P out the back. We put our sleeping bags in the loft and made driftwood furniture.

It was a tiny house, little more than a shack. Yet even that small project impressed me with the difficulty of getting anything done in the wilderness, so far from the nearest store. Every time I visited my friend's house on the point, I was amazed at the dimension of what they had taken on, flawed though it was.

In the early 1970s, forest service leases were running around twelve hundred dollars a year, and there was a good possibility that the lessees would eventually be able to buy their leased land at very reasonable prices. And not only was there land, there was good fishing close at hand.

Most of the newcomers took up hand trolling, towing arrays of salmon baits, plugs, and spoons through the water, cranking the fish aboard with little winches called hand gurdies. The small vessels that fished this way were baby brothers to the power trollers, larger vessels that fished four lines they hauled up by engine power.

Most fishing boats in the region have at least modest quarters and a stove of some sort, for most of the fisheries involve a stay of days or weeks away from town. But many of the young settlers in places like Port Protection could only afford open skiffs, puddle jumpers as they were known locally. A Briggs & Stratton air-cooled engine was connected to the propeller shaft with an arrangement of belts and pulleys to provide affordable propulsion. When the fishing wasn't good at Baker, these men packed up their gear, and sometimes their families, and tented, following the fish up and down the coast.

This was an echo of the past, of the twenties and thirties, when hand trollers fished and traveled in fleets, setting up tent cities on remote islands and following the fish. Often far from the nearest settlement, they depended on fish-buying vessels for gas and supplies.

In those days, many fishermen couldn't afford engines of any kind, and they worked their boats with long oars which they employed by standing up and facing forward.

Sure, for you boys in your big power boats, you don't think nothing of going down to Noyes Island, or up to Icy Strait, if you get a tip that's where the fish are . . . jes set the auto pilot, get a cup of coffee, put yer feet up and enjoy the ride, cruising along at ten, eleven knots. You ought to take a trip down with us, taking every long cut we can to get out of the weather, going along at six knots, standing out there in your oilskins with no toasty oil stove to belly up to. You ought to try finding some place to beach yer skiff and set up your tent and get some hot grub in ya some evening with the rain pouring down, after y' been fishing since maybe four or five that morning.

—A friend

In an average to better year, a good hand troller working out of Point Baker, home in his own bed every night, might be able to catch six or eight thousand dollars' worth of fish.

Fishing was pretty much done by the first of October, and money was hard to come by after that. Trolling for kings was still open, but those winter kings were generally few and far between. If a guy hadn't made his season in the summer, the long dark months between October and April could be pretty hard. A person could always go into town (Wrangell or Ketchikan) for the winter and work in the pulp mills or sawmills, but trapping was about the only other local alternative for money.

We ended up trapping for most of the winter. Most of the good trapping territory around Port P was pretty much already taken, so we ended up quite a ways away. That meant we had to live in the little bow-picker [a twenty-six-foot gill-net boat], instead of our little cabin. Luckily there were plenty of minks and martens where we ended up, but it was a cold old winter, and that bow-picker wasn't really set up for it.

We didn't have a diesel stove, just the little propane cooker, so it was always cold. The worst of it was that the walls weren't insulated, so after we turned the stove off and went to bed at night, all that moisture would condense on the walls and freeze. It didn't bother John too much, he's got short hair, but about every other morning, I'd wake up and my hair would be froze to the wall. I couldn't even move until John got up, heated up some water, and melted the ice. I didn't mind the rest of it, but that part wasn't much fun.

—A friend

But still, where else in the whole country could you get a piece of land on the water, start building your house, buy a fishing boat, and start making enough money to live on, all for less than five thousand bucks?

Plus, part of the deal with leasing one of the lots from the forest service was that you got to cut ten thousand board feet of lumber free, plenty to build a small house with. In 1977, one of the young settlers brought in a small sawmill powered by a Volkswagen engine and the land rush was on.

The first to be built on were the lots along the shore, followed by those in the second or third row back, where the trees were monsters, six and eight feet in diameter, eighty or a hundred feet to the first branch. The new settlers cut just enough to clear a house site, putting crude plank boardwalks across the boggy places.

To walk among the back lots in the mid- and late 1970s was like stepping back in time: crude plank houses were taking shape among the dark forest giants, with the wood smoke rising into the dripping canopy above. They looked like the photographs of early settlements in Alaska, Washington, and Oregon.

Most of the older folks more or less welcomed the younger fishermen to the community and shared with them their experience and their knowledge of the fisheries. A few resented the newcomers.

That first spring I started out halibut fishing out of my skiff. It was just a 16-footer with a Briggs & Stratton for power, and I only had three skates of gear. [A skate is a unit of halibut gear, usually a hundred hooks, six hundred feet of line, and a buoy and anchor at each end.] I tried to go out where there wasn't any other gear set, you know, so I wouldn't step on anyone's toes, being a newcomer and all, but I kept losing gear. I'd set out my gear, come back the next day; and it wouldn't be there. At first I thought it might be the tide sweeping the buoys under, so I went out at slack water looking, but still, no buoys. I was wild, the only thing I could figure was that someone was cutting me off, that they didn't want me fishing there.

So finally I took my rifle out with me and camped on my gear; I put up a tent in woods, where I could look out and see my buoy. I hid the tent pretty well, and took my skiff way up around a bend in the creek, so you'd never see it from the salt water, and just waited. Sure enough, just at first light the next morning, this boat came around the point and stopped right by my buoy. I'd set so that the buoy was pretty close to the shore, so he wasn't more than fifty yards from where I was hiding in the woods. I'd already sighted in my rifle on the buoy the night before. The guy grabbed a gaff hook, and he was just getting ready to pick up my buoy, and I put a shot into the water about ten feet off his stern. That was all it took. He looked around, real surprised like, and put his gaff slowly back on the deck. You know, I'd see the guy around town sometimes, and he'd nod to me like everyone else, but I didn't have no trouble after that.

—A friend

A few hundred yards away from our cabin was the place where the tidal currents boil as Sumner Strait turns a sharp corner. These eddies churned plankton to the surface and were a favorite spot for humpback whales in the summer. On a still evening, when there was no wind to rustle the trees around our cabin, you could clearly hear the whales blowing as they surfaced after a few minutes underwater.

The eddies were a popular fishing spot, where I suggested my parents go to catch a salmon when they visited one summer. My skiff that year was a typical puddle jumper, powered with a Briggs & Stratton engine. It ran well, but I hadn't finished installing the controls, so the speed could only be controlled by turning a screw in and out on the carburetor. I started the engine for them, and sent them out to the tide rip, while I remained at our net float, working on gear. "Oh yeah," I said as they departed, "there's a bunch of whales that fool around in that tide rip, but they shouldn't bother you."

A little later I heard what sounded like screams and looked out to see my parents and the skiff more or less surrounded by a pod of whales, coming up all around them. When they finally made it back to the float they were pale from their experience. The engine had stopped, and before they could get it restarted, the whales were playing all around them; what had looked fascinating from a distance was terrifying up close.

Although our cabin was on a secluded cove, it was only a ten-minute skiff ride from neighbors and the settlement at Point Baker. At night the darkness was broken only by the flashing light at West Rock, where Sumner Strait turns the corner.

In the summer, cruise ships would pass, floating cities like the four-hundred-foot *Spirit of London*. They'd come around the point, filling up the darkness with light and the odd, out-of-place noise of music and voices. They'd pass beyond the other point, and there would be only the dark and the sigh of the wind or the rush of the tide.

Just inside the harbor entrance at Point Baker was a bar and general store built on a log raft, with plenty of room for vessels to tie up. In this fashion, the nasty problem of having to negotiate a steep and slippery ramp down to one's boat after having a few drinks was avoided. The Point Baker floating bar was the closest drinking spot to good fishing grounds in all of Alaska. Of course, for people used to more urban bars, like myself in 1972, the Point Baker floating bar took a little getting used to. We tied up there after an eight- or ten-day trip from Seattle; I thought I'd stand the couple on the boat traveling with us, our "running partner" for the trip, to a round of drinks.

The bartender turned from the rough-looking fellows at the other stools and came over to us.

"What'll it be, fellas?"

"Let's see," Susanna said, "maybe I'll have a stinger. How 'bout you, Joe, want your usual rum and tonic?"

"Look here, pals," the bartender replied, "we got whiskey and water, whiskey and Coke, and whiskey and Tang. What's it gonna be?"

The cook in the back occasionally wore boots. As time passed and the logs became waterlogged, the building would ride a little lower in the water, and on a busy night with a lot of customers aboard he might be ankle-deep in salt water.

Behind the building that housed the bar lay the sixty-foot tug and onetime fish-buying vessel *Dividend,* which the owners used to transport supplies out from Petersburg. The walls and floors of the fish hold were carpeted, because the vessel had served as their home until they were able to move into more roomy quarters ashore. One summer, when there was an unexpectedly large run of fish in the area and a shortage of fish packers, the *Dividend* was pressed into service, carpeting and all.

"Yeah," the owner laughed later, "those were probably the first fish in Alaska to go to town in a *carpeted fish hold!*"

It may be no surprise that a bar so close to good fishing attracts its own sort of people. One rainy night, I had tied to the float to sleep for a few hours before going out to make the daylight set with my gill net. Before I hit the bunk, though, I put on my rain gear and stepped out onto the float to take the dog for a walk. The dimly lighted windows of the bar provided but the faintest visibility, and as I walked past what I thought was a bundle of trash on the dock, a hand reached up and grabbed my leg. I stopped, startled, and looked down. Another hand reached up to me with a pint bottle of whiskey.

"Hey, young fellow," a throaty, rasping voice called out, "care for a snort?"

I recognized the prone shape as one of our senior local fishermen, who was taking a little rest on the float before he got into his skiff to row off in the dark to his cabin. It was an awful mean night, so I took him up on his kind offer.

Most people in these remote communities were there because they liked it the way it was. When the forest service announced a plan to expand the network of logging roads to serve Port P and Point Baker, it stirred up a hornet's nest of opposition. Alerted by the residents, national environmental organizations got involved.

The most vocal opponent of the proposed roads was a young man whose skiff we had taken to calling the *Widow-Maker*. In Southeast, *a widow-maker* is a logger's term for a dangerously leaning tree or an overhanging branch that could fall on a careless or unlucky logger. In this case, it was the young man's Boston Whaler, which was dangerously overpowered with a very high horsepower Mercury outboard he had hung on it, and doubly dangerous for the way the controls were set up, or not set up. You steered with the steering wheel in the middle seat, but the engine controls were not connected there, so the engine could only be controlled from the stern. What this Port P resident usually did was point the boat straight, start the engine, get it going full speed, say forty knots, and then clamber over the seat to the steering station as the craft was pounding over the choppy bay. Also, because the Boston Whaler is basically unsinkable, and because it rains a great deal in Southeast Alaska, he usually left the boat at the dock with the drain plug out, so the water would seek its own level and flow out the plug whenever he used the boat. As everyone in the community basically wore knee-high rubber boots, or "Alaska tennis shoes," when they were out and about, having four or five inches of water in one's skiff wasn't a problem.

One afternoon I happened to be on the dock when a chartered floatplane arrived with representatives of both the National Audubon Society and the Sierra Club, dressed in city clothes. They seemed taken aback when they realized their ride to the next bay, where the locals were trying to stop the siting of a logging camp, was the *Widow-Maker*. They came back paler still. Later I got the story of their skiff ride across the bay.

I was just trolling along off the mouth of the back channel when I sees the *Widow-Maker* screaming through with these two dudes all dressed up in city slicker clothes fer passengers, lookin' scared out of their wits and holding on fer all they was worth. They got about halfway across, and all of a sudden the driver sees a bunch of ducks starting to get off the water ahead. He always kept a shotgun aboard, like we all do, but because of where those controls were and everything, he knew that if he took the time to get back to the controls and slow down, those ducks would have been history. So he just grabbed the shotgun, let go of the steering wheel, stood up and started blasting away at the ducks, and them dipping along full bore. Man, I didn't know who those dudes were, but even I could tell that they weren't really ready for *that!*

—A friend

The story may or may not be true, but it gives a sense of the gulf of perception and understanding that sometimes existed between the people of the outport communities and the people on the outside who became involved in their affairs.

In the summer, most of my neighbors and I were busy fishing. Sometimes we'd be gone from Baker for weeks or months at a time, following the fish up and down the coast. It was in the fall and winter that we had time to visit.

The woods were so thick that even to visit a neighbor, most people used their skiffs. Many of our friends were in Port Protection, which we reached via a winding and rocky channel. On one November visit, we stayed later than anticipated. What had begun as an impromptu visit became a full-fledged dinner party—two chickens went to the block—and our friend, a colorful tugboat operator turned gill-netter, showed us around his place. Over the previous winter he had constructed a big barn and filled it with his possessions, which previously he had stashed here and there all over Southeast Alaska. The whole building was filled with . . . stuff. Old engines, old nets, pieces of boats, boxes of magazines, broken furniture. Our friend walked us through it and proudly waved around at the incredible collection.

"And it's all here by *choice*!"

When we stepped outside to head home, the night was cloudless and extremely dark. A mist lay on the surface of the bay, through which we made our way.

I had forgotten the compass so we navigated by sound. Two of the families had little generators popping away, making electricity for their freezers and lights. We'd travel a few minutes, then shut off our outboard and listen to orient ourselves. When the sound of the generators became faint and finally died away to nothing, it would be the sea, washing softly on the rocks of the shore, that we'd listen for.

When we came to the back channel, the tide was extremely low. Parts of the channel were wide enough for two boats to pass at high tide but barely wide enough for our skiff at low tide. At night, by flashlight, with kelp-draped rocks looming unnaturally large all around us, it seemed totally unfamiliar. For part of it we had to shut off the outboard, tilt it up, and push ourselves through, the water was so thin.

"You know where we are?" Susanna's question only reinforced my doubts. The channel which I thought I knew so well suddenly seemed not familiar at all. We stopped again and again for a long listen, for we should have been near some of the other houses at Point Baker; I hoped to see a light, hear the sound of a generator. But it was late, the generators probably shut down, and there was only the distant rush of the tide in the strait, and the wet sounds of rain in the woods close at hand.

Then we heard our dog barking, and we followed the channel until our flashlight revealed the slippery rock bank below our cabin, and we were home.

WILDERNESS PEOPLE CAN BE WILDER than the WILDLIFE

IT TAKES A pretty hardy soul to take on Alaska on its own terms. Particularly when a person gets away from the streets of Anchorage or Fairbanks, Alaska can be a force to be reckoned with. Beautiful, yes. It's a land where every vista is a Kodak moment. But that beauty is hardly safe. Alaska's untamed and dangerous beauty is exactly what draws real Alaskans into the backwoods and tundra. They crave the challenge that the land gives them. Whether they face angry bears, hungry wolves, winds so bitingly cold that unprotected skin freezes within seconds, broken ice and freezing waters that can kill in an instant, they have found what they came to Alaska for—a land that's as wild and free as they are. Naturally, such people lead lives that are as epic and unpredictable as Alaska itself. These are some of the stories they tell. . . .

LARRY KANIUT

◈ LARRY KANIUT is the author of the classic books *Alaska Bear Tales, More Alaska Bear Tales, Cheating Death,* and *Danger Stalks the Land.* He's also the editor of this book—though his contributions to this volume were picked by his co-editor, Denise Little, because he's much too self-effacing to include his own work. This story can also be found in Larry's forthcoming book, *Swallowed Alive.* More about Larry, his many books, and his very interesting life can be found at www.kaniut.com. ◈

WHAT IF?

*T*HOUSANDS OF STAMPEDERS *headed for the Throndiuk River in Canada's Yukon Territory in the late 1890s. That was its geographic name before the newsmen got hold of it, changing the Indian word meaning "hammer water" into Klondike. The locale was a place of trapping salmon by way of hammering wood posts into the streambed. The Klondike discovery was made and the rush was on.*

Some years later Harry Boyden followed his predecessors to the gold fields near Dawson City, arriving in 1908. Four years after that he joined gold stampeders flocking to Chisana in the Wrangell–St. Elias country, a couple of hundred miles south of Dawson City. Harry prospected and freighted cargo in the White River–Nabesna area before moving to McCarthy in 1936.

He later returned to the Chisana area, where he ran a trading post at Nabesna until 1957. He then built a cabin at Chistochina Flats and resided there until his death in March 1968. During the last thirty years of his life Harry gained fame as a guide. The same legendary Alaska guide tells this story.

I t didn't look good. It never does when a man goes solo into the wilderness and is caught out back of beyond with little food and gear, especially when the weather is well below zero. It was 1925, and the trekker was in a pickle. He was deep in the White River country near the Alaska-Yukon border, a savage and unforgiving land. Only by piecing together the evidence he left—scrawled notes, equipment, clothing, tracks, and his own remains—would the survivors be able to guess at what happened on his journey.

H e was in the Wrangell Mountains. Thoughts of *what if* plagued him. *What if I'd brought more gear? More food? An extra horse? What if I'd come two weeks earlier?* as he looked off into the black of night, his tiny fire brought some solace. He sipped weak tea and planned the next twenty-four hours.

While wet snow pelted his rain pants and slicker, he cursed the white stuff that was already a foot deep. He'd been in more jams than he cared to remember and knew he'd find a way out of this one. His journey had been compounded by a dead horse, lack of food, and now the snow.

He'd ridden horseback into the mountains, but the horse had wandered off one night. For several days he'd searched for it, finding no sign of the animal. Then he saw a flock of ravens circling downriver a couple of miles. He went to investigate and found his horse at the base of a cut bank. It looked like the horse had dropped from the fifty-foot bluff and broken its neck. The discovery was disappointing, but it was not a cause for great concern. Just one that demanded a change in strategy.

The man turned and headed for camp, noticing the southern sky beyond blotted out by gray snow clouds. It was only October 10 and somewhat early for snow. *It probably won't stay,* he thought.

He pressed on, tried not to think about the necessity of getting out and the problem it posed. He was some fifty miles from his cabin. To reach it he'd have to climb to higher elevation in order to cross the mountain pass, which would have at least twice the snow on the ground as his river camp.

He knew that crossing two to three feet of snow would be extremely difficult without snowshoes. Without webs he'd be nearly helpless.

Another factor to consider was the probable temperature drop of thirty to forty below. Momentarily he thought about staying, hoping that someone would come looking for him in this desolate country. But he knew better. *Who would come out here this time of year? There is absolutely no reason for anyone to come here now.*

He was positive that no man lived in the valley. He'd seen no one in his recent search nor any signs of human activity, and he knew no Indians resided here. Trapping season was three weeks away. He knew he had to make a move soon or it might be too late.

His situation demanded a survival strategy. He knew the necessity of remaining calm and assessing his situation.

I'm a gamer. I can do it. I've been in other jams and worked my way out. More food, warm clothes, and snowshoes would make it easier, but I'll have to make do with what I've got.

He knew the first ten miles through timber would be the easiest and that the next thirty in the barren plateaus east of him would be the toughest to negotiate. *Those rolling hills will be covered with two to three feet of snow. There won't even be a twig for building a fire.*

He also knew that the wind following the storm would come howling out of the north, cutting through clothing like a sandblaster. To be caught out poorly clothed in below-zero weather in screeching winds would be like committing suicide . . . slowly.

He turned in, knowing that the trip was unavoidable. He lay cozy in his sleeping bag. And he cursed himself for making an impulsive decision and preparing so poorly. At home he'd be snug and warm and his sixteen horses would be feeding near his cabin in the meadows. He was angry that he hadn't brought a spare cayuse.

He hadn't intended his trip to turn out the way it had. Originally he'd planned to scout new game country for four, maybe five days, push ahead for new territory. But it seemed that every new valley and distant ridge was more tantalizing than the last, and he kept traveling deeper into the mountains . . . eventually losing his horse.

When he awakened the next morning, he roused out of his sleeping bag. Eighteen inches of snow had accumulated overnight. He prepared some of the last of the tea he'd hoarded, boiled a few strips of dried moose meat, and chomped a piece of pilot bread. It wasn't much but it was better than nothing.

He dug into a saddlebag and extracted seventeen shells for his .22 single-shot rifle, thinking he might get a crack at the moose that had left the tracks he'd seen while searching for his horse.

Leaving camp with his rifle and skinning knife, he headed for the horse carcass, planning to extract what he could for his sustenance over the next several days. During the night the stomach had been torn open and part of the entrails eaten by a wolverine. Ravens had picked a large hole in one ham.

The frozen flesh compounded the use of the sharp knife; however, he carved off fifteen pounds. The horse had put in a long season in the mountains and was lacking fat, but the man sliced off as much as he thought he'd need, knowing it was necessary to provide body heat in the days ahead.

When he returned to camp, he prepared a cup of tea, ate from his dwindling supply of moose meat, then cut four eight-foot green willows from which to fashion snowshoes.

He spent the next morning finalizing his snowshoes with rawhide strips of horsehide. Then he placed them near the fire to shrink-dry them. Next he took the saddle blanket and constructed a backpack. Then he made a sling for the .22 rifle.

The following morning he placed his saddle in a tree where it would be safe from rodents and rabbits. *Better carry the snowshoes through the timber so they won't get damaged. I can put them on when I leave timberline.* He shouldered his pack, grabbed his rifle, and set out on his journey over the mountains.

Exhausted near dark, he reached the edge of the timber. *Not as good as I'd hoped, but it'll have to do.* He selected a large spruce, dropped his gear at its foot, and broke off dry branches below its overhanging limbs. He scrounged enough dry firewood in the area to build a large fire. *This will be the last heat I feel till I get through the pass and over the barrens. Might as well enjoy it as much as possible.*

The temperature plummeted during the day, and he knew he'd feel its effect this night. When the northern lights twinkled and hissed overhead, it was laughterlike, mocking and leering down at him. *Almost a live thing making fun of my stupidity.* He was angry with his situation. Again, it caused him to question his lack of preparation.

He shivered through the night, rebuilding the fire before daylight. It hit twenty-five below overnight, all the reason to cherish his last piece of moose meat that he boiled with a hunk of horse fat. He savored the meat with his last piece of pilot bread.

Finishing his meal, he gathered up his pack, rifle, and webs and struck out for the open country beyond. He struggled onward through the crotch-deep snow, fighting exhaustion and the tangled alder thickets. With two hours to go until nightfall, exhaustion again embraced him as he topped the last ridge and looked out across the bleak, snow-filled land known as the barrens. Snow three feet deep leered at him over thirty miles of rolling hills on the plateau. The white stuff, untracked by another human, lay before him, both beckoning and mocking.

He guessed it was thirty-five to forty below, as his nose hairs and beard frosted over. But he had chosen his path. He tied on his snowshoes and trudged onward.

As he labored along, the webs lacking the usual upturned front caught a lot of snow. It was a grueling trek, each step sinking noseward on a snowshoe and exacting a tremendous amount of energy to bring the tip above the snow for the next step.

He guessed that he'd covered two miles in the final two hours before darkness engulfed him. He selected a gully to get out of any potential wind and scraped out a depression with his snowshoe. He spread his sleeping bag in the dip and covered it with the piece of canvas, then placed a foot of snow on it for insulation. The canvas would keep any melted snow from him.

Planning ahead, he carried a hunk of horse meat into his bag with him, hoping it would thaw during the night next to his body. But such was not the case. When he awoke the meat was still half-frozen.

He gnawed on the meat awhile before setting out into the waist-deep snow. He traveled this way for two days. Then he repeated the mundane process: right foot step, sink, lift the front of the left web from the snow and step with it while the right snowshoe sank; lift the front from the snow on the right snowshoe and shake it off before stepping again. Onward without end.

Two days and two nights witnessed the same activity . . . stop for the night, scrape snow to form a depression on the ground, spread his sleeping bag and canvas, cover them with snow, arise in the morning, gnaw more raw frozen horse meat, and attack the day.

By nightfall of the second day he knew the frost was penetrating his extremities. *Can't keep my hands warm. Think they're freezing along with my face. Must be about forty-five below.* Adding to his troubles, a frigid wind out of the north cut like a knife.

The rifle was extra weight. That night he thought about jettisoning it, but he reasoned that it could bag ptarmigan or a caribou should he get the chance. It was a tough decision. The weapon could save his life.

The wind woke him the third night. Wind-driven snow scoured the landscape. Like a high-powered sandblaster, ice particles blistered the barrens and everything in their path. There was no letup. His situation gripped him with fear. *What if I'm buried by the drifting snow?* All night he listened. And the snow in his depression built up.

At daylight he dug his way out, hearing the howling wind the whole while. Once he was clear of the snow, the icy hand of death pummeled him from every side. Visibility limited him to a handful of yards. The bitter wind and blowing snow, combined with the forty-five-below temperature, drove him back to his nest. Gripped by fear and hopelessness, he knew that he was hamstrung by the elements. *No landmarks. Will have to stay here till I can see. Maybe the wind will let up soon.*

He lay in his nest gnawing on the frozen meat and wondering and hoping. *How long will the ten pounds of meat last? How much longer will the wind pin me down? If I stay warm and conserve my strength, I may get out.*

One day turned interminably into the next until a week had passed. He left his cocoon only to grab another hunk of frozen meat or to relieve himself.

For seven days the wind prevailed. She played a cruel joke on him.

When he awoke on the morning of the eighth day, he arose to silence. *The wind stopped.* He struggled from his sleeping bag and gazed upon the sun. For as far as he could see, a frigid, white world loomed to the horizon. Ridges poked up all around, but the gullies were choked with snowdrifts, some as deep as twenty feet.

At that point he cooked his goose.

Though reasoning may have been beyond his capabilities, he thought of a solution: *My meat supply is nearly gone. If the wind starts again, I'm dead. Back at the river I can have wood, a fire, and heat. I can get more horse meat. I might find that moose or get some rabbits. Maybe I can make a better pair of snowshoes and walk out.*

This proved by far his most trying wilderness test. A tough customer, he hated to admit defeat, but the cold, the wind, and the snow had whipped him. He accepted it and chose to regroup and to try again. He turned back.

After three grueling days he reached his river campsite. He immediately made for the horse carcass, expecting to find meat. But a wolverine and a pack of wolves had beaten him to it. They'd left nothing but some bone fragments, hooves with the shoes on, the skull plate, and strips of hide. *Not even enough here for a thick broth.*

Over the next week he hunted hard for the moose but failed to find it . . . or any other creature.

Although he was protected from the wind by the forest, the cold and hunger brought him closer to death's door each day. Starvation sapped his strength.

Late November found him checking rabbit snares. That's when tragedy struck. Thin ice and the cold teamed up to destroy him. While crossing ice he plunged through into the water below and got drenched to his crotch. From the time he freed himself from the frigid water and reached his camp, his hands and feet were frozen.

Death stalked him now as never before. He shivered the night away trying to get warm in his sleeping bag next to the dying fire. Camp bound because he could not walk, he watched his hands blacken, then turn gangrenous. *I can't walk, hunt, collect wood, or eat. How long till the Grim Reaper calls my number?*

By day he watched the gangrene get worse. He wasted away, becoming weaker with each sunrise. By night he languished in his sleeping bag, shivering and agonizing because of the physical pain. Who could know the depths of his despair?

Slowly but surely, starvation pinched his spine. December witnessed his hopelessness. And Old Man Death knocked on his door, welcoming him with open arms.

And surely the *if onlys* must have plagued him to the bitter end.

DANA STABENOW

➢ Best known for her long-running and wonderful Kate Shugak mystery series and her regular contributions in *Alaska* magazine, Dana is a superb writer of both fiction and fact. Her first Kate Shugak novel won an Edgar Award, and the fourteenth book in the series, *A Taint in the Blood*, was released in September 2004. She is also frequently laugh-out-loud funny and is a fabulous observer of humanity who is not afraid to get out in the scrum and get her hands into whatever adventure presents itself—even when it means climbing to an insane height on a bad trail. She edits anthologies, cohosts the radio book club *Book Talk Alaska*, is the cochair of Bouchercon 2007, and obviously has no life. ➢

A Time Machine Called the Chilkoot Trail

What the HELL was I thinking?
—entry from Happy Camp log, Chilkoot Trail

I had a plan.

I wasn't going to let anyone rush me. I wasn't going to let *me* rush me. I was going to take it one foot at a time, one boulder at a time. I was going slow, I was going careful, I was not going to slip or fall, there would be no Stabenow blood shed in the Chilkoot Pass that day.

That was my plan. I slithered across the snowfield to the foot of the Scales and got chest to chest with a boulder taller than I was. Slowly, carefully, one fingernail at a time, I thought my way over it.

One boulder behind me. A thousand to go. I stretched out a toe that was suddenly and inexplicably prehensile for the next.

What the hell was I thinking, saying I'd hike the Chilkoot Pass with my friends Rhonda Sleighter and Sharyn Wilson? I didn't even know what the Sheep Camp ranger meant when she told us the pass was a class three rock scramble. Who was I, overweight, out of shape, someone who voluntarily quit camping when she was twelve, who was I to think I could hoist myself over a mountain pass which Henry De Windt had described in 1897 as, "difficult, even dangerous, to those not possessed of steady nerve"?

Plus, I was carrying half a tent, and at the end of every day of the five-day hike, I had to help pitch it. Adding insult to serious injury, I then had to sleep in it, because there are no cabins on the Chilkoot Trail, a situation I felt should be remedied. Preferably before I got to the trailhead.

At least I wasn't one of the women of 1897, who wore an average forty pounds of clothes each. The prospect of getting over the pass with a full pack was intimidating enough, never mind getting over the pass with a full pack and a bustle.

One image, according to Pierre Berton in *The Klondike Fever,* tells the entire story of the Klondike gold rush. It is a black-and-white photograph of "a solid line of men, forming a human chain, hanging across the white face of a mountain rampart." Alaskans are as familiar with this image as we are with our own faces, it is part and parcel of our history, it has been transmuted into legend, it's even reproduced on the Alaska license plate.

In the winter of 1897–98, twenty-two thousand people crossed the Chilkoot Pass in a reckless quest for their share of the gold discovered by George Washington Carmack in the Klondike the year before. At some point, each one of the twenty-two thousand had stood in that solid line. Jack London lived it, Robert Service wrote verse about it, and now Rhonda and Sharyn and I were taking our place in that same line.

It was all Rhonda's fault. Ever since we were college roommates, I've known her to be hooked on old photographs. "Don't have to know a soul in them," she admits cheerfully. She had wanted to hike the Chilkoot Trail, to cross from Alaska to Canada in the footsteps of the stampeders, ever since she went to Dawson City and saw the old photographs of the gold rush days there. In a weak moment I agreed to accompany her, and when Sharyn heard about it she foolishly said she wanted to come, too. So we three flew into Skagway on a Saturday in July 2000, packs and sleeping bags and boots in hand, ready for adventure. Mind you, I hadn't had the pack on since a couple of overnight hikes the year before, but I was going to have to hump it over thirty-three miles of trail and it seemed to me that I'd know how to carry it by the time I got to Bennett. I'm not big on training.

There is a slide show on the Chilkoot Trail at the National Park Center in Skagway, and that evening we committed the cardinal error of watching it. Most of the photographs were of vertical rocks, in fog. Most of my comments were unprintable.

We returned at once to the hotel to re-evaluate what was in our packs. "We don't need bowls," Sharyn said, "we can eat out of our mugs." "I don't need camp shoes," Rhonda said. "I don't really need to change my underwear every day," I said.

At the Trail Center when we picked up our permits that afternoon, Ranger Jim Wessel had told us, deadpan, "The rangers are happy to haul your packs over the pass." Pause. "For a hundred bucks." He told us that every year the park rangers fall heir to all manner of stuff jettisoned before the summit, three-pound bags of M&Ms, six-packs of beer, bagels, zucchini. He should have been in our room that night.

The next morning we took Dyea Dave's taxi to the trailhead, where the Sharyn Wilson Solution to the Chilkoot Trail was born: Get run over by Dyea Dave in front of the trailhead outhouse, and you don't have to hike at all. The first half mile of trail is twelve hundred feet straight up and then twelve hundred feet straight down. "There's nothing wrong with this section of trail that a couple of sticks of dynamite wouldn't cure," Rhonda said, and then added, "but I have the can-do attitude, so I will be fine." It was our mantra afterward, we were the Rhonda Sleighter Chilkoot Trail Party in the year 2000, we had the can-do attitude, and we would be fine.

Four miles later we lunched at Finnegan's Point, where in 1897 Pat Finnegan and his two sons built a bridge and charged a toll of two dollars until the press of stampeders rolled right over the top of them. We camped that first night in Canyon City, in a muggy, buggy rain forest with trees so tall we couldn't see the sky. Before dinner we walked the half mile to the ruins of Canyon City, the southern terminus of the aerial tramway, completed in 1898, which would haul freight the fourteen miles from Canyon City up and over the Chilkoot Pass, the gold rush predecessor of air cargo. At seven and a half cents a pound, the cost was out of reach of most stampeders. All that is left today is the boiler that provided its power. There are the rusty remains of a stove, too, hauled in by some enterprising stampeder—a woman, perhaps?—who set it up and sold pancakes for ten cents each.

What can I say about the bear pole at Canyon City? It wasn't Klondike Kate but it certainly provided the evening's entertainment. Any bear who figured out how to get all those packs and stuff sacks down after they'd been strung up would also have been too smart to try in the first place. Unlike us.

"Now there's a Chilkoot Trail job crying out to be filled," Sharyn said thoughtfully.

"What?"

"Shot putter."

"Also masseuse," Rhonda said, stretching and wincing.

The next day, more rain forest, more bugs, a sheer cliff face that had Rhonda rethinking her great idea ("But I have the can-do attitude, I'm fine"), and we arrived at Sheep Camp, an idyllic spot on an island in the middle of a shallow, rushing river, where that evening Ranger Suzanne gave a talk.

First she made what she called the August 1st Team Chilkoot introduce itself. There were two large groups, one a guided hike from Vancouver led by Len Webster, who was on his tenth Chilkoot hike and who has that Canadian twinkle in his eyes. (When asked at Canyon City what there was to see at Sheep Camp, he replied solemnly, "Nothing. Except me.") There was a mother from Wasilla who thought hiking the Chilkoot would be empowering for her two daughters, both of whom were along, as was their godmother, who showed extreme good sense in preparing for the next day's hike by sleeping through the ranger talk in their tent. There were two guys from Belgium who smiled a lot and were always first out in the mornings, a couple from Toronto on their honeymoon who were still speaking to each other by Bennett Lake, which augured well for their continued future together, and another couple in their seventies hiking the pass with their daughter and son-in-law. For the whole five days, the daughter kept saying, "Where's Mom?" and she'd look around and say, "Oh. She's right here." There was geologist Cara Wright of Anchorage, who felt it was part of her job to hike the Chilkoot, making the trip with Karen, Linda, and Michelle, who, I noted enviously, were very well supplied with small bottles of liquor.

Ranger Suzanne warned us about bears, they were all over the place, she said: "If you see one, don't run from it, and don't feed it." We promised we wouldn't. Then she gave us the weather report, as follows: "Evening showers, partial clearing by midnight, partly cloudy tomorrow," and added, "This is the first forecast this year without the word *rain* in it."

She described the next day's hike. Three miles to the boulder field called the Scales, another half mile to the pass, where came the "class three rock scramble" remark, another five miles to the next night's camp, Happy Camp. She demonstrated methods of climb, using both hands and feet. She mentioned snow, and wind, and rain, and sleet, and hypothermia. She explained that fluorescent orange markers would guide us if fog settled in. It would be a long day. We should start early.

I went to bed that night fantasizing about Sherpas. I got to sleep only to have nightmares of broken bones and blood at the bottom of the Golden Stairs. Sharyn said later that her legs were shaking the next morning as she took down her tent, and she kept asking herself, "Why am I doing this? Why am I putting my life in danger?" Her nightmare was that the weight of her pack would pull her backward down the Scales. The most Rhonda will admit to is that she was "concerned." You'll understand when I tell you that the Chilkoot Trail was the first hike of her life.

No one's mood was improved when we discoved that in the mad rush to lighten our packs in Skagway we had miscounted and left a dinner behind. If the weather went contrary to forecast, if the temperature dropped, if it rained or snowed, Rhonda's Lipton Cup-A-Soups, Sharyn's herbal teas, and my tiny bottle of honey would go only so far. How could we have been so stupid?

"It's okay," Sharyn said.

"We'll be fine," I said.

"Because we have the can-do attitude," Rhonda said.

First light and fear jerked me awake at four-thirty. I woke Sharyn and Rhonda, thinking to get a really early start on the day, but Len's group was up before us. The Belgians of course had already left.

The first three miles were an uphill grind, crossing and recrossing the same creek. We left the tree line behind and were at the foot of the Scales, a steep slide of boulders the size of minor planets with edges like steak knives. I looked up and thought, *What's a class four rock scramble, the West Buttress of Denali?*

Some of the boulders were teetery and tippety and some were not and you never knew which was which until you stepped on or grabbed one. I had a brief, rose-colored vision of one of those tough, surly Tlingit packers who hired themselves out to the Klondike stampeders to pack goods over the pass, who were known to sit down in the middle of the trail on strike for better wages, usually just before the summit. The Scales got its name because this was where the packers would re-weigh their loads and jack up their prices.

Whatever they charged, it wasn't enough.

Although . . . a third of the way up I realized I was kind of enjoying myself. My pack was still heavy, with a tendency to hit me in the back of the head every time I bent too far over, but I was moving upward, slowly, steadily, undeniably upward. I had a few bruises, and one moment of real terror when I got stuck on the wrong side of a patch of homicidal shale, but came the moment when I realized there were more boulders behind me than were ahead of me, that the sun was beaming blindingly down, that the view seemed to go all the way back to the Lynn Canal, and I was about to kick the Scales' ass, in the best tradition of that long, solid line. Only I was doing it in color.

"You're doing great!" Ranger Suzanne said over her shoulder as she streaked by. "Isn't this a beautiful day? This is the first time I've seen this view in six weeks!"

Rhonda was waiting at the top with a grin the size of Galveston and a handful of gorp. What I really wanted was champagne.

Now only forty-five degrees of Golden Stairs lay between us and the summit.

During the winter of 1897–98, two enterprising stampeders carved steps in the snow covering the pass and collected eighty dollars a day in tolls, which after six weeks they promptly blew on an extended drunk. This was summer, and to me the Golden Stairs looked like just another, albeit shorter Scales. "Rhonda," I said, "Samuel Benton Steele is waiting for me at the summit, right? In his red uniform, with his Mountie hat on and his arms wide open, saying, 'I've been waiting for you, babe'?" Steele being that magnificent Mountie who saved so many lives during the gold rush by refusing to admit stampeders into Canada without their supplies, who saved more lives by keeping strict track of the boats that sailed to Dawson from Lindeman and Bennett, who kept Soapy Smith's gang bottled up on the U.S. side of the border, and whose enforcement of Canadian customs at the Chilkoot Pass established a de facto international border that stands to this day.

"I don't know, Dana," Rhonda said, and I said, "Just say he is, Rhonda," and she said, "Sam's waiting for you on the summit, Dana," and I said, "Okay, then, let's go."

Another snowfield, another boulder climb, and there was the summit. No, wait, it was a false summit. Bad word. Another snowfield, another boulder climb, and the summit, but no, a second false summit. Very bad word. Another snowfield, and then there was the summit, the real summit, the last, the final, the one true summit of the Chilkoot Pass.

"Rhonda, I can see the Canadian flag!" I shouted. I don't even remember the last rocks I stumbled over to get to the border. The Lion of the Yukon wasn't waiting for me, only a warden in a Parks Canada uniform, but I was so happy to see her that I flung out my arms and belted out the first line of the Canadian national anthem as we crossed into her country. The wind was kicking up and it was nippy, but the sun had never been brighter, the sky bluer, the Canadian flag more beautiful, no orange had ever tasted better, and I had never loved Rhonda and Sharyn so much.

"I can't believe what my body just did," Sharyn said.

"It's a great accomplishment," Rhonda said.

"We've still got five miles to go," I said.

They looked at me in disgust. They didn't say I had no soul, but they were thinking it.

We were triumphant at one crossing of the pass, but the stampeders had to haul enough supplies to support themselves in Canada for one year without outside help. This amounted to about a ton of goods. Some of them had to climb the Chilkoot Pass thirty-five times to bring it all across. Through seventy feet of snow, a glacier fall in September that killed three, and an avalanche in April that took more than sixty lives, not to mention Soapy Smith's gang waiting to rob and frequently kill them from Skagway all the way to the pass.

Thirty-five times. I couldn't bend my mind around that number before I climbed the Chilkoot. Now, I find it even more unthinkable.

We set out again, through a broad valley filled with a careless spill of deep sapphire lakes and rimmed with wedges of mountain that seemed to have risen whole from the center of the earth, chilling into single monoliths when they reached the surface. We passed the Stone Crib, the northern anchor for the aerial tramway. It was beautiful, but the trail here was a seemingly endless series of snowfields, boulder fields, and creek crossings and we were exhausted before we began. By the time we got to Happy Camp we were literally staggering with fatigue. It was after five o'clock, we'd been hiking for almost eleven hours, and the campsite, hewn from an alpine slope, looked like kitty corner from heaven.

The log at the Happy Camp warming cabin was filled with comments written by people who hadn't had the luck of good weather. One man who crossed the pass the day before us wrote, "I've never seen it rain uphill before." I, on the other hand, was sunburned. Len's group didn't make it in until after seven, and Sharyn said she had watched Len guide someone step by step up the pass—"Okay, you're doing great, put your right hand here, your left hand there, okay, terrific, now put your left foot here . . ." It turned out he had three people in his group who were afraid of heights. His assistant, Deb, who has a mountain goat somewhere in her ancestry, climbed the Scales three times carrying someone else's pack. Happy Camp was the first time I saw either one of them tired.

Cara's group celebrated crossing the pass with Yukon Jack. "It seemed appropriate," she explained. I wished I'd thought of that.

We had enough energy to make camp and dinner. Rhonda had some two-two-twos, Canadian aspirin with codeine. I downed two and rolled into my sleeping bag at 8:00 P.M. I woke up in exactly the same position eleven hours later.

The weather held, sunshine all the way to Lindeman City, a glorious hike that follows first a mountain ridge with a view that puts you at eye level with the surrounding mountains and then the narrow edge of a deep gorge filled with a jumbled, tumbling mass of rapids. There are cairns at every turn of the trail, rocks piled in the shapes of Buddha, a malevolent toad, an eagle, even a woman standing in front of a counter kneading bread. It is a sobering testimonial to how long Canadian wardens have been hiking the Chilkoot Trail back and forth in search of errant hikers.

The final mile into Lindeman was enlivened by a bear sighting sign. Rhonda and I sang "Sixteen Tons" and "Mercedes Benz" and "Chapel of Love." Loudly. Sharyn led us in a spirited rendition of "Why'd the Bear Go Round the Mountain." We neither saw nor heard any bears, but at Lindeman a warden displayed a stampeder's homemade crampon a bear looking for ants had dug up the day before, and a lot of pictures.

A smile spread across Sharyn's face as she pointed to a black-and-white picture of the Pass, circa 1898. "We were there."

It rained that night, but not for very long, and after that the wind blew. "Air fluff," Rhonda said, "no heat." The tents were dry by morning.

The last day was a seven-mile hike over an up-and-down trail made mostly of sharp-edged granite. It isn't fun, and neither is the last half mile, a long hill of sand with a lot of signs on it, all pointing the way in the wrong direction. "It's a good thing I have a can-do attitude," Sharyn said, "otherwise I'd be in complete despair." If I'd known, I would have offered my body to the Lindeman City warden in exchange for a boat ride to Bennett and eschewed the last day's hike entirely.

That night we were down to one freeze-dried package of Santa Fe Chicken. Fortunately, the honeymooning couple had a spare package of corn tortillas. The tortillas were dry and tough and ambrosial. Sharyn remarked on how clever it was to get the couple to carry the tortillas for us all the way to Bennett Lake.

Bennett is where a tent city sprang up overnight in 1897, where the stampeders built their boats to sail the seven hundred miles to Dawson and gold. There isn't much left but a stove made of three sheets of rusted iron held together with bent nails, a lot of broken glass, and St. Andrew's Presbyterian Church.

But at Bennett the earth rises up and folds in upon itself in abrupt granite inclines and precipitous descents of rock and boulder and shale that I did not have to climb, only appreciate. The lake is a narrow, inland fjord, made a grayer blue than the pass lakes with glacial silt. The sun was reluctant to set, painting a lingering glow on the mountain faces raised to it.

The next morning we broke camp for the last time, and arrived at the train station a little before a troop of Boy Scouts, most of whom were limping. There may have been some snickering on the part of the (adult) non-limpers. There are historical exhibits inside the depot, but they don't unlock the door in until the train gets there and all the cruise ship passengers get off to eat their box lunches inside, and by then it's time to go. The hikers are sequestered in the last car in line, so as not to pollute the air of the cruise ship passengers.

"I'll take a cup of coffee and two doughnuts," somebody said to the brakeman.

"I'd rather you take two showers," the brakeman replied.

It was another glorious day, the White Pass filled to the brim with sunshine, but I must admit that our admiration of the view from the track winding down through the mountains from Bennett to Skagway was, well, a bit distracted. "I just want a beer," I said. "A long, cold beer, and keep them coming."

"I want a shower," Rhonda said.

"Why can't you have your beer in the shower?" Cara said.

Worked for me.

At our B&B in Skagway, after showering (I had to shampoo twice to get my hair clean), we inventoried our food supplies. Between the three of us, this is what we had left:

> Four (4) sticks of gum (Spearmint)
> Five (5) teabags (Lemon Zinger)
> Two (2) Lipton Cup-A-Soups (chicken noodle)

Looking back on the hike, I felt as though we had walked backward through time. The same mountains and lakes and passes that we crossed, the same path we walked are in the photographs of the Klondike gold rush. The trail is strewn with the debris of those who went before us, shoes, boats, stoves, boilers, saws, cans, machine parts.

Did they look up, the stampeders? Did they look up in Bennett from their packs and their sawpits and their boat-building, from their frantic preparations for the last leg of the journey to the Klondike gold fields? Did they look up and see the beauty of the mountains, of alpine vale and sapphire lake and rain forest, of hanging glacier and endless sky and rushing stream?

I hope so.

Except from *Tales of Alaska's Bush Rat Governor*

JAY S. HAMMOND and JIM REARDEN

❧ A Yankee minister's nonconformist son, after serving as a Marine fighter pilot in the South Pacific during World War II, flees the demands of civilization for a life of solitary self-sufficiency in Alaska's wilderness . . . only to become the nation's most unlikely and perhaps most innovative governor from 1974 to 1982, during the nation's oil crisis. Beginning in 1946, JAY STERNER HAMMOND lived a life of high adventure as a bush pilot, trapper, commercial fisherman, and wilderness guide. But neither his crash landings and midair engine failures (thirteen of them!), broken bones, and blizzards that stranded him in remote corners of Alaska, nor his encounters with murder, mayhem, and angry brown bears—all of which he writes about with entertaining irreverence—prepared him for the predatory power politics he also describes with humor and insight. This is an extraordinary story of a man in love with his adopted land and grateful for the life it provides. In nearly half a century, Jay Hammond has stepped lightly on the land, hardly leaving a permanent footprint—except for the log cabin homestead he built on the shore of remote Lake Clark, far from the nearest road or neighbor. Yet the unique Permanent Fund he championed as governor, with its annual dividends, has helped send thousands of young people to college, brought a share of the oil wealth to all Alaskans, and changed his state forever. This title is available at www.epicenterpress.com. ❧

❧ A fifty-year resident of Alaska, JIM REARDEN has written seventeen books and more than five hundred magazine articles, mostly about Alaska. Recent books include *Shadows on the Koyukuk,* the life story of trapper, businessman, and public-service leader Sidney Huntington (the coauthor); *In the Shadow of Eagles,* on the life of barnstormer/bush pilot Rudy Billberg: *Koga's Zero,* the story of the first Japanese Zero airplane captured and flown by the United States during World War II; *Alaska's Wolf Man,* relating the wilderness adventures of Frank Glaser (for the Alaska Historical Society); and a novel, *Castner's Cutthroats,* about the famed Alaska Scouts of World War II. Rearden earned a B.S. degree in fish and game management from Oregon State College and an M.S. in wildlife conservation from the University of Maine. In Alaska he has served as a federal fishery patrol agent and taught wildlife management at the University of Alaska–Fairbanks, and was fisheries biologist in charge of commercial fisheries in Cook Inlet for ten years. He has also been a commercial fisherman and a registered big-game guide. He served on the Alaska Board of Game for twelve years and is a private pilot. Rearden was outdoors editor for *Alaska* magazine for twenty years, and for twenty years he was also a field editor for *Outdoor Life* magazine. He lives in Homer with his wife, Audrey, in a log house he built. *Tales of Alaska's Bush Rat Governor* and other titles by Jim Rearden are available at www.epicenterpress.com. ☞

No one tried harder to pitch me back into my Lake Clark briar patch than powerful Teamster boss Jesse Carr. So potent a force had Carr's Teamsters become, most businessmen and politicians believed, with good reason, it was the kiss of death to earn their disfavor. For survival, many chose to engage openly in osculation of quite a different sort. Despite suspicions of my environmentalist leanings, too many business people had already been clubbed by Carr's heavy hand. That I wasn't in his hind pocket, but a burr in his britches, had perverse appeal to many.

These people wrote such things as, "I don't know much about you, but anybody who's got the Teamsters against them must be okay!" Often these were unsigned, just in case.

During the course of the '74 campaign, and long after, Jesse Carr and his Teamsters exhibited far more devotion to my defeat than did I to victory. My every public appearance was attended by Teamsters, busily handing out anti-Hammond flyers or putting them on car windshields.

"If Hammond's elected there'll be a Right-to-Work Law!" "Hammond is Anti-Growth!" Or, "Protect Your Jobs/Re-Elect Bill Egan!" And later: "Can Salmon—And Hammond!"

These ploys were effective. Combined with my own diligence, hard work, and indecent public exposures, we managed to whittle my discomforting lead down a few points each day. Though somewhat nervous, I remained confident I would lose handily, as in the campaign's final weeks, polls showed the rise of Egan/Boucher and the fall of Hammond/Thomas to be mutually accelerating.

As salvation seemed imminent, I began to relax. My chief regret was the one TV spot I wanted to run, never did. After months of assaulting long-suffering viewers with high-decibel political ads, in atonement I'd hoped to air one showing a tranquil mountain lake, with my voice-over saying simply: "The following thirty seconds of merciful silence are brought to you courtesy of . . ." Instead, my staff insisted on ads showing me engaged in pursuits with which most Alaskans like to identify: splitting wood, fishing, or laying up logs for a wilderness cabin.

Courage and innovation went into some of these ads. One was made by filmmaker Tim McGinnis, who imprudently subjected both his camera and cranium to undue hazard, placing them on my chopping block beside a chunk of wood I was splitting. If Tim's confidence in my accuracy with an ax was only barely justified, his "Woodchopper" ad is still considered an Alaskan campaign classic.

Another camera crew visiting our homestead came to understand more than most my reluctance to win the governor's chair. Arriving by floatplane one balmy late summer evening, they sighted two moose in our cove and a large brown bear just up the beach. The setting sun was turning the surrounding snow peaks into improbable hues of calendar art, reflected in the mirror-like waters below.

As we stood on the shore, a crew member shook his head and asked, "Why would you ever leave this to run for public office?"

I confessed this rude thought surfaced often, around three in the morning.

During the general election campaign I continued to drum my "healthy growth vs. malignant growth" theme. Unless an economic development project was environmentally sound, good for a majority if not all Alaskans, and could pay its own way, rather than become a burden to the state, I would oppose it.

"Heresy!" howled growth-for-growth's-sake advocates. To suggest *any* economic development should not be embraced automatically was anathema to those who would profit, even at the expense of other citizens.

Some hostility toward my "malignant growth" warnings was promulgated by Alaskans' increasing frustration with federal regulations emerging in the wake of the nation's growing environmental concerns. None of my opponents was more outraged by such "unnecessary obstructions" than crusty old Fairbanks miner Joe Vogler. Incensed with constant federal intervention, Joe had created the Alaskan Independence Party, and was running in the general election on a secession platform.

At our first confrontation in one of those interminable "debates," I was impressed by an impassioned tirade from Vogler which from the mouth of a less gifted orator would have been gibberish. Joe was a master at sweeping his audience spellbound into a torrent of vitriolic castigation of bureaucrats. Even I found my feet slipping in the tug of his hypnotic delivery—until the echo of jackboots and "Sieg Heils!" brought me back to reality.

But the audience, by now thoroughly saturated, responded with wave after wave of applause that seemed to crescendo when Joe referred fondly to me as "a posey sniffing swine!" I say "fondly," for as we filed from the hall after the debate, he growled to me, "If I can't win this thing I kinda hope you do, Hammond. You seem the least worst of those other guys."

Later I was asked my reaction to Joe's verbal attack. "Anyone who can come up with language like 'posey sniffing swine' can't be all bad." I still believe this and harbor affectionate memories of Joe, who mysteriously disappeared from his cabin one spring day in 1993.

As November's first Tuesday grew closer, I was confident my ordeal was about over as we fell steadily in the polls. Though I felt some remorse in being about to disappoint those who had worked so hard for my election, it was submersed in belief that the most merciful thing that could happen to me would be to just barely lose. Then, as the years passed, those disenchanted with what had happened to Alaska might be inclined to say, "If only Hammond had been elected!" Indulgent? Perhaps. But only those who were present in Alaska at that cataclysmic time are qualified to judge.

Bill Egan, on the other hand, exuded confidence. With several thousand ballots being distributed among newly eligible trans-Alaska pipeline workers—mostly Teamsters—a huge block of votes not reflected in previous polls was predicted to elect Egan by a comfortable margin.

And then it was Election Day. When my campaign staff and I arrived at "Election Central"—a non-partisan Election Watch tradition at an Anchorage hotel after the polls close—I managed with difficulty to mirror their morose demeanor. Covertly, I was relieved. Convinced the nightmare was over, I could hardly wait to shuck the neckties, social obligations, and the horrendous demands imposed on those who subject themselves to campaigning for public office.

As the evening went on, however, it was evident something had gone badly awry. Egan and I remained almost neck and neck. Each time a tally was registered showing me slightly ahead, my supporters would whoop and holler, while I attempted to look as though I shared their elation. Conversely, when we dropped a few votes behind, I tried to look somber.

That election night was one of the most painful ordeals I ever experienced. I not only felt like the monstrous fraud I was; I repeatedly verified this to myself by adjusting my outward expression to contrast with what I was feeling within: abject dismay!

When it was announced I'd won by less than a thousand votes, I couldn't believe it. My supporters went ballistically berserk. I went mentally bilious. As they thumped my back and cavorted, I wondered what in the world had gone wrong? Above the din, I could almost hear cell doors clang shut behind me.

Bill Egan not only shared my shock and disbelief, he quickly did something about it. Charging "improprieties," he demanded a recount. The first reduced my lead by half. Good. He ordered another. My lead was cut in two again. Great! Yet despite my rooting for the incumbent, it was not to be. When the smoke finally cleared, we had won—by 221 votes.

More accurately, I learned later, Egan lost because secessionist candidate Joe Vogler had taken five thousand votes that certainly would have gone to Bill. How bitterly divided the state had become over land and resource issues was fortunately lost on me in the moment of "victory." If I'd known the full range of problems that would boil to a head in the next four years, I might have conceded before the final recount was tallied.

As it was, weeks went by until then. Ballots from remote villages came in slowly. I was used to this; as a legislator I often didn't learn election results until after Thanksgiving. By then, I hardly cared any more. This time I cared a lot, clinging to the hope I could still have my "cake" in helping set Alaska's agenda, but, Heaven forbid, not have to eat it!

The heartburn of that alarming eventuality increased with each passing day during the recount, each day's delay allowing less and less time to select a staff and cabinet in the short transition period when one is supposed to learn at least the existence, if not the functions, of the "ropes." Then it was frighteningly official. I'd won.

Later, I was told how Red Boucher, who as lieutenant governor supervised the Office of Elections, had performed an act of considerable courage which, if true, gave him ironic revenge on me. Boucher, according to a reporter present, had refused to surrender ballots in his care to some political operatives not under his charge. If true, my subsequent friendship with Red has enabled me to forgive him.

On Dec. 2, 1974, I was sworn in as Alaska's third governor. No less than *Ripley's Believe It or Not* pointed out that I had defeated every other governor in the state's history to win. Construction on the trans-Alaska pipeline was about to begin. The Greatland was about to undergo enormous change. "The Last Frontier" would soon become, according to author Peter Gruenstein, *The Lost Frontier.*

And like it or not, one who had come to seek solitude in Alaska's wilderness would find much less of either in the tumultuous years ahead.

I don't know if I'm the only person who ever ran for governor literally praying he'd not be elected, but I suspect a multitude of Alaskans joined me in that supplication. To my prayers, however, I'd always add: "Lord, should it be your wish that I give up a good life for the burdens of public office, please help me accept it with good grace if not gusto."

While I don't for a minute believe I was elected by divine ordination, I'm no longer certain it was meant to be the divine retribution I originally thought.

In my first months as governor I was miserable, in temperament and performance. Not only had I been thrust into a job for which I was ill-prepared, I resented enormously my loss of freedom and privacy. Compounding this misery, unlike any Alaska governor before or since, instead of the normal three-week transition period between Election Day and the Oath of Office, I had just three days.

Seventy-two hours allowed little time for indoctrination. I had only a thirty-minute audience with my less than effusive predecessor before he reluctantly vacated his office. Once alone, I opened the governor's desk drawers and found them stripped clean, save for a lone postcard, facedown. Flipping it over I was greeted by the picture of a closed fist, mid-finger rampant, above the hand-written salutation: "Good luck—but not too much." It was unsigned.

Outgoing lieutenant governor Red Boucher, a tough, dynamic opponent who became an ardent supporter, later told me he'd felt it was "a bit tacky" for Egan to clean his desk of everything but an obscene postcard and "the exploding cigar." Exploding cigar? I didn't remember an exploding cigar. Later I learned I'd given it to stogie-chewing Ed Orbeck, a former pro football player who, despite my "gift," survived the detonation to become my loyal and able labor commissioner.

Though I retained some Egan appointees in my administration, most had departed, along with their files and wealth of counsel. This was no fault of Bill Egan, who didn't know he was leaving until three days before compelled to. In any event, we assumed office in almost total ignorance.

About the only intelligence I'd gleaned from my brief summit meeting with Bill was learning to distinguish between three identical doors in the governor's office: the middle door led out to the reception area; the left was an "escape hatch" to the governor's conference room. The third door opened abruptly into the governor's toilet. To those unfamiliar with this layout, the similarity of these doors could be disorienting.

The first to verify this was Fran Ulmer, an extremely competent and lovely young woman who visited my office for a job interview. I was very impressed and somewhat intimidated by her exceptional poise and intelligence. Confident she'd made a good impression, Fran rose to make a dignified exit—only to stumble into the "john." Her embarrassed emergence and subsequent laughter thawed what reservation I might have had. Not "too good to be true" after all, she became my director of policy development and planning.

In addition to selecting a staff and cabinet, I had to write three major speeches on matters of which I had limited knowledge: an inaugural address to a bitterly divided Alaska, a state of the state message, and the annual budget report to the legislature. As I had never employed a speech writer, I did these on my own. That they were completed on time was remarkable. That they were pretty well received was astounding. Of my inaugural address, international journalist Lowell Thomas Sr. had this to say in his January 20, 1975, national broadcast:

I wonder if I have attended more conventions and inaugurals than anyone? My first was Teddy Roosevelt's "Bull Moose" convention in Chicago in 1912. Speeches at these are not always as memorable as when FDR told us "the only thing to fear is fear itself." Back at the 1936 Cleveland GOP convention, John Hamilton held his audience spellbound when he nominated Alf Landon. One of the most impressive; perhaps the most impressive of them all, was the Inaugural address I just heard in Alaska, delivered by an unusual political personality, Jay Hammond . . .

Lowell Sr.'s overblown accolade can be forgiven. His only son, Lowell Jr., was sworn in as my lieutenant governor at the same ceremony. Still, I especially treasure this comment from a hard-bitten international journalist who'd seen and heard it all.

Unfortunately, Thomas's abundant praise served not only to encourage ever-widening flights of oratorical fancy, it persuaded me no one else could write speeches with which I was comfortable. As a result, I too often drowned my audiences in flurries of mixed metaphors, scrambled syntax, and what the irreverent termed "Hammondese." True, some speech would occasionally soar, but not a few simply "stalled out." Still others left my audiences far behind as I swooped and swerved over the linguistic landscape, unaware no passengers had stayed aboard.

By my own measure, for the first few months—some would say longer— I was a lousy governor. Too much time was spent wallowing in self-pity and resenting loss of freedom to the shackles of office.

While my sense of dread and doubts of omniscience may not have been unique—even to candidates who'd never admit to them—unlike any others I've known, I failed to find sufficient offsetting compensation in the power, prestige, and other trappings of public office. I simply viewed them as additional burdens.

Though I functioned poorly, a dedicated staff and cabinet kept my head above water, barely. After stumbling blindly through those first painful months, at a cabinet meeting I reflected that if everyone present was serving "at the governor's pleasure," as the saying goes, "How come I'm not getting any?"

The heaviest burden of all was a backbreaking load of guilt over my negative attitude. I felt like a monstrous fraud. Throughout the campaign, after the election, and during those first months as governor, I'd played the role of eager candidate, then grateful recipient of the gubernatorial mantle, who now wore it with comfort and competence. I detested myself for this deception but couldn't shake it.

I tried to do penance by working ever harder at understanding all facets of government. In the process I tinkered too much with minor nuts and bolts of administrative machinery best left to department mechanics. Floundering about for extra hours each day and night, working almost every weekend and holidays, like Jimmy Carter, I learned almost too late how the fast footwork required to stay atop shifting sands of bureaucracy can ultimately trigger an inundating avalanche. Only by turning over the tools to those who could better use them did I avoid being buried.

In those awful first months I not only felt trapped in a job for which I was unprepared, I seemed unable to neutralize the character-corroding acid of self-pity in which I was saturated. About three-thirty each morning I'd wake up wallowing, thrash around for a couple of hours, mentally chewing on some indigestible problem, and at 7:00 A.M. unenthusiastically take the short walk from the Governor's House to my office on the third floor of the Capitol building. Naturally, such a negative attitude did little to add luster to my performance, let alone the public's perception thereof. My major success in this period was proving what I'd believed all along: I should have run for the hills instead of the state's highest office.

I did my best to obscure this from my staff and the electorate, but my best was inadequate. New evidence cropped up daily. Fortunately, there was one on my staff who could empathize. Bob Palmer, my first executive assistant, had been well aware of my reluctance to run. He also felt a bit guilty, not just for helping to talk me into filing, but for managing a successful campaign. No one did more to propel me into office than Bob, and I had occasion to credit him publicly in a speech soon after the election.

"There's no doubt about it, if there's one man to whom I owe the privilege of appearing before you today as your governor, it's Bob Palmer. And someday I hope to forgive him."

The audience chuckled indulgently, certain I was joshing. Bob knew better. He came to my office later and we apologized to each other. It was apparent to us both my downbeat attitude was beating up my staff and any chance to leave a "Hammond Years" legacy any could point to with other than ridicule.

That meeting proved the turning point. If we couldn't erase my poor attitude, we could at least better obscure it. In my case, each morning in consultation with my Maker, I asked to be shown how. Gradually, things began to improve.

Around this time I came across a quotation from some ancient philosopher: "Only he deserves to lead who just as soon would not." Hmm. Maybe it wasn't so despicable after all, not to have that fire in the belly that seems to motivate those who seek positions of power and leadership.

My staff and cabinet included some thoroughbred talent which, when given rein and adequate fodder, took the bit and carried me over many a hazardous jump. In spite of myself, I began to find certain aspects of the job rather enjoyable. Opportunities to solve some little guy's problems by shredding red tape or bruising some bumptious bureaucrat were especially zestful. Less to my credit, I also found in myself a surprisingly large slice of "ham" which, when slathered with the condiment of public applause, piques the appetite of most politicians. That this condiment was often sparse, or laced with opprobrium, only increased the savor of those times when it came unadulterated.

Because my speeches invariably reiterated themes I'd articulated in the campaign, and Alaskans were becoming increasingly divided over such issues as lands, resource development, and money, applause—if and when it came—was very well received by me. Speechmaking, of course, like theater, provides the best chance to exhibit one's ideas and sample live, public response. Speech *writing* was a chore laced with love and hate. I hated the obligation of preparing a speech; but once I had, if it succeeded, self-satisfaction leeched into my shameless soul.

Occasionally I'd write a speech that alarmed staff members assured me would outrage or insult my audience, only to have the latter applaud in wild approval. Conversely, speeches designed to placate or pander to some special audience would elicit a backfire of boos. This challenge of the unknown made speechmaking all the more intriguing.

Of course, my speeches frequently flopped with no help whatsoever from the audience. I'd said in my campaign those people who expected special treatment should not vote for me. Many had taken this advice. When they later appealed for special treatment anyhow, I felt the least I could do was to keep my end of the bargain. Consequently, to avoid the appearance of genuflecting, I bent over too far backward to craft barbed speeches for such audiences. It did little to improve communications with most special interest groups.

M y first serious conflict as governor involved Jesse Carr and the Teamsters. Having been catered to in the past, most of these stalwarts had complied when I suggested those who found equal treatment a comedown should not vote for me. While searching for a way to keep my side of this bargain, I was presented a platter on which Jesse's head might be served. Of course, only a vindictive, mean-spirited soul would seek such a trophy ahead of justice. So I sought both. Justice would be served—hopefully along with Carr's cranium.

My attorney general catered the affair. One morning Av Gross came to my office with a clutch of papers, spreading them before me with a reverence accorded the Magna Carta or Dead Sea Scrolls.

"Boy, is this hot. These are lease papers drawn up between the state and the Teamsters long before you were governor. The lease terms are, to say the least, most favorable to the union, but payments to the state are far in arrears. They owe a bunch of money. What do you want to do? You can foreclose and kick them off the property or sue, demanding payment plus penalties and interest. If you do the former, of course, there'll be the perception you're seeking revenge. If you do the latter, you'll simply compound the outrage of your worst enemy. What's your choice?"

"Well, Av, as you say, it's a tough choice. I'd prefer not to make it. Can't we do *both*?"

At first Av blanched. Then, presuming I was joking, he smiled. Before he could conclude the contrary, I asked him how he would handle the situation if it was anyone but Carr and the Teamsters.

"Why, we would sue," he replied.

"Then let's do it. I promised Jesse before I took office he'd be given exactly the same consideration as anyone else, no more and no less."

Informed in Anchorage of the state's lawsuit, Carr's detonation reverberated six hundred miles away in Juneau. Jessie Dodson of my staff was still blinking as she related an expurgated version of his diatribe demanding an immediate audience. Since I'd never seen, much less spoken to the man, I agreed to meet with him on my next trip to Anchorage.

A few days later I was led into my Anchorage office by an unusually large contingent of state troopers, shouldering through a crowd of glowering Teamsters carrying placards: "Don't Blame Me—I Voted For Egan!"

Once inside my office, my uneasy escort grudgingly withdrew, leaving me by myself. A few minutes later, Jesse Carr was ushered in by a secretary who beat a hasty retreat. For the first time, Jesse Carr and I confronted one another in person.

A short, powerfully built, bulldog-jawed man about my age stood splay-legged facing me; dark, gun-barrel eyes bored in on mine. For a moment we stalked each other around opposite sides of the large conference table like two pitbulls. Growling in what passed for acknowledging the other dog's presence, each tried to establish dominance by every means short of lifting a leg or scratching hind paws on the carpet.

At least he doesn't have crystal clear glacial blue eyes, was my first ridiculous thought, remembering past experiences with blue-eyed con-artists. *Maybe he can be trusted.* In that vein I recalled what people who knew Carr well had told me. "Whatever else you think of Jesse Carr, when he tells you something, you can take it as Gospel—at least the Gospel according to Carr. He wouldn't say it if he didn't believe it." Jesse was the first to bite and shake the bone of contention between us.

"Look," he growled, "I was in the Marine Corps so I respect the uniform if not the man who wears it. You may be governor, but I want you to know I'm not going to take any crap from you for something that's completely aboveboard and legal. We've done everything 'according to Hoyle' and we have all the papers to prove it."

"That's fine, Jesse," I responded with what I hoped was exasperatingly patronizing, unflappable reason. "I was in the Marines too, so I appreciate your marching straight to the point. And if you can prove that point with documentation showing you have indeed done it according to Hoyle, you'll get no grief from us. On the other hand, if you can't prove it, we're going to take you to the mat."

For a moment I thought he was about to grapple with me on the spot. Instead, his face turned an apoplectic magenta, which—the idiotic thought leaped into my mind—clashed hideously with his expensive silk tie. Blasting me one final time with those gun-barrel eyes, he stormed from the room muttering obscenities undoubtedly gleaned from his days in the corps.

When I emerged from my office a few minutes later, wide-eyed reporters schooled in, one almost tracheotomizing me with his microphone. "What in the world did you say to Jesse Carr to make him call you an S.O.B.?"

"I'm sure he meant 'Sorry Old Bureaucrat,'" I responded. "If he meant something less charitable, I'm surprised. Jesse and I were both Marines but I didn't think he thought we had anything else in common."

Until then, I'd supposed the feud between Carr and myself was a purely Alaskan affair. But now it slopped over into the national arena. A few days after this confrontation, CBS's Dan Rather arrived from New York to interview first Carr, then me, for a *60 Minutes* segment on Teamster power-brokering Alaska pipeline construction. In my interview, Rather asked, in essence, "Some people say Jesse Carr has more to say about running Alaska than even the governor. Apparently you're the first politician up here not willing to give him a free hand. Obviously he doesn't like it. What makes you think you can 'thumb your nose' at Carr and his Teamsters and survive?"

"Well," I replied, "while I'd like to have you think righteous indignation and guts shored my spine, the truth is: one, I'm too 'stove up' to grovel gracefully; two, I'm not terribly entranced with holding this office; and three, if Jesse Carr helps send me home to the hills, it might be considered a favor."

Referring to news reports of Carr's publicly impugning my ancestry, Rather asked, "I understand this was your first encounter with Jesse Carr. Tell me, what's your impression of him as a man?"

"Actually," I admitted, "aside from what he says and does, I rather like the fellow—but I don't think my Mother would."

When that *60 Minutes* program aired in Alaska, rumblings from Carr & Company rattled windows, and the ensuing shards of excoriating editorials in union publications so alarmed my staff they insisted on beefing up security. I was no longer allowed to travel without a trooper escort, new alarm systems were installed in the office and at the Governor's House. Visitors were subjected to careful scrutiny. All this probably bothered me more than it did the troopers and visitors. Until then, I had always traveled without escort, and previously—to the surprise of many callers—Bella, daughters Heidi and Dana, and I answered the phones at the Governor's House.

Word of my conflict with Carr and the Teamsters carried all the way to the White House. It was still there when President Jimmy Carter called the nation's governors to an emergency energy conference. When I arrived, the president apologized for the short notice and asked if I, as most other governors, had come in my personal plane.

"No," I replied.

"You do have a plane, don't you?" the president asked.

"You bet," I said.

"What is it, a Learjet? Saberliner? Queen Air?"

"Nothing like that, I'm afraid. All I've got is an old, single-engine 1953 Cessna 170."

"Really!?" asked the president, surprised. "Don't Alaskans worry about you flying around by yourself in an ancient aircraft like that?"

"No," I explained. "In fact, I'm encouraged by many to do so. During my campaign, Jesse Carr's Teamsters even offered to contribute a hundred gallons of aviation gas, and throw the sugar in free."

Carter looked at me blankly for a moment but laughed when I explained the effects of sugared gasoline on the digestive tract of combustion engines.

D uring my time in office, at least once a year some state or federal agency would advise that the Teamster leadership was being investigated and indictments would soon be issued. To my knowledge, none ever were. Nevertheless, Alaska's Teamster boss found his power eroding as time and truth took their toll. Some say our successful challenge of the Teamster leases was the beginning of this decline. Perhaps. But even those previously antagonistic members of both management and labor who'd been warned Hammond's policies would bankrupt them couldn't escape the fact they were prospering beyond precedent under, or perhaps in spite of, my administration. This conclusion eventually made it much harder to march to the discordant drumbeats of anti-Hammond propaganda thumped out by Teamsters and the *Anchorage Times*.

But before this evolved, most Alaska union leaders had conditioned their members to believe I was the Prince of Darkness. This myth was exacerbated when my refusal to cave in to demands made by the Alaska State Employees' Union precipitated two painful strikes.

While inconvenient, these strikes hardly brought the state to its knees. But they did help publicize salary schedule inequities, illustrating how well paid were the strikers compared to other employees, in and outside government. The ineffectiveness of the first strike prompted one embarrassed official to wonder: "What *if all* state employees went on strike and nobody noticed?"

Not until I'd endured the second strike did I figure out how to deal with the problem. Calling in my old cohort Clem Tillion, I gave him a resolution I'd drafted which, if approved, would have the legislature direct the governor how to deal with employee salary demands.

The resolution went something like, "We, the Alaska State Legislature, hereby inform the governor we will refuse to fund any collectively bargained salary increases for employees whose salaries have kept pace with inflation, until such time as members of other bargaining units doing comparable work have achieved parity. Therefore, the governor is directed henceforth, *not to agree to any salary demands at odds with this objective*."

Clem introduced the measure. Delighted to be "telling the governor how to do his job," the legislature passed it with hardly a ripple. When I cited this legislative directive as my grounds for rejecting the latest union proposals, labor's angry backwash splashed on the legislature, not me. Delightful. I was beginning to like this job after all!

With Clem's enthusiastic assistance, I used this process on more than one occasion when I wished to involve the legislature in business they preferred to avoid.

Having alienated Republicans and unions alike in my first term, once again I managed to irritate Big Business. In Alaska, there was no bigger business than that involved with the trans-Alaska pipeline.

Due to legal delays, pipeline construction still hadn't begun by the time I took office in December 1974. But not even by then was it politically permissible to discuss the project with candor. Any rude questioning of propaganda pumped out by pipeline promoters only showered the questioner with abuse. Being a very slow learner, I once more stuck my face in front of the nozzle.

I was on an airplane when my seat companion, ex–House Speaker Gene Guess, told me the pipeline could be delayed at least a year and cost as much as $9 *billion* rather than the $900 million promoters had claimed. Gene was privy to data I was not. But since his data paralleled my own conclusions, I reiterated them to a news reporter who asked about pipeline schedules and costs.

To my astonishment, all bedlam broke loose. Editors, pipeline officials, labor unions, and oil companies all shrieked I was totally wrong. They agreed pipeline costs had risen "modestly" but assured us it wouldn't cost one penny more than $3 billion! Declining comment on the "modesty" of an increase from $900 million to $3 billion, I listened politely as they vowed construction schedules were "right on track" and any pronouncement to the contrary was absurd.

Meanwhile, my imprudent airing of suspicions reverberated off the canyons of Wall Street. Oil stocks plummeted. In an effort to undo the damage, pipeline owners bundled me aboard a helicopter for a grand inspection tour. One after another, key pipeline officials assured me everything was right on schedule and costs would be contained within $3 billion.

I, in turn, relayed their assurances to the media who converged like iron filings on a magnet when our helicopter touched down in Anchorage. Subsequent headlines trumpeted that I had admitted my error and agreed everything was right on schedule! Nothing I'd said should have conveyed that conclusion. They heard what they wanted to hear. Such imprecise reporting was, unfortunately, not uncommon. I'd merely reported reassurances given by those who should know. I did not say I agreed with them, nor did I. I was not the slightest surprised when the pipeline was, in fact, delayed a year and construction costs soared to almost *$10 billion.* I suppose I should have learned from my resolutions regarding pipeline routes and potential delays how intellectual integrity and political prudence are often incompatible bedfellows.

O n a later tour of the pipeline in 1976, I enjoyed the company of President Gerald Ford, Henry Kissinger, and Barbara Walters. Best recalled from this trip is how the windchill exuding from Barbara—unhappily out of her element—was exceeded only by that blasting off the Arctic Ocean. Henry, by contrast, insulated from both by keen wit, down parka, and "bunny boots," prompted warm laughter. No one appeared more ludicrously out of place than Kissinger clad as polar explorer. His sonorous pronouncements and professorial demeanor were as out of sync in this clime as seal oil and muktuk (whale blubber) at a white tie diplomatic reception. Only his portly figure and gait seemed not to clash with the surroundings; the U.S. Secretary of State easily could have passed for a penguin.

As I was returning to Anchorage with President Ford on *Air Force One,* we discussed other matters of warmth and cold.

"Tell me, Governor, where did you live before going to Juneau?" asked the president.

"A small village called Naknek," I answered.

"What's Naknek like? Describe it."

"Well," said I, "it's a little, windswept, almost treeless. Bering Sea fishing community of about three hundred shivering souls, all but devoid of redeeming virtues. It's a great place to live, but I wouldn't want to visit there."

The president did a double take and then laughed. "Why? Does it get as cold as, say, Fairbanks?" (Which can fall to seventy below.)

"No, but it can get pretty chilly. A while back it got down to twenty below with a forty-knot wind. I had our furnace going full blast and couldn't get the house above fifty degrees. But when I read your energy conservation plea to keep thermostats at sixty-five because of the energy crisis, I vowed to meet your mandate, even if I had to install a second furnace to do it."

TRAPPED ON THE BEACH

Frank W. Johnson decided to go trapping. When Frank needed help seal hunting, fishing, or completing similar work, he had previously engaged in business with his friend The Kid. In the fall of 1971, they decided to partner up and go to Southeast Alaska's Dry Bay, fifty miles south of Yakutat. What began as an ordinary hunting and trapping trip turned disastrous.

Although the old-timer had been reluctant, The Kid had assured him that game was plentiful, that he needed meat for his family, and that he'd do all the work trapping and hunting. It sounded too good to be true, which should have raised some red flags.

The plan was for Frank to cook, take care of camp, and keep The Kid company. The youngster figured they'd make $3,000. Frank would be happy to go home with five hundred dollars clear. He had spent the bulk of his seventy-nine years outdoors, so he knew very well what conditions they might meet, but still he decided one more winter wouldn't hurt, in spite of his better judgment.

Frank made arrangements with Dick Nichols to fly him, The Kid, and their gear to the trapping area. Then he got busy rounding up $300 worth of food and supplies. They left for an Alsek River cabin on Dry Bay November 4, 1971.

When they first laid eyes on it, they knew they had their work cut out for them. The cabin would need heat. An oil drum was needed in order to construct a stove. The Kid spent the day hunting while Frank worked on bringing the cabin up to his standards. Even though The Kid reported ample moose and furbearers in the vicinity, he didn't bring home any meat.

Frank encouraged his partner to build a few line camps right away. These were basically shelter lean-tos consisting of a ridgepole with evergreen boughs forming the "A-frame" roof. The lean-to would provide crude shelter overnight—a day's trapping journey from the next one. Once the snow covered the roof, it would provide ample shelter for the trapper.

From what Frank could tell, The Kid never built a line camp, and by the time the plane returned two weeks later to check on the men, the youngster still had no meat in camp.

Ten days later snow arrived in a large dump. With all the snow on the ground the partners knew the wheel plane wouldn't be landing at the camp again until spring. Yakutat usually receives 130–200 inches of precipitation a year but that year received 400 inches of snow.

Anticipating a few days in Yakutat at Christmas, Frank decided they could wait for the plane at the beach where it would be able to land at low tide. It was roughly six miles from the cabin to the mouth of the Alsek. They could walk overland or float downstream during high tide. Choosing to ride rather than walk, Frank began building a plywood boat.

Forty days after their arrival and before the boat was completed, The Kid seemed impatient and told Frank they should just go on and walk to Yakutat. Frank figured he had cabin fever (a condition wherein the sufferer felt trapped and needed to get away). He told The Kid they could readily hike to the beach or else take the boat when it was finished, but that it would be more prudent to catch the plane than to walk the fifty miles to Yakutat.

Since the trapping was abysmal—yielding only a marten, a squirrel, and a weasel—their camp meat consisted of two ducks; the men were hardly speaking to each other. Frank thought maybe a trip to Yakutat was well advised.

They loaded some gear into the boat and started downriver, which turned out to be rougher than either of the men had expected. Ice choked the river, requiring them to pull the boat over and around it.

The first day they reached only the halfway point. It took them all of the second day to cover the remaining three miles. They finally reached the beach that night.

Both men had good sleeping bags and tarps. The high tide came all the way up to the snow line. Because it was getting dark, Frank chose to build a snow wall for protection from the incoming tide as opposed to building a snow house.

That night Frank slept well. He was happy with his surroundings and felt he could have stayed a month. Food was not a problem. Had they needed more, they could have returned to their camp on the incoming tide. They had time since the tide was high.

The tide book indicated the tides were scheduled to be higher each day.

The next day following breakfast the men discovered a cabin that Frank had left years before.

Sand had drifted against the door effectively blocking the window and door. Using tools he found at hand—a board, a gallon can, and an ax—Frank began removing the gritty material in order to gain access.

In the midst of digging he felt a cold chill, felt slightly light-headed, and lay down to see if the feeling would go away.

Evidently The Kid had had enough of the waiting game, and while Frank rested, The Kid abandoned him. He hiked to a food-stocked cabin located between them and Yakutat where he was found in good health three days later.

Frank awoke to find his partner gone and a storm brewing. He felt he could safely stay at his beach camp another night and complete the cabin digging the next day.

During the night he awoke once and realized he needed air. He had taken a poke stick with him to his sleeping bag. This was an old habit. Often in the past he'd used similar sticks to open a breathing hole in snow if necessary. So he poked a hole to get air.

Daylight brought both the dawn and a dilemma. Frank lay on his left side unable to move his sleeping bag frozen solidly to the beach sand-gravel. An unexpected phenomenon had trapped him on the beach. Ocean spray had

blown a thousand feet across the spit and settled on the hapless man. The settling mist froze, effectively "welding" Frank to the ground.

No matter how hard he tried, he could not move enough to apply any
pressure to his sleeping bag. He lay there listening to the seas building, knowing that the tides would be higher that night. Thoughts about his chances of
surviving the incoming tide flooded his mind and he wondered whether the
tide would free him, drown him, or take him out to sea.

His only hope lay in the tide's thawing the ice to enable his escape or in
the timely yet nearly impossible arrival of someone coming to his rescue.

He went to sleep, but during the night the heavy breakers washed over
him, hammering his position for half an hour. Every receding wave brought
cold, salt water into his sleeping bag through the breathing hole he'd opened.
The water drained away through the open zipper.

The ice had softened some from the water's immersion. Although cold
from the repeated dunkings, Frank began kicking at his tomb. He kicked,
rested, slept, and awakened to kick again for the next thirty-six hours.

The third night a higher tide brought bigger waves, which kept Frank
busy for three hours. First he heard the wave coming. Then it washed over his
bag and drenched it. He managed to trap enough air in his bag between waves
to allow him to breathe. The constant washing of the waves had nearly freed
Frank's cocoon.

By noon he'd managed to kick a small hole in the bag and plastic tarp. As
he was able only to free the lower part of his body, the icy grip still held him
tightly. Knowing that the fourth night's higher tide would cover him and keep
him from acquiring air to breathe, Frank was now desperate. The below-zero
temperature caused the bag to freeze and he couldn't get back into it. He knew
that the incoming tide allowed him only an hour and a half before his final
breath.

That's when Frank heard the sound of an aircraft in the distance. As the
noise drew nearer, it was the sweetest music he had ever heard. The name
came from two aircraft. As he later found out, one carried Dick Nichols and
the marshal; the other was a Coast Guard plane.

The planes circled, then landed. Before long helping hands freed Frank and carried him to a waiting plane, which medivaced him to Anchorage's Providence Hospital. Frank spent nine months in the hospital and in a rest home. He lost five toes.

The long nights on the beach had given him time to think about his partner and their venture. He didn't think he'd be partnering up again anytime soon with The Kid.

Excerpt from *On the Edge of Nowhere*

JAMES HUNTINGTON and
LAWRENCE ELLIOTT

JAMES HUNTINGTON is the quintessential Alaskan. The son of
a white trapper and a Athabascan mother, he grew up far from civilization in the Kuskokwim region of Alaska. When his mother died young,
he helped raise his siblings, and he learned how to survive in the wilderness almost before he was old enough to walk. He was the first person to
win both the Anchorage and the Fairbanks sled dog race championships in the same year. He later served on the Alaskan Fisheries
Board, one of the toughest jobs in Alaska, since it decides the policies for
the conservation and utilization of one of Alaska's most important resources: her commercial, subsistence, and sports fisheries.

LAWRENCE ELLIOTT, who has written several books and numerous magazine articles, was the *Reader's Digest* correspondent for
Alaska and western Canada when *On the Edge of Nowhere* was written
in the mid-1960s. Elliott now lives in Luxembourg. This title is available at www.epicenterpress.com.

There was plenty of fur that year, and I didn't want to leave my traps.
It was March before I got back, and by then my baby daughter was
two months old. They had named her Christine, and when Cecelia
put her in my arms I was afraid to breathe, she was that tiny. Then I didn't
want to let her go.

After a while Cecelia said, "You told me you'd come down before she was born."

"We're a family now. We need money," I said. "I figured it was more important to build up a stake for us than to waste a lot of time mushing back and forth visiting."

She nodded. I think she understood.

In June, we went a hundred and fifty miles up the Hogatza to the mouth of Caribou Creek. I had heard about some abandoned gold diggings that were open for new staking, and since there was supposed to be a heavy salmon run up that way, it seemed as good a place as any to make a summer camp. Now I was really looking to put together some cash. I loved the trapping life but it was beginning to look as though it was over for me—how could a man go off and leave his wife and daughter every winter? And so my father's old dream of running a little trading post somewhere slowly took hold of me. All I thought about was getting enough money to start.

I spent long hours putting up drying racks and emptying the fish wheel. One day, when the smokehouse was almost finished, we heard a gas boat coming up from downstream, and I sent Cecelia to put up some tea. It was the bishop of the Episcopal Church making his annual trip to the camps and villages along the river. We were sure glad to see him, for now the baby could be baptized. Afterward, he gave Cecelia and me Holy Communion, and we had a nice tea. Then he was off again on his long, lonely trip.

We ate well that summer. There was plenty of bear around the camp, and since fresh meat doesn't keep more than a few days in the July heat, there was no sense in saving any. We ate the best of the salmon, and one day I shot a couple of geese, and Cecelia made a good stew. It was fine living—except for the mosquitoes. We had to keep a net over Christine.

When the salmon run was past its peak, I walked back out to the creeks. Gold colors showed almost every place I panned, but I was a long way from getting excited. I knew enough from listening to Dad to realize that a man working alone couldn't take enough out of these creeks even to pay for his labor. The only chance to make a dollar was to get some big mining outfit interested and sell out. I strolled around, taking plenty of time, and staked the eight claims I was allowed, four for me, four for Cecelia. When I got back to camp,

I wrote a letter to the Commissioner in Fairbanks telling about my claims, then got in the boat and went forty miles downstream to the mouth of the Hogatza where the mail boat went by once a month or so. I stuck a pole into the bank, hung a gasoline can on it, and put the letter inside. I sure hoped they noticed it.

A couple of Eskimos came up the river in a canoe one August afternoon and we made a lunch for them. Things had changed a lot between the Eskimos and Indians since my mother's day. We didn't exactly consider ourselves blood brothers, but at least we didn't shoot each other on sight. These two, a boy of fifteen or so and an older man named Henry, were on their way home to Kobuk, where the Pah River bends north of the Arctic Circle, and they still had a long portage to make. I asked them what they were doing in Indian country, and they said they'd come down to see how the hunting was.

That ticked me off. I know it's a free country, but I didn't like the idea of somebody scouting the game and then bringing back a whole pack of Eskimo hunters. But what really got me mad was the older one's bragging about what a good shot he was with that Luger pistol tucked in his pants. "I killed a bear with it yesterday," he said. "One shot."

I asked him where the meat was. I didn't see it in the canoe. He shrugged. "We left it. No sense packing meat when there's so much around."

I just looked at him. I think the younger one knew what was on my mind because he got nervous and edged away from the fire. Finally I said, "The game in this country was put here to feed the people—the Indians. We don't kill it just to prove what good shots we are, and nobody else is going to kill it for no reason, either." I stood up and he scrambled back, as if he thought I was going to hit him. "This party's over, Mister. You can make your camp down on the beach, but you better be way upriver when I wake up tomorrow."

Cecelia was afraid he'd try to hurt us during the night, but I knew better. I'd seen men like that before—Eskimos, Indians, and white men—the kind that do everything with their mouths. When you make them shut up they're finished. I felt sorry for the boy, though.

In the morning they were gone. But we weren't done with them yet, not quite. In that hour of the evening when the mosquitoes are still, Cecelia and I were sitting on the bank smoking and watching the last of the salmon struggle up the river. Suddenly I felt her stiffen beside me and when I looked upstream I saw why: the Eskimos' canoe had just come around the bend, and the boy was paddling hard toward our camp. There was no sign of the other one.

I got up and started for the beach. Cecelia tried to catch me. "Take your rifle," she said.

"I don't need any rifle. They're in trouble."

They sure were. Henry, the older one, lay in the bottom of the canoe more dead than alive, his clothes all torn, and his body, too, what you could see of it. Most of him was caked with dried blood. The boy's face was white as snow, but he kept his voice steady when he asked if I would help them. "He went into the woods after a wounded bear," he said.

He didn't have to tell me that. There is a certain look to a man, or what's left of him, when a bear gets through mauling him. This was it. "Let's pack him up to the bank," I said.

He groaned when we fetched him out from the bottom of the canoe. He tried to talk, but it was hopeless: his mouth was torn open from the left corner to the socket of his left eye, and his tongue just flopped around in that big, bloody opening. Cecelia took one look, then shuddered and turned away. I told her to boil up some hot water.

We laid him on a piece of canvas and I cut his clothes off to see if there was any sense in prolonging his agony. Some times the kindest thing you can do for a man who's tangled with a bear is to speed him on his way. I had a hunch that maybe that was what the Eskimo was trying to ask me for when I lifted him out of the canoe.

His right arm was laid open from the shoulder to the wrist. His right thigh was torn, too, and full of holes where the bear had bitten him. There were deep claw marks at the back of his neck. Then the bear had really dug in and all but torn the scalp from his head. It looked as though he had a couple of broken ribs, too, but that would have to wait.

When the hot water was ready, I stirred a cup of table salt into it and began washing the wounds. That's all we had by way of medicine, but I figured it didn't much matter: if God wasn't with this man, all the medicine in Fairbanks wouldn't help him. When I'd cleaned him as well as I could, I poured more salt into the deeper wounds. He moaned, but that wasn't the half of it. I had to stuff it into those holes in his thigh, and my fingers went all the way in, and he screamed and passed out. That was the best thing for him since I hadn't even started to sew up his face.

I was going to use caribou sinew, but when I went to get some Cecelia told me it would rot in his skin and come apart. She said to use the hair from his head and she gave me a bone needle that she used for sewing moccasins. But she didn't come out of the tent.

I pulled a bunch of hairs out of his head, taking care not to rip the rest of his scalp off. His hair was just right, nice and thick, and I threw it into the boiling salt water, along with the needle. Then I took a good long look at his face and the top of his head, trying to figure out the best way to sew him together. All this time the boy hadn't said a word, only watching and helping me whenever he could. But as soon as I pulled those two flaps of mouth together and stuck the needle through, I lost my helper for good. He clapped a hand over his mouth and ran for the bushes, and I could hear him being mighty sick.

I sewed away until the sun was low on the horizon, and I couldn't see too well anymore. Then I called for Cecelia to bring the coal-oil lamp. She wasn't happy about it, but she stuck right with me, even when she had to hold the lamp close enough so I could see to take the last few stitches inside his mouth. Altogether it had taken nearly four hours. Henry wouldn't be any beauty—if he lived—but I had done the best for him that I knew how.

I got the boy to help me fix his bedroll on the ground and lift him in. We put a mosquito net over him, and sat there for a little while listening to him struggle for breath. The boy asked me if I thought he was going to die. I said I didn't know, but that there wasn't anything more we could do about it, either way.

"I'm sorry I ran away," the boy said.

"Forget it. Next time you won't." I asked him how it had all happened.

They had come on the bear about twelve miles up the river, he said, a big blackie slapping salmon up on the beach. Before the boy could stop him, Henry had that Luger out and shot the bear in the side. The bear went roaring into the woods, and Henry went in right after him, not even waiting until the bear had stiffened up some so he couldn't move so fast. The boy had to tie up the canoe, then followed with a .22. He heard the bear charge and Henry screaming, and he'd run toward them, firing the rifle in the air and yelling as loud as he could. It worked. When he reached the place where his partner lay, the bear was gone, scared away. But the damage had been done. Henry was ripped and mangled as only a bear can do it, and the boy dragged him back to the canoe and made for the nearest help, our camp.

"Even among my people he is known as a big mouth," the boy said now, looking at the ground. "But he is one of my people. I thank you for him."

"Let's wait to see if there's anything to thank me for," I told him. "Anyway, there's one good thing: I don't think he'll be coming down this way to hunt anymore."

Very early in the morning the boy shook me awake. "I think he is dying now," he said.

I went out to have a look. Henry's breath was coming in noisy little rasps. He seemed to be choking and was burning up with fever. I put my arm under his shoulders and raised him as much as I dared. Then I sent the boy for some water, and managed to get a couple of spoonfuls into him. Once he'd swallowed whatever was backed up in his throat he breathed a little easier.

I made the boy some breakfast. His eyes were dark with strain and exhaustion, and I guessed he'd stayed up all night, watching his friend. He wanted to know if I thought it would be better to put Henry in the boat and take him down to the Yukon, maybe to the hospital at Tanana.

"That's a three-week trip," I said, "and he wouldn't last three days on the river. His only chance is to stay right where he is."

We built a lean-to over him to keep the sun off. The boy squatted right by his side, hour after hour, wiping the sweat from his face and shooing the mosquitoes off. On the third day the fever broke and Henry opened his eyes. "My chest hurts," he said.

I was surprised that he could talk. His face was so swollen that you couldn't tell where his mouth ended and his eye began. I tore some strips of canvas and bound up the broken ribs. Then he wanted to see himself in a looking glass. I told him he looked better than before but that he'd have to wait until I took the stitches out to see. Cecelia cooked up a fish broth and fed it to him, and he seemed to enjoy it.

On the fourth day we helped him get to his feet so he wouldn't stiffen up. He could move pretty well with only a little support. Next day I pulled the stitches out and gave him the looking glass. He didn't look so bad: the scar was nice and straight, except that I didn't get the corner of his mouth quite right so that he seemed to be forever grinning at something. But he was satisfied.

"Where'd you learn about sewing up a person?" he asked.

"By working on you," I said. "The hard way. Same as you learned about hunting bear."

He had nothing to say to that.

In another ten days he felt strong enough to travel. Of course he was in no shape to make that portage over to the Pah, so I told them to go downriver and have the doctor at Tanana make sure I hadn't done anything wrong. When they left, Henry shook my hand and said, "If you're ever in my country, I'll try to thank you the right way."

At the end of August Cecelia and I went back to Cutoff. There was no letter waiting for me with good news about my claims so all I could do was go back up to the winter cabin at Hogatza and trap fur again. This time, though, Cecelia said that she and the baby were going with me. "It can't be any worse than staying alone," she told me.

We went by dogsled not long after freeze-up, Christine all wrapped in blankets and fur. It wasn't too bad: it never got much colder than twenty or thirty below, and there was a fair number of mink around. When the trapping tapered off we decided to go back to Cutoff for the Christmas potlatch, and to stock up on some supplies.

But there was bad news waiting for us at Cutoff. The store had burned down and, except for some fresh meat the men brought in, there was no food in the whole town—no flour for bread, no potatoes or canned vegetables, and, worst of all, no milk for the babies. Nor would any come in until breakup, unless someone went and got it.

That night Cecelia and I talked it over. I remembered that the Eskimo boy had told me about a trading post not far from Kobuk. If I got some other men to go with me, we could take three or four dog teams up and bring back the things people needed. It was probably a hundred miles each way, but with good weather we could do that in a week. Meanwhile, Cecelia and the baby could stay with her parents.

There was no shortage of volunteers. None of us had ever been up in Eskimo country, and this seemed like a good opportunity to look it over: we had skins to trade, and since the one called Henry owed me his life, his people ought to be pretty nice to my people. Early next morning five of us driving four teams headed out. We didn't know the way so we just followed the Dakili River north, then crossed over the divide to the head of the Selawik. That was the end of the timber country. Up ahead the snow and the slow rolling hills stretched out to the sky. It seemed as though you could see forever, and there was nothing to see, only that endless white land. We were just about at the Arctic Circle now and figured it was fifty miles more to the Kobuk.

We camped under the last trees and cut enough firewood to carry for the trip. In the morning, when we'd been on the trail about three hours, we saw our first caribou. They were less than half a mile away, a good-sized herd of them, moving slowly across the hills in front of us. I led the teams into a hollow and told three of the men to keep the dogs quiet and out of sight. The other man and I grabbed our rifles and started trotting toward the herd, bent low to the ground so they wouldn't spot us. We didn't know the first thing about hunting caribou—you just don't see them in our part of the country—but we meant to give it a try because the people in Cutoff would need all the fresh meat they could get.

When we were still three hundred yards away, the herd turned in our direction. We hit the ground and, lying prone in the snow, lined them up in our sights. I thought, *This is too good to be true.* It was. Whether the dogs had caught the caribou smell or were excited by something else, I never did find out, but all at once you could hear them howling clear across the tundra. My partner and I each had time for one quick shot before the herd swerved to the west and took off like a brown blur on the snow.

We stood up to see if we'd had any luck when, suddenly, the howling was right on us and we spun around to see two teams of dogs flying by, sleds and all. They were hell-bent for those caribou—and the caribou were hell-bent straight down the Selawik Valley with not a tree or a rock or a bush to slow them down. I have never seen game travel so fast—and the dogs were gaining on them!

Our troubles had only begun. Down in the hollow, we could hear the other men fighting to hold the rest of the dogs in, and we ran for all we were worth to give them a hand. We had already lost two teams, and if the other two got loose in this godforsaken land we'd really be in for it. I dived for the nearest sled and dug my heels into the snow to brake it. But those dogs had gone absolutely crazy. They yowled and pulled for all they were worth, and the towline broke and away they went and all I had hold of was the sled. I jumped to my feet—too late. The last team had just broken away from the three men hanging onto it. We now had forty-six dogs running wild across the open tundra.

For a while we just stood there, five dummies trying to work up the ambition to take out after our teams on foot. Then the dark specks strung out along the white valley seemed to grow darker, bigger. The caribou had begun a cautious swing to the left.

"We must have dropped their leader," I said. "They're coming back."

We came running up out of the hollow and, from the next hill, saw the dead caribou: one of the two shots we'd fired had made a lucky hit. When we got close enough we could see that it was the leader. He had a tremendous rack of antlers and the scuffed, hairless neck of a fighter. The rest of the herd was a mile away, the dogs maybe four hundred yards behind them, and they were still coming on.

I sent the other men to hide behind the crest of the hill and I dropped down behind the dead animal. I made myself hold fire until the herd was less than fifty feet away. Then I opened up, squeezing off shots until my rifle was empty. Back up on the hill, I could hear the others pumping away just as hard, and I saw three, maybe four caribou drop. But it was like trying to turn back a blizzard with a fly swatter. By the time the leaders veered off, the rest of them were all over me—and those crazy, yapping dogs came swarming right up their backs.

The other men, unable to shoot anymore for fear of hitting me, were running off the hill with their knives out. I never had a chance to go for mine. All I could see was flashing caribou hooves and I burrowed in under the dead one trying to protect myself.

Then the dogs hit—forty-six raving, rattle-brained malamutes, tangled in their towlines and fighting and biting anything they could sink their teeth into. One of them even went to work on my leg and that was his big mistake of the day. I clouted him on the head with my rifle stock and jumped to my feet, just as wrought up as the dogs were now, swinging at every one I could reach. Pretty soon I had half of them laid out, and all the fight had gone out of the others. The caribou were gone and I stood there in the sudden deathly quiet, breathing so hard it hurt and feeling the sweat soaking my under-clothes. All around, where the men had fought the caribou with their knives, the snow was splattered with blood. We had killed six of them. The dogs were flung over a fifty-foot area, but they weren't going anyplace, not even the ones who were still conscious. They had their lines so hopelessly snarled that it would take us an hour just to separate the teams.

My legs turned all rubbery and I sank down in the snow. Man, I thought, we were a great pack of hunters! Losing our dogs! Fighting caribou with knives! I made up my mind to warn the others that we'd better just keep this whole mess our little secret—as soon as I could talk again.

One of them had made a fire and brought me some melted snow to drink. That was a big help. "I was on my way over to give you a hand with the dogs," he said. "But the way you were swinging that rifle around I figured I better stay put."

That reminded me of my leg. I hiked my pants up to have a look and found three neat little holes where teeth had gone through. I stuffed some table salt in them and tied the leg with a strip of flour sack, and it hardly both-ered me at all.

I sat there coaxing my strength back while the other boys untangled the dogs. They were sure quiet now, pretending to be friendly as pups. After the lacing I'd given them they'd have jumped a foot if anybody said, "Boo!" Once they were straightened out, all of us went to work skinning out the caribou. We cached the meat and marked it for the return trip, then had some tea and a lunch and set off again.

We had to make only one more camp. By that first afternoon, we'd come on an old dog-team trail and followed it straight to the river. Next day we were in Kobuk.

The people seemed friendly enough. They poured out of every house and alleyway and swarmed around us, jabbering and gaping as though we'd come from another world. In a way, I suppose, you could say that we did. One thing for sure: this place and its people, the first Eskimo town we had ever been in, was as strange to us as we were to them. Everthing was different. You didn't see a single thing made of wood. The houses looked just like the round igloos you see in picture books. Later I found out they were actually built up with squares of sod, and that snow blocks were laid on for extra protection. Even their dogs were hitched in a different way.

Suddenly, in that great babbling mob, I heard someone call, "Jim Huntington!" It was the boy who had been in our fishing camp the summer before, looking twice as big in his parka and wolverine ruff, grinning as he elbowed through the crowd and pumped my hand. "What are you doing up in this country?"

I told him we were after supplies, and he said the trading post was only eight miles up the river and would have everything we needed. Then he said, "Now you come to my house and eat a meal." I tried to explain that I had to take care of my dogs, and that there were four other men with me. But it seems as though you don't tell the Eskimo anything when you're in his country: you just do what he says. The boy said something to his people in their language, and the next thing I knew our dogs were led away and each one of my friends was being escorted to a different igloo.

We had to bend real low to get into the boy's house, going through a long tunnel that came out in a fair-sized room lit with a seal-oil lamp and full of the people of his family, from little tots to a grandmother who must have been old when the Russians owned Alaska. Everybody kowtowed to her. The boy told them who I was and then we sat down to eat—dried salmon, muktuk, caribou meat, crackers, and a good strong tea. The old grandmother asked me how come I was so far from home. I told her about the store in Cutoff burning down. I said I came to buy shells and food and milk for my baby.

She rolled a cigarette and lit it, never taking her eyes off me. "What's the matter with your wife, no more milk?" she said. "How old him baby?"

"She is a girl baby. She is two years old."

"How long you and wife stay together?"

"Three years."

"Three years, only one baby come? Ha! Maybe you don't stay home enough. Maybe you work too much."

I told her I was out on the trapline most of the time.

She blew smoke in my face and said, "Maybe you stay home two moon. After that, ha, some more baby come. Then you don't have to buy milk in store."

I said I would give it a try. I figured I had to be polite to her. I even thanked her for the advice. But I was sure desperate to change the subject. I turned to the boy and asked, "How's your friend Henry? What did the doctor in Tanana say about my sewing job?"

The igloo got very quiet. I thought for sure I'd put my foot in it again. Finally the boy spoke: "The doctor said you did a good job. There was no more he could do."

I felt better. I said, "Well, where is the great bear hunter? I'd like to say hello."

The boy shook his head. "Right after the first frost he took a team out on the river. Nobody could tell him anything, that the ice was still thin. You know. He went in less than a mile from here—dogs, sled, and all. The only thing we ever found was the hole."

Man, that made me mad—after the way I'd worked to keep that man alive! But all I said was, "That's too bad."

The grandmother spoke up again: "He was looking for death. If not bear or ice, he find some other way to die. He a man who not meant to grow old."

I nodded. She was a smart old lady, after all.

Pretty soon some other people came and said that now I had to go eat in their house. Just to be nice I ate some more muktuk and drank some more tea. I had no more than finished when they took me to another house, and still another, and in each one there was a big feed. It got so that all I could manage to get down was the tea. I drank so much tea that I felt as though my back teeth were afloat. I asked them where the bathroom was, but they didn't seem to understand. I tried every word I knew—*privy, restroom, toilet*—but all I got was a blank look, so finally I told them in plain English what I needed.

They laughed and laughed. "Oh, anyplace outside," they said.

I went outside, but there were kids playing around everywhere so I kept going until I'd walked all the way to the river. And there were still people around. Pretty soon I came across two of my buddies with the same problem. "Say, where's a guy supposed to go in this place?" they asked.

I told them that the Eskimos had given us permission to use any part of the arctic land for that purpose, and I stood there as though I were admiring the view and did what I had to do; not one person even looked up. Later I discovered that the Eskimos always did the same. They weren't troubled by any two-faced modesty, and let's face it, in a land where there wasn't a bush or a bit of cover, that makes a lot of sense.

As I wandered along the riverbank looking for our dogs, a big, strong-looking man with a vaguely familiar face came up to me. He said that my bedroll and things had been taken to his house, that I was to spend the night there. In the morning, he would put me on the trail to the trading post. I told him that that was okay with me, it didn't make any difference where I stayed, but that I had to buy some dried fish for my dogs first.

"Dogs already eat," he said. "We take care."

I thanked him—that was really service! We walked by the dogs on the way to his house and I got the barest wag of their tails as I passed, that's how contented they were.

Excerpt from *Cheating Death*

LARRY KANIUT

AT THE RIVER'S MERCY

TALL TALES ABOUND on the last frontier—fish grow in size at nearly every fisherman's telling, weather worsens every time a pilot relates a harrowing experience. But nearly all Alaska tales have at their heart the immensity and grandeur of a land that, even unembellished, still sounds fantastic. This story of the Copper River, completely true, is so wild it borders on the unbelievable. In the pages that follow, Kevin Smith tells his own story.

The Copper River has historically presented a challenge to Alaskans. It was a primary obstacle to railway pioneers and miners at the turn of the century. Nearly nine decades later, this same river challenged my good friend Blake Call to plan a float trip on its waters. I joined him in 1987, along with his parents and two other friends. It was to be a casual six-day float downstream from Chitina for about one hundred miles through some of the most spectacular Alaskan wilderness.

Let me tell you a bit about myself and the other folks on the trip. At six-foot-two and 215 pounds, I'm larger than most of my friends. I was raised as an active outdoorsman and have been in Alaska since the pipeline days in the mid-1970s. I didn't work on the oil pipeline, though; I was only twelve when construction got under way in 1974.

I met my rafting partners when I was attending the University of Alaska Fairbanks. Kurt Wold and Blake Call both were close to my age. Shelly Call, Blake's mother, is a whitewater canoe instructor in Fairbanks. David Call, Blake's father, is also a river-running veteran. Both had run the Copper River before. Barbara Cotting was a friend of David and Shelly and, like me, had done some rafting and canoeing but had never faced water the size of the Copper River.

The six of us slipped our two rafts into the Copper River at Chitina at mid-morning on a Wednesday. The trip had barely begun when we spotted the largest bull moose I have ever seen in my years in Alaska. Continuing through Wood Canyon and beyond, we became the audience for a symphony of wildlife and scenic splendor. Trumpeter swans, grizzly bears, bald eagles, and more gave a private performance for the six of us floating lazily by.

We floated, rowed, camped, and ate. The weather was fine—in fact, too fine. The sun, beating down on nearby glaciers, weakened a glacier dam. Late Thursday, the dam of snow and ice burst, sending a surge of pent-up water into the Copper River. The rise in the water level was slow, but the effect was dramatic.

We met the water almost a day later at legendary Abercrombie Rapids. At the rapids, this flowing giant of a river crams all its force into a gorge that is no wider than a few hundred feet. The rapids consist of large oceanlike swells bordered on one side by a house-size rock and on the other by small standing waves. This day, however, only the very top of the rock was visible as water repeatedly broke across it. The rapids were a mass of swarming, standing waves whose size we couldn't determine from a distance.

We surveyed the rapids as we approached and agreed to go in, but we still couldn't figure out how big the waves were. I knew that bushes on the side of a mountain that appear to be only knee-high can, upon closer scrutiny, prove to be twelve-foot-high alders.

So it was with the waves at Abercrombie Rapids. My estimate, before entering the rapids, was that the waves were cresting at about the height of my thigh. But as we hit the first wave, my error became frighteningly obvious.

We never got beyond the second wave. A wall of water that dwarfed our sixteen-foot raft tossed it end over end without hesitation.

Shelly was trapped beneath the raft, hanging onto the rowing frame, with her head in the airspace created by the foot compartment. David, the helmsman, managed to hold on to the lifeline. I was not so fortunate. My 215-pound frame was catapulted out of the raft and into the current, and I was swept away.

As Kevin Smith fought to stay above water, Blake Call's raft was trailing behind. Blake's raft, with him at the oars, also carried Kurt and Barbara. They were seventy-five yards behind the lead raft, and they had watched carefully as that raft entered the rapids. When the lead raft closely approached the first wave, Blake was stunned. The water was enormous. The standing waves were twenty feet high.

The lead raft crashed over the first wave and landed, bottom flat, on the uphill surge of the second wave. There it seemed to hover, on a mountain of water, before it was tossed end over end, dumping his parents into the frothing torrent and launching his friend Kevin through the air.

"Row for your life!" Blake shouted, and they did. "They've flipped!" he screamed. "They've goddam flipped!"

They rowed wildly away from the most intense part of the rapids, skirting the waves as best they could on the right. As they rowed away from the main current, the overturned raft moved away from them. Once around the most dangerous part of the rapids, Blake, Kurt, and Barbara rowed with what strength they had left into the current to catch up with the overturned raft. Waves bounced up and down, obscuring their view of the capsized boat. Could the others live through this?

As they approached the other raft, only David could be seen clinging to the lifeline.

"I think I see your dad," Kurt reported. Then the head of Shelly Call appeared beside her husband's as he helped her out from beneath the upside-down boat.

But there was no sign of Kevin Smith.

Through the enormous waves, they finally reached the overturned boat and pulled David and Shelly into the raft. The sound of the river around them was deafening.

"Where's Smith?" Blake yelled.

"The last I saw him, he was floating high," Shelly shouted back. Supported by his life vest, Kevin was last seen being swept to the river's left.

They lashed the capsized raft to the side and rowed into an eerily calm eddy, a kind of whirlpool. It reminded Barbara of the eye of a hurricane. Still the river roared, and the force of the water was so strong just behind the flat spot that the river flowed crazily uphill. The group paused only briefly to make certain everything was secure before trying to enter the raging current again.

But they couldn't break the grip of the eddy. The raft slipped downhill and swirled to the back of the whirlpool. Again the crew paddled madly at the water, trying to reach the outside of the whirlpool, but again failed. Shifting positions for optimum efficiency, and powered on adrenaline, they tried again. This time the raft train broke loose from the eddy and was once again at the mercy of the fast-moving water. Still there was no sign of Kevin.

I must get to the raft, I told myself as I fought against the current, but it was wasted effort. I was in the river and the river was in control. My paddle—the last vestige of a raft I had already lost sight of—floated toward me, and I grabbed it. This was to be my security blanket for the ordeal that followed.

The water was so big that I felt that I must ride as high as possible. Afraid that the water and silt would fill my rubber boots and hold me down, I kicked them off. As I crested the next wave I surveyed my situation, then took a deep breath and held it as I plunged twenty feet down to the trough and rode back up the next wave for some more of the same treatment. Breathe and survey. Hold on for dear life and plunge.

Fortunately I was dressed as well as I could be for the rapids. I wore wool long underwear beneath my wool pants. I wore a T-shirt, a long-sleeved shirt, and a wool sweater beneath my Woolrich jacket. Wool gloves, wool socks, and a life vest finished my outfit. But even though I may have been wearing a family of sheep, the frigid water of the glacier-fed river penetrated my every pore and set my teeth to chattering.

After riding to the top of several waves, I could understand what awaited me downriver. Below me and to my right was an island flanked on the right side by a line of hungry-looking rocks. If I was to make it to safety, I needed to get well beyond the jagged teeth of the rocks and into the eddy in front of the island. Not a foot less would do, or the current would drag me across the teeth, chewing me up and spitting me out on the other side.

I paddled for all I was worth, but I wasn't doing much good. I picked a spot on the other bank, off to my left, and began to paddle and pray.

I was swept safely past the rocks and continued to paddle toward the other shore, alternately praying and singing "Going to the chapel, gonna get married," a promise I had made to myself and my fiancée of two weeks. Already the frigid water was cooling my body core and hypothermia was setting in; I could hear my voice slurred and thick. I could not feel my feet.

I reached the point where I had hoped to paddle ashore, but I drifted past, unable to get there. I stuck the paddle under my knees, pulled myself into a cannonball, and let the river carry me where it wished.

Thoughts flooded my mind as I realized that I was dying. My life didn't flash before my eyes. It was more a reflective review on what I had done, whom I had loved, and what my purpose in life had been.

I don't hate anyone, I told myself. *This is good. I hold no grudges. I have not seriously wronged anybody. I am doing what I love to do, and I am paying a price that comes with that.*

I thought too of what was supposed to be. Former daydreams of my future swept through my mind. As any bachelor might, I began the trip wondering if getting married was something I was ready to do. Now, floating in the river and about to die, I knew that getting married was exactly what I wanted to do.

I looked around. *This country is beautiful*, I thought. *It truly has the fingerprints of God all over it. If now is the time that I must go, then nowhere could be a more fitting place.*

All the rationalization in the world, however, could not erase one nagging thought: *While I am prepared to die, I am not yet ready to die.*

Meanwhile, the five other members of the expedition rode the current around the island and pulled in behind it, onto the main shore. As they pulled toward shore, they spotted one of the rubber boots Kevin had worn, swirling in a whirlpool behind the island. Everyone saw the boot, but no one called attention to it. Each chose to file the sight silently away rather than alarm the others. But the seed of doubt about the chances for Kevin's survival was beginning to grow.

Blake and Kurt set off with binoculars to look for Kevin; one walked upstream, the other downstream. It was now forty-five minutes since the raft had thrown Kevin into the river.

As Blake searched, he spotted a dot in the water. He drew his binoculars to his eyes expectantly and focused—but it was only a seal. Again and again this happened, and each time his frustration grew.

Kurt also scanned for signs of life. He spotted movement on the far shore and checked through his binoculars. He saw a huge brown bear tossing and shaking something in the air. He closed his eyes and could only hope he had not found Kevin.

Of course I prayed. I prayed to God to forgive my indiscretions. I prayed for strength to survive.

A seal popped up beside me in the river. This animal with dark, mysterious eyes seemed to know instinctively that I was out of place and in trouble. Curious, the animal floated near me, examining me in his element the way I have examined seals in a zoo. He moved closer, with what seemed like a sense of compassion. It was entirely plausible in my mind that the seal could help me.

Becoming seriously hypothermic, I felt I was about to black out. I drifted in and out of thought. I fought the urge to close my eyes and sleep. My vision got darker and darker, like backing into a long tunnel and seeing the light at the entrance getting smaller and smaller. The light became just a flicker, a point, while darkness surrounded me. My eyes closed—and I bumped into the bottom of the river.

I bounded upward and discovered that I could stand. The water was only about a foot deep. Facing upstream, and shaking uncontrollably from the cold, I planted my paddle in front of me and surveyed the situation. The river was very wide. On either side of my shallow stance, it was at least half a mile to shore. My guess was that I had floated more than three miles down the river.

The warm air felt good. From the position of the sun, I guessed it to be about 6:00 P.M. I realized I should be dead by now. Since I wasn't, and I was standing on the bottom, things were looking fairly good. The seal surfaced near me again, and I made an appeal for help. It looked at me quizzically and slowly sank into the river.

After about twenty minutes I was warm enough to remove my hood and to shout weakly for help. Weakly, indeed. I was startled at how insignificant my cries sounded in the middle of this muddy giant of a river. Upstream I saw no one. I realized it would be up to me to save my own life.

I tried to move laterally across the river toward the right bank. I knew the chances of finding only foot-deep water all the way to shore were remote at best. Within five or six steps, I was in chest-deep water and the current was forcing me backward. I tried to return to the shallows but couldn't regain the ground I had lost. I managed to get back to water that reached only to the middle of my stomach.

Once again I was shuddering uncontrollably. I planted the paddle in the riverbed and let go to zip my coat up further and replace my hood, knowing I would probably lose the paddle—my security blanket—and too cold to care. I had just taken two steps toward the other bank when the freezing, muddy water sucked me up and once more carried me away.

Upstream, the five rafters had decided on a rescue plan. Blake, Kurt, and Barbara would remain in the area where they were. They would search the side of the river they were on from the rapids downstream and then move to the other side of the river and do the same. Nearly two hours after the accident, it seemed clear that if they were to find Kevin, he would have to be on shore. Staying alive in the frigid waters of the Copper River for more than forty-five minutes was a near impossibility. Chances were slim that a live person would be found very far downriver.

The plan called for Shelly and David to take the other raft and head down the river, keeping a watch out for Kevin as they floated down to the Million Dollar Bridge. At the bridge, a popular summertime tourist spot and the first possible point of human contact, they could try to find help.

Before splitting into two parties, they divided up the gear and food. Very little was lost in the upset because most of the gear was lashed down in watertight bags. Only a few items fell victim to the river: some tent poles, the propane tank for the camp stove, perhaps a case of beer.

They agreed on a system of fire signals. If David and Shelly spotted Kevin but were unable to get to him, they would light one fire at 10:00 P.M. If they actually picked Kevin up, they would light two fires at ten o'clock. If there was no Kevin, there would be no fire.

David and Shelly pushed off in their blue raft at 6:30 P.M.

B ack in the current, I once again needed to conserve body heat. This time, however, I had no paddle to help me in keeping my knees to my chest, and I was too weak to do so without an aid. I grabbed a piece of driftwood floating by. I stuck the driftwood under my knees and used it to help pull myself into a cannonball.

I bobbed along in the current with the other flotsam picked up by the new high water of the Copper. The seal floated next to me and dived. I prayed again.

I looked up anxiously as I approached the looming Miles Glacier, which was calving off big chunks of ice into the river—loudly and often and in the direction that I was being carried.

My vision was again waning. Stronger than ever was that familiar desire to close my eyes—to succumb to the darkness and let go of the little point of light at the end of the tunnel that was my consciousness and my life. Now severely hypothermic, I was slow in my thinking when I thought at all. My sole task was to keep my eyes open.

As I approached the glacier, icebergs entered the mainstream, joining me and the high-water driftwood in the fastest part of the river. The approach of the first iceberg gave me an idea. I swam awkwardly to meet the ice.

The first iceberg was the size of a coffee table. I reached out with my last remaining strength over the top of the ice, pulling myself near. As I attempted to mount the iceberg, it slowly rolled over and floated bottom-side up. The bottom was smooth and clear from melting in the water and was even harder to try to climb up on. So I rolled the iceberg back over and carefully pulled myself up onto its surface, spreading my weight as evenly as possible across the berg.

Exhausted, I lay on the iceberg, shivering, feeling even colder than when I was in the water. I could feel the heat being sucked from my body like power from a battery.

Towering above me, the snout of Miles Glacier calved again and sent a large wave my way. The wave rolled slowly over the river toward me, closer and closer. It hit me gently and spilled me back into the river, rolling my little iceberg back upside down. I climbed on again, but each time the glacier calved, it sent waves that tipped me into the icy water. This happened four or five times. Each time, it became more difficult for me to swim back to the iceberg and climb aboard.

We continued to approach the glacier, my iceberg and I, closing in and passing other icebergs. I spotted a larger, more spacious, and more stable iceberg. I rolled off my little piece of ice and breaststroked toward the larger, slower-moving berg. This iceberg was big enough, about the size of a large desk, to permit me to get completely out of the water. Cold as it was, it was a definite upgrade.

Reaching from the iceberg, I pulled up pieces of driftwood to put underneath me, to insulate myself from the cold: a piece of wood for a seat, sticks for a floor, and a couple of extras just in case. I was completely out of the water for the first time since I was thrown from the raft, and I was alive!

David and Shelly floated down the river. Binoculars in hand and shouting Kevin's name, they drifted and they rowed, scanning both shorelines. They had already come four miles and nearly as many hours from Abercrombie

Rapids, and they knew that the fate of their friend Kevin was all but sealed. They discussed the impossibility of Kevin's survival and the possibilities of what would happen to his body. Still they held to a ray of hope and continued to search in the remaining light.

The three people upstream spent the evening until nearly dark searching the shore for Kevin. Disheartened, they silently packed their raft and rowed to the island, each immersed in private grief. Blake, Kurt, and Barbara set up a makeshift camp and checked frequently for signal fires from downstream. Each time they checked and saw nothing, their spirits dropped lower.

*W*ell, *this is great,* I thought, as visions of riding an iceberg heroically to safety filled my head. I would simply jump off at the nearest shore as I floated by. Better yet, I could ride the berg to the Million Dollar Bridge and step off, bowing to the tourists. I was alive, getting warmer, and floating toward civilization. Things were definitely looking brighter.

At that moment, the iceberg ground to a halt on the bottom of the river. The silt of the river assaulted the iceberg, sandblasting away at it. I could hear the sound of the sand as it scoured by, and I knew I was in trouble.

Now in Miles Lake, only four hundred yards from Miles Glacier, I sized up my predicament. The glacier rose out of the water on my left as I faced the downstream shore a mile or more away. That was the closest shore. Across the lake, the other shore was at least two miles away. Upstream, only one hundred yards away, was a sandbar. But with this current, I knew that having the sandbar one hundred yards upstream or one hundred miles upstream was pretty much the same: it would be impossible for me to get to it.

I heard a crack, felt a rumble, and out of the water next to me shot two pieces of ice about a foot and a half in diameter. The iceberg began to list, and I adjusted my weight accordingly, desperate to prevent it from rolling. Standing against the current, my iceberg was beginning to fall apart.

I began looking at nearby stationary icebergs that were more stable, icebergs that were at least the size of a small house. One of these would have to be my next destination. The possibility of spending the night on an iceberg became a very real one.

It was now about 8:30 P.M. The sun was low and a ray of sunlight spread from the distant shore across the lake and onto the Miles icefield in a narrow beam. I sat and pondered my fate. I prayed—and I heard a voice.

Unsure, I removed my hood and looked around. I shouted, "Hello," and listened. I thought I heard a shout from the far shore, and I turned just in time to see a flash of blue pass through the narrow beam of waning sunlight. Blue was the color of the overturned raft.

D avid and Shelly's raft drifted silently across Miles Lake. Could it be possible? Had they heard a voice? Or was it just an echo from their last cry?

Shelly yelled, "Hello." The reply came back, "Hello." It was just an echo; it must have been. The lake was bordered on three sides by glaciers and high mountains, a perfect echo chamber.

Shelly called again. "Hello," she shouted. "Hello," came the reply. "Hello," she screamed. "Hi," came the answer. David and Shelly looked at each other in disbelief.

Then they heard the distant voice again. "Hello . . . hello . . . hello . . ." followed by a message that they couldn't make out, a message overpowered by echoes, distance, and the river. It had to be Kevin, but how, and where? The voice sounded as if it might be coming from the far side of the lake, about three miles away. But there was no shore there, only the vertical face of Miles Glacier rising out of the water. Where else could it be coming from?

They finally decided the voice must be coming from across the lake, glacier or not. They paddled toward the glacier.

H appy in a way that I cannot describe, so incredibly happy to be alive and to see rescue coming, I forgot entirely about being cold. Adrenaline pumped through my system as I saw the blue dot get larger and larger. I danced on my iceberg island, waving my arms and shouting to my rescuers: "I'm over by the glacier on an iceberg, and my iceberg is melting!"

I continued to shout to help David and Shelly find me in the fading light. I sang, "Row, row, row your boat," the echoes helping with the rounds. I told them how happy I was. I also tried to explain that the iceberg I was on was deteriorating and likely to go at any time.

As the raft drew within a mile, they spotted me. Waving back, Shelly yelled, "We see you. Save your energy."

"I don't think you understand," I shouted back. "I'm on an iceberg, and my iceberg is breaking up!" They didn't understand. They thought I was on a sandbar or something. The idea I could be standing on an iceberg never entered their minds.

When they were within half a mile of me, they suddenly figured out the situation. Once they understood, they rowed faster.

About forty-five minutes after I first spotted the raft, it pulled up to my iceberg.

"So that's Abercrombie Rapids!" I said. "What a wild ride!"

"We've never been so happy to see anyone in all our lives!" came the reply.

Then I felt a rumbling under my feet. Now an experienced iceberg pilot, I knew this was the moment. I yelled, "It's breaking up!" And with that I lunged into the air toward the raft.

As I did so, the iceberg I was standing on broke apart, with a sound like a rifle shot. With a couple of oar strokes, the raft was on me, and David and Shelly pulled me into the boat.

Unbelieving, they looked at me. "You're one tough son of a bitch," David said.

"You're right," I replied.

Shelly helped me while David rowed toward shore.

"How do you feel?" she asked.

"I'm afraid I may lose my feet," I said. Shelly put dry socks on me and stuck my feet between her legs as we traded accounts of what had happened since four that afternoon.

It took nearly an hour and a half to reach the closest shore, a sandbar at the base of a steep mountain. I stripped immediately and climbed inside two sleeping bags. David scrambled to find enough wood to light two signal fires. It was well past ten, the prearranged signal time.

Not enough fuel lay on the sandbar to make the fires very large, and it was too dark to collect more wood. But what David's signal fires lacked in communications ability, they more than made up for in warmth. Wearing socks and a sweatsuit and draped with a sleeping bag. I huddled near a fire while a tent was assembled. I tried to eat but couldn't, and I settled for the comfort of the fire.

Later, in the tent, lying between Shelly and David inside two zipped-together sleeping bags, I felt the warmth of their bodies flow into me like I had felt the ice suck it from me. Within ten minutes, Shelly was shivering from having gone to bed with an ice cube. But all of us were exhausted, and we quickly fell asleep.

Sleep didn't last long. Our sandbar was only fifteen feet wide, and the water continued to rise. About three in the morning we awoke to the sounds of water lapping at the tent. For one groggy moment I feared I was still in the river. We quickly pulled the tent as far as we could up the sandbar, tied the raft securely, and went back to sleep.

U pstream, the three other rafters continued to look in vain for some signal from David and Shelly. The next morning, at first light, they moved to the other side of the river and chose a site suitable for landing a helicopter. Then they began the search for Kevin again.

Blake hiked upstream to the rapids and started working his way back. Kurt hiked downstream but soon hit a tributary that blocked his progress. Looking across a long, desertlike sandbar, he could see for miles, and nowhere was there a sign of Kevin. Barbara remained at camp and built a fire as a signal for an eventual helicopter.

Kurt and Blake returned to camp at noon, exhausted and depressed. Without enthusiasm they went through the motions of eating. They tested the helicopter signal fire, sending a billowing smoke signal into the noontime sky. Twenty hours had passed since the raft overturned. Still, each tried to keep the others' spirits up.

Just before the weary band turned in for a midday nap, Blake prophesied, "At two o'clock Smith will come around that corner and say hello."

Hello!" boomed a voice that woke all three members of the upstream search party. Kurt, Barbara, and Blake stumbled out of their tents, squinting their eyes in the afternoon light. It was two o'clock.

Then they heard another shout.

"Hello the camp!"

Scanning the horizon over the scrub brush and the sandbar, they spotted Blake's mom, Shelly, dwarfed by the owner of the voice, none other than the missing Kevin Smith!

Kurt, Barbara, and Blake ran toward the tributary that earlier had blocked Kurt's progress. Blake led the way, flipping handstands and jumping up and down.

"Smith, are we glad to see you!" they hollered. Shouting from across the stream at each other, the two groups agreed on a time when Blake and Kurt would bring their raft to the tributary. Kevin and Shelly would first go back and get David, who was downstream at Miles Lake with the raft.

It was one of the happiest moments I'll likely ever be a part of, that moment when all six of us were reunited. We feasted and drank, shared our thoughts and fears and experiences, and celebrated life until late into the night.

The next morning, we had a visitor for breakfast. A tiny little sparrow, usually a spooky bird, landed near the campfire and begged for crumbs. Within minutes the tiny bird was flitting from person to person, sharing breakfast with each of us.

As we packed the raft with all the gear, making room for the three extra passengers, Bird remained. Jokingly we referred to the bird as my guardian angel. Jokingly, I say, but I still wonder.

Much of the trip still remained ahead of us. We recovered the second raft. We still had two days of travel before we were to reach our takeout, including floating by the enormous face of Childs Glacier, right next to the Million Dollar Bridge.

This glacier is truly spectacular, but a bit dangerous. The glacier has been known to calve pieces of ice large enough to send a wall of water up over the ten-foot bank on the other side of the river and claim vehicles parked near the shore. We hoped to merely glide past the glacier. As we began to do so, Bird fluttered to our raft and sat on the oarsman's head, undeniably a good omen.

Although the glacier did calve, the wave was small. It missed our raft entirely and merely pushed the other raft to shore, where David, Shelly, and Barbara easily shoved it off again. Bird remained with us for the rest of the trip.

Author's note: This title is available at www.epicenterpress.com.

Bush Pilots—
The Lifeline
of Alaska

ALASKA IS THE only state that is largely unscarred by roadways. Outside of the major cities, it's rare to find a paved road of any length. Only the Alcan Highway goes from one end of the state to the other. At the best of times, the vast distances involved mean that Alaska's people get around in bush planes when they want to cover any respectable amount of mileage. In the winter, most of Alaska's traffic moves by snowmobile, dogsled, snowshoe, or plane. Whether it's ferrying pregnant women to the hospital or a basketball team to the next village for a weekly game or a hunter in search of a trophy, Alaska's bush pilots are what knit the state together. In the process they face some of the wildest flying conditions on the planet. These are a few of their stories. . . .

Excerpt from *Arctic Bush Pilot*

JAMES "ANDY" ANDERSON
and JIM REARDEN

JAMES L. ANDERSON, born in 1922, grew up in the coal-mining town of Montcoal, West Virginia. He became an Eagle Scout, played on the high school football team, did odd jobs, and worked in the Montcoal electrical power plant. He enlisted in the Navy five days after Pearl Harbor and in six years of service advanced from apprentice seaman to lieutenant (jg). After flight training, he was assigned to the aircraft carrier USS *Princeton,* from which he flew Curtiss dive-bombers in combat. In 1946 he returned to civilian life and for a year became a Civil Aeronautics Administration flight controller at Bettles in the Koyukuk Valley of northern Alaska. Realizing the need for bush plane service in the Koyukuk, he resigned from the CAA and, backed by pioneering Wien Airlines, almost single-handedly established regular, dependable air service for villages, mines, and travelers in a vast region of northern Alaska. He built a roadhouse, or lodge, at Bettles, which became the focal point of commerce in the Koyukuk region. In the seventeen years he flew from Bettles Field, Anderson accumulated thirty-two thousand hours of logged flight time in a wide variety of single- and twin-engine airplanes. After twenty years of aviation in Alaska, he retired to a Pennsylvania farm, where he lives with his wife, Betty. Be sure to check out more about him at www.epicenterpress.com.

I often made medical evacuation flights at night or during terrible weather. Sometimes both. Why, I never understood, but medivac flights seemed more frequent in nighttime or during the worst possible flying conditions. Weather stations and navigation aids were spaced so far apart they were almost useless to me. As a result I had to learn the area, including the location of every mountain ridge, every lake, and every possible landing site.

One midwinter night a radioed request came from Allakaket for me to fly a young woman in labor and expecting her first child to the Alaska Native Service hospital at Tanana. It was snowing, with a blustery wind, and the temperature was well below zero—a nasty night; even a daylight flight would have been questionable.

There were no lights at the short dirt runway at Allakaket. I had to depend on a Good Samaritan to stand at the approach or touchdown end of the runway with a flashlight pointed in the direction I was to land. This allowed me to fly so the landing light on the aircraft could guide me in landing—light from the flashlight helped me to determine how close I was to the ground. On a long airfield there would have been some leeway, for then I could have felt my way down, gradually allowing the plane to descend. But long runways were an almost nonexistent luxury in the Koyukuk. The hummocky strip at Allakaket was no exception. Even today the airport facility directory warns pilots landing at Allakaket to "watch for children and dogs on runway" and that "river floods south end in spring."

On the forty-mile flight to Allakaket I flew through the snow and wind a few hundred feet above the white, frozen Koyukuk River, bordered by dark trees. Someone, I never knew who, was waiting in the dark with a flashlight to show me where the end of the runway was. I let down and managed to stop. Several villagers were there with the frightened young mother-to-be wrapped in furs and blankets.

I didn't get out of the plane or stop the engine. Someone helped the young woman in and I pulled the lap belt across her upper legs and snapped it in place. I tried to reassure her with a smile, swung the plane around, and roared down the runway with the snow flying every which way.

That 150-mile night flight from Allakaket to Tanana was one of the most hazardous I can remember. There are no predominant landmarks along the route, which consists of rolling hills interspersed with wooded areas. Here and there is an occasional treeless, windblown opening.

On my right was 3,500-feet-high Utopia Creek Mountain. Peaks on my left were four to five thousand feet high. To be sure I was above all of these I started climbing. I was almost instantly flying on instruments, with no sight of the ground. I climbed above five thousand feet and took up a compass course, praying there was no ice in the clouds where I flew.

The radio range at Tanana was not very reliable from fifty miles out, and my low-frequency receiver left a lot to be desired. For me to receive any signal at all I had to reel out forty feet of trailing antenna.

As we flew in the clouds and snow, I continually inspected the wings with a flashlight, praying ice wouldn't develop, and it didn't. I had no idea of wind direction and velocity at my altitude. Turbulence bounced the plane like a sock in a washing machine. My entire being was concentrated on flying and on the radio range signal. It gradually became stronger, indicating I was nearing Tanana.

After flying as if inside a bottle of milk for more than an hour, and with the radio range signal coming in loud and strong, I called CAA flight service and requested the runway lights be turned to high intensity. I caught a glimpse of a glow below and cautiously descended in a tight circle, keeping the glow in view. I broke out of the clouds a few hundred feet directly over the runway. Landing was no problem.

A Jeep arrived to pick up my passenger, who had not said a word. I assumed she was justifiably frightened half out of her wits. She did manage a wan, "Thank you, Andy," as she left. She delivered a healthy baby boy just ten minutes after arriving at the hospital.

"You have to leave immediately, Andy," one of the attendants said. "The community is under a medical quarantine."

I figured I had used up all my luck that night and I wasn't about to try to fly the 190 miles back to Bettles in the snowy darkness. It was too cold to sleep in my plane, so I persuaded the man on watch to isolate me in the CAA building, where I grabbed a few hours of sleep. At daylight I was able to return to Bettles.

I flew so many women in labor to the Tanana hospital that the doctors there gave me instructions on how to handle a birth and provided me with an emergency kit to keep in the plane. Happily I never had to use it, for no baby was ever born on any of my flights. However, birth was too near to suit me on a number of occasions.

I finally announced to everyone in the region that I would no longer consider a woman in labor a medical emergency. This resulted in my flying expectant mothers to the hospital in advance of expected birth dates, and these flights were made in decent weather and during daylight.

When I flew on a cool, crisp autumn day, with the land below me in splotches of vivid orange, red, and gold, with the air as smooth as silk, the joy within me seemed to overflow. In the crystal air of the Arctic I could sometimes see for a hundred miles or more. The beauty of the land under my wings always gave me pleasure.

The Brooks Range of northern Alaska was, and still is, the wildest, most remote, and least-hunted of the important big-game areas in North America. This rugged, untouched wilderness, the northern extension of the Rockies, spans six hundred miles across northern Alaska and has a north-south depth of about one hundred miles.

During the 1950s and 1960s, increasing numbers of adventuresome hunters arrived at Bettles, asking me to fly them into this lonely land. Vast herds of roaming caribou are found there; I've seen caribou crowded so closely together I would have had difficulty in finding an open spot among them for landing an airplane. At times on clear fall days I could see the snowy white necks of the bulls from a distance of twenty miles.

Grizzly bears also wander along the mountains, mostly at or beyond timberline. Some are blond, some dark. Others are blond on the back, with dark legs. Shiny black bears also roam the south slope of the range.

Pure white Dall sheep—North America's most northerly wild mountain sheep—dot the high ridges. Early in fall on grassy peaks, they look like popcorn scattered on green cloth. After snowfall, the only way I could see them was to find their tracks; their bodies are nearly invisible against snow.

Moose are most abundant on the south slopes of the mountains, although these huge deer are also found on the North Slope. As I flew above them, their salt-and-pepper and dark bodies stood out against the spruce, birch, and open tundra. Often the bright, clean antlers of the bulls flashed like mirrors in the distance. Sometimes I looked down in wonder at these big, ugly-handsome deer as they stood with heads submerged in lakes, feeding on aquatic plants.

Wolves were especially abundant in the Koyukuk Valley, for they are found everywhere there are moose or caribou, their main food.

Warren Tilman, an old-time Alaska guide and one of the few who hunted these mountains in the 1930s, once said, "In the Brooks Range the game dies of old age and the country remains just like God put it there."

Wien Airlines and I started to promote hunting in the region. Within a few years as many as sixty to seventy hunters and guides were chartering my float-equipped airplane to reach isolated spots of the mountains each fall. Hunting season ran from the first of August until late September. Whenever the nonresident hunters or guides didn't want the meat of big game they killed, I flew it to the nearest Native village, where it was welcome indeed; none was wasted.

Some hunters arrived at Bettles unprepared for camping in mountains where snow can fly every month of the year, and I often loaned them the proper equipment. Timberline in the Brooks Range is at about two thousand feet, and much of the range is above and beyond the last timber. There are twenty-four hours of daylight in the range during early August, but even then the temperature can drop fast; August weather is comparable to that of early October in the northern contiguous states.

High-country lakes often freeze over in early September, halting float-plane landings. After a few years I ruled that my hunters had to be out of the high-country Brooks Range by September 1. If they weren't, I told them, I refused to be responsible if they became frozen in. In this event, their only recourse would be to walk out, and a hundred-mile hike through snow-covered mountains could be deadly. (My annual changeover to skis on my airplanes usually came in October or November—too late to benefit any hunters who failed to beat the freeze.) Happily, no hunter I flew into the mountains ever had to hike out—thanks, I believe, to my September 1 deadline.

Some of Alaska's top guides came to Bettles Field with their hunters. I recall providing charter service to Hal Waugh, Warren Tilman, Jim Rearden, and the famed partners Bill Pinnell and Morris Talifson, and there were many others.

My most famous passenger was General James Doolittle. He had been a hero to me ever since his famous bombing raid on Tokyo early in World War II. One fall he was a guest at an Air Force hunting camp not far from Chandler Lake. The Air Force had its own registered guides and floatplanes there, so I remained clear of them except for an occasional drop-in visit to check on their well-being.

On one such visit I learned that Doolittle was the only hunter in camp who had not taken a trophy Dall ram. I offered to fly him and his guide to nearby Shebou Lake, where I thought he would have no difficulty finding a trophy. I named this small, high-country lake Shebou, a combination of sheep and caribou, because of the constant abundance of trophy rams and caribou bulls.

The general and his guide climbed into my plane, and after a short flight I eased down for a landing on Shebou. This was long before Alaska's current regulation that prohibits hunters from hunting on the same day they are airborne. The two men headed up a nearby ridge while I waited. Later that day the ecstatic general, who was then in his seventies, and his guide appeared with the general's trophy ram, which we loaded into the plane and flew back to the Air Force camp.

Doolittle tried to pay me for the flight. This I refused, because my service was but a token of my appreciation for his wartime heroism. I did ask for and receive from him a one-dollar bill with his signature on it, which I treasure to this day.

The waters of the Brooks Range are a strong attraction to sportfishermen, drawn to the thousands of miles of clear-water streams and hundreds of untouched lakes.

Grayling abound in the clear rivers and most of the lakes. This handsome, flag-finned, rainbow-hued fish is usually eager to take a fly, a spinner, spoon, or small plug. White-fleshed and mild-flavored, it is a favorite of Alaska's sportfishermen.

Lake trout are plentiful at virtually every lake inlet and outlet across the range. They also cruise the shallows in summer. Some weigh up to twenty pounds, and they too make for fine eating.

Arctic char are found in most of the high-country lakes. This beautiful cold-water fish, related to the Dolly Varden, will strike at almost any lure. That toothy predator the pike, some up to thirty pounds, is abundant mostly in lakes along the south slope of the Brooks Range.

Sheefish, a close relative to the salmon, winter in coastal estuaries. They migrate annually to freshwater spawning grounds far up the clear Koyukuk River. Unlike the Pacific salmon, sheefish do not die after spawning. I often anchored a boat just above a riffle on the Koyukuk River and cast my lures just below the riffle. When sheefish were there, I would seldom cast without getting a strike. In the course of an afternoon I have caught upward of four hundred pounds of these delicious, white-fleshed fighters. I enjoy sportfishing, and sheefish are among the best of fighters. But when I caught these fish it was to acquire a supply of them for winter use. No fish is tastier.

Whenever I returned to the roadhouse with sheefish, I removed the entrails, cut off the heads, removed the scales, wrapped the fish in aluminum foil, and dropped them into my freezer. They kept perfectly, and we could eat what passed for fresh fish all winter.

Koyukuk River salmon are mostly chums, or dog salmon, not normally considered a sport fish, for they rarely hit a lure. At spawning time when both grizzly and black bears flock to the tributaries to feed on these oily fish, I often flew low over these streams, enjoying the sight of these grand animals dining on their favorite food.

During my later years in Bettles, tourists occasionally arrived to charter my plane for a scenic flight. Those who accompanied me on such flights usually returned with stars in their eyes after viewing the splendors of the upper Koyukuk River country.

In all my work at Bettles, my principal obligation was clear: to offer transportation in return for a fee. When a customer called for service, he didn't want a weather report or a reason why I couldn't fly him or his freight. Nor was that customer concerned about the condition of my airplanes. He usually wanted one thing only: for me to fly him or his freight from point A to point B as quickly and safely as possible.

That was my primary goal for the seventeen years I flew from Bettles. However, in time I learned there was a bit more to it than that. My life became intertwined with that of my customers. Many became my close friends. Their triumphs and tragedies became my triumphs, my tragedies. On many flights, money was the last thing on my mind.

On a scheduled mail run one winter, I landed at Chandalar Lake high in the Brooks Range. While waiting for the postmaster, I saw a couple of large sled dogs trotting across the frozen lake, pulling a sled that resembled an undersize television dish.

As they drew closer I made out a person sitting in the dish. He was heavily bundled in clothing because of the forty below temperature. Frost on his parka ruff framed his face in white.

The dogs trotted to my plane and stopped. The man leaped to his feet, stuck out his hand, and said, "I'm Amero. I guess you're Andy."

His full name was Alfred W. Amero (pronounced AM-uh-row), but most people called him Old Amero. He was a Klondike goldrusher in 1898, making the journey on money from his mother. He didn't get rich in the Klondike, and he arrived in Alaska on the Kobuk River Stampede, a gold rush in 1898–99.

Amero mined on the Kobuk River, the adjacent Noatak, and then the Koyukuk—and by the time I met him he had ranged all over the north. He was reputed to have been the best woodcutter in Beaver, where he had cut wood for the steamboats that once plied the Yukon River. He could take two pack dogs and go for weeks, even months, wandering in the mountains, searching for gold. Another old-timer once said Amero would size up a fat ground squirrel like it was a side of beef.

In 1946 Amero sold one of his claims for enough money to visit his old home in New England, the first time he had been south of the Yukon River since 1898. In all that time he had never been to Fairbanks, the only city within 250 miles. In his extreme old age he lived in the Pioneers' Home at Sitka.

We became friends. Although he was in his eighties, he moved, talked, and behaved like a much younger man. I even started calling him Amorous Amero, because he still had an eye for the ladies.

On one of my flights to Chandalar, he arranged for me to fly him to the Arctic Village area, about a hundred miles to the east. As a youngster he had worked for a mining company there, and the outfit had done well. Amero thought it might be worth reworking the claim.

He remained in the Arctic Village area for more than a month. When he returned to Chandalar he made no mention of his experiences at the old mine. Curious, I asked Red Adney, also of Chandalar, if Amero had found anything in the old diggings.

"Naw. All he found was a bunch of old horse manure," Red said.

The company Amero had worked for had used horses in their mining, and all Amero had found was what the horses left behind. He was proud of his ability to find gold, and his find at the old mine embarrassed him. He wasn't about to tell me about it.

A nother Chandalar miner I made friends with was Ellis Anderson. In his eighties when I first met him, he had arrived from Sweden about 1910 and acquired several mining claims. On one claim, at Squaw Creek, about eight miles from Chandalar Lake, he built a log cabin situated well above timberline. He laboriously dragged all the logs several miles to the site.

About 1949 he went to Fairbanks to work and make some money. He returned in winter, landing at Chandalar Lake without snowshoes. He had a terrible struggle in the deep snow in walking the eight miles home. When he got there he found a bear had torn a corner off his tiny cabin, which was now filled with tightly packed snow. It took days to shovel it out.

Ellis had a suspicious nature, harboring the notion that anyone who made friends with him was trying to steal his claims. I often flew over his cabin to check on him. He was so suspicious of those flights that he refused to leave the cabin to wave at me or to see who was buzzing him.

One winter I didn't see any tracks in the snow at the times I flew over his cabin, although a trace of smoke was usually curling from the stovepipe. This puzzled me, and I worried about the old man. One day that spring I landed on the shore of Chandalar Lake and found Ellis waiting for me.

He had broken his leg during winter and had somehow survived until spring. Then he had struggled eight miles on crutches he had carved to where I would find him and could fly him to the Fairbanks hospital. No one had been aware of his broken leg.

Doctors broke his leg a second time and reset it so it healed properly, permitting him to walk again. When his leg healed he returned to the wilderness to continue mining.

I often wondered how Ellis survived such an ordeal. His everyday tasks such as preparing food were difficult even under normal conditions. How had he managed with a broken leg? How did he keep from freezing?

He never bothered to become a U.S. citizen and could not get the Territorial retirement pension. He eventually sold out for ten thousand dollars and lived frugally in Fairbanks for the rest of his days.

I marvel at the tenacity of such independent old-timers. Most sourdoughs like Amero and Ellis Anderson stubbornly refused to ask anyone for help or to borrow anything.

Soon after Alaska statehood in 1959, schools were established in most Native villages. This called for many new teachers, many of whom came from Outside (that is, from the South 48 states), attracted by generous salaries. Living quarters were generally provided in or near the schools.

A major drawback for many of these newcomers was the loneliness. They were strangers in a strange, unforgiving land. Often it was difficult for a city-bred teacher to adjust to life in a wilderness village. This was culture shock to which many simply couldn't adjust.

Icy winter temperatures usually discouraged visiting outside the village during the school year. Consequently at the end of the year, many of these teachers were anxious to get out of the villages and were ready to talk to anyone who would listen.

After one school year, the middle-aged teacher at the sixty-three-person village of Hughes was anxious to return to her New York home. I made a special flight to Hughes because she wanted to get an early start.

That poor teacher talked incessantly during the flight. I nodded at what I thought were appropriate intervals, not paying much attention. At one point, I radioed a Wien DC-3 that was in flight, requesting that the plane stop at Bettles for the teacher. I had to plug in my earphones for the call.

When I clamped the earphones on, I apparently offended the jabbering teacher. She reached up and yanked them off my head, tossing them onto the floor, angrily announcing, "You're going to listen to what I have to say whether you want to or not."

Loneliness does strange things to some people.

O ne of my strangest charters involved a former Alaskan, an engineer, who had moved to California and married a woman who was a judge. He was addicted to smoking, but so fearful of cancer that he had his mouth scraped periodically in an attempt to prevent cancerous growths. He decided to break himself of the tobacco habit by isolating himself in the wilderness of the Koyukuk.

He wrote, asking if I could fly him and his wife to a place where they would have no contact with people.

"No problem," I responded.

The couple arrived. The food and equipment they brought was more than adequate, so I agreed to fly them to a lake about sixty-five miles from Bettles.

Their gear was piled, ready for loading into the plane, when the man requested, "Andy, please go through our stuff to make sure there are no cigarettes."

His addiction was so serious he didn't trust himself not to hide cigarettes in his personal gear.

I flew the couple to the lake aboard a floatplane. Three weeks later when I landed, taxied ashore, and shut the engine off, the man leaped onto a float, opened the door on the passenger side, and climbed in. He was in a panic.

"Andy, you can shoot me, but I am not getting out of this airplane. I must have a cigarette. I'll pay for the charter to Bettles and return. Just don't ask me to get out."

The flight to Bettles Field took about forty-five minutes. I landed on the Koyukuk River as usual and taxied to the dock and shut down. The prop was still revolving when the engineer leaped ashore and ran full speed the half mile to the store.

His wife understood. No way could her husband stop smoking. When I flew the engineer back to the lake, the couple broke camp and returned to Bettles with me. He happily chain-smoked cigarette after cigarette as they waited a couple of days for the DC-3 to pick them up for the first leg of their flight back to California.

One day in the late 1950s, two middle-aged men arrived at Bettles on the mainliner flight from Fairbanks.

"We're prospectors," one of them said, "and we need to check out a few areas. Can you fly us?"

"Sure," I said. "How do you plan to pay?"

"I left a signed blank check with your traffic department in Fairbanks to cover all expenses," one of them said.

I called Fairbanks and was told they were holding the signed blank check and that I could fly the pair wherever they wanted to go.

I flew those two all over the country. I'd drop them off for a time, then pick them up and fly them to another spot they picked from a map. They had built up a couple of thousand dollars' worth of flying and roadhouse bills when I received a frantic call from Fairbanks. "Their check is no good; they don't even have an account at the bank. Provide no more services."

I later learned that these men had no prospecting experience. They were gamblers, scam artists. They had heard there was gold in the Koyukuk country and thought they would bluff their way into getting control of a gold mine and pay their expenses from whatever gold they might find.

A peculiar-appearing stranger climbed off the mainliner DC-3 one fall day and walked into the roadhouse. I suppose he would have been called a hippie in those days. A long scraggly beard half-hid his face. His greasy hair was tied into a ponytail and fastened with a piece of string. His clothing looked slept in.

He introduced himself to me. "I'm the teacher you've been corresponding with."

I could scarcely believe it. This was the schoolteacher I had been trading letters with for the past year? The one who had told me about his desire for a new lifestyle? His beautifully written letters bore little resemblance to this apparition.

"I want you to fly me to a place where I'm completely isolated," he said. "I don't want anyone near me. Nobody!"

I left the man—I'll call him Edward—at an abandoned mining airstrip where there was a warm cabin and plenty of nearby timber for firewood. The food he brought consisted mostly of pemmican—ground meat mixed with fat and other substances—that he had prepared.

Edward's last words as I left him standing on the little airstrip were, "I really want to be left alone."

I flew over the spot occasionally to check on him. After a couple of weeks, I saw he had put out a flag, the signal for me to land. He appeared to be safe and healthy, so I didn't land until I had the time a day or so later.

"Where in hell have you been?" he demanded to know. "I've been signaling you to land for days."

"You convinced me you wanted to be left alone," I explained, feeling a little guilty at having pushed him so far. I was certain he was ready to return to civilization.

To my surprise he handed me a list. "I'm sick of pemmican. Here's a grocery list. Bring the stuff as soon as you can."

It turned out Edward was sincere about wanting to live in the wilderness, and he stuck it out.

Within a year he had moved to a nearby lake, where he built himself a nice log cabin. He bought a trapping license and was working toward becoming a registered big-game guide. At that point his lovely wife and young son joined him. I hadn't been aware he had a wife and son.

Both Edward and his wife were ambitious, hard workers. They were diligently settling in to become longtime bushrats—the Alaska term for people who prefer the independent, isolated life.

It all ended abruptly one day in a tragic accident when Edward stepped into the whirling propeller of an airplane that was preparing for takeoff. He died instantly.

The body was returned to his home state and buried in the family plot. Soon after, recognizing the futility of trying to live deep in the bush without Edward, his wife and son left Alaska.

Prospective bushrats in all flavors arrived at Bettles Field. One March a middle-aged couple from the South 48, recently married, with the bride's two pre-teen sons by a previous marriage, arrived at Bettles on the Wien DC-3.

"We've read all about Alaska and have decided to live off the land," the man announced.

They had sold everything they owned, and with no outdoor experience had chosen Bettles in March as their jumping-off point.

They planned to live in a tent heated with propane and had brought a small tank of propane and a burner more suitable for cooking than heating. Their supplies included potato chips, soft drinks, candy bars, and loaves of bakery bread—food mostly unsuitable for a long stay in the wilderness. Their sleeping bags were summer-weight. They did not have an ax or tools of any kind.

Deciding to give them a taste of the land they had reached, and yet ensure their safety, I offered to loan them a cabin I owned at a lake within an hour's flying time from Bettles. Before taking off for the first of two charter flights to the cabin, I asked, "Do you have snowshoes?"

"No, we won't need them. We have galoshes," the man said.

Galoshes are worse than useless in the Arctic's deep snows.

I landed my ski plane on the lake, taxied near shore, and shut the engine down. The father opened the passenger side door and jumped into snow up to his hips.

"Think you could use snowshoes now?" I asked.

He looked thoughtful, but didn't reply.

That night the temperature dropped to 50 below. Fortunately for them there was a good supply of firewood, so they remained warm.

That family lived on the lake for some time, eventually moving into another cabin. I continued to fly supplies to them when I could conveniently veer from a mail flight.

About a year after these folks arrived, I was returning to Bettles with an empty plane. I decided it would be a welcome change for the family if I treated them to a weekend visit at the roadhouse, a hot bath, good meals, and a Saturday night movie. I landed and made the offer.

"There'll be no charge," I said.

"We'd love it!" the woman exclaimed.

"Me too," both boys chipped in.

"You three go ahead. I'll stay here and keep an eye on things," the man said, rather sourly.

I flew the woman and two boys back to the lake the following Sunday. Luckily for me I took a friend along for the ride. As I stepped out of the plane the man met me and poked a .38 pistol in my face.

"You're trying to steal my wife!" he screamed.

I'm being a gentleman when I say merely that the woman was past her prime. The accusation was absurd.

Luckily my friend was a diplomat who understood the seriousness of the situation. I was in a mood to do battle. I thought the pistol was empty and the nut behind it was waving it for effect. After soothing words by my friend and backup from the woman and boys, we all retreated to the cabin for coffee.

During our friendly coffee klatch I had a chance to examine the .38. When I broke the cylinder and saw six live cartridges, I turned pale. Anderson's rule No. 1 after that: "Never invite a lady to your home for a visit unless she's accompanied by husband."

BRAD MATSEN

For twenty years, Brad Matsen fished and traveled the Alaskan fishing grounds, publishing his stories in *National Fisherman, The Alaska Fisherman's Journal, Audubon,* and *Oceans.* Among Matsen's books are *Reaching Home: Pacific Salmon, Pacific People; Shocking Fish Tales;* and *Planet Ocean. Fishing Up North* can be found at www.gacpc.com and at fine bookstores everywhere.

I first heard about the DC–6 crash when I was standing around the coffee urn in the galley of a processing barge, not as interested in the thin coffee as in the jive and rumors that flow wherever fishing crews eat together. The galley of the *Bering Star* is an ingenious, miniature cafeteria with seats for fifty in a claustrophobic tangle of chrome-and-yellow-plastic tables. It is mug-up, a break from work when only a few people take the time to shuck their gory oilskins, as they must to enter the galley. Most grab their coffee from a cart on the processing deck and take it out on the catwalks that rise in tiers along the deep-blue sides of the barge.

The few visiting fishermen, tendermen, and off-shift workers who are in the galley are gathered around a guy wearing sweats and the most revolting, gurry-spattered baseball cap I've ever seen. I can barely make out the red Viking ship in a circle that is the logo of Icicle Seafoods. He's demonstrating his trick: he can breathe Jell-O. With a substantial red mound in a bowl on the table, he locks his hands behind his back, dips his head forward, and *schlupppppp*. Gone. That fast. He does it three times and everybody cheers.

The barge is at anchor off Clark's Point in the mouth of the Nushagak River on the west side of the Bay. Mothered by the strong, brown flow of the river, this spot is usually one of the most productive, but this season that part of the run is weak and nobody knows why. I hear the east side is crackling, though, with strong runs to the Ugashik and Egegik Rivers drawing most of the gillnetters, packers, and planes.

Bristol Bay is almost always called simply "the Bay," and only the greenest of North Pacific fishermen will be puzzled by the reference. It lies on the chart in the crotch between the pocked alluvial fan of the Yukon River and the volcanic Alaska Peninsula, which runs west to the nether world of the Aleutian Chain. For eight weeks every year, upward of 40 million red salmon rush through the distant passes of the Chain into the Bering Sea and then to Bristol Bay. There, they merge with thirty thousand fishermen, packers, pilots, and hustlers in the biggest spawning frenzy on the planet.

So anyway, during the Jell-O sucking, this woman with dark hair, high-mileage eyes, and a red tee-shirt comes up to me there in the galley of the *Bering Star* and draws her own cup of watery coffee. She's the cook. We watch the performance, and after a couple of minutes of "whaddya doing up here on the Bay," she asks me if I heard about the big plane crash. It involved, she said, a four-engine DC–6 freighter, fifteen tons of salmon, the Moonies, and a forty-foot bluff on the lee edge of the beach at Egegik. A real disaster, but the Bay is always dangerous. A renegade thought momentarily pulls my mind to another lee shore where, almost thirty-seven years ago to the day, on July 5, 1948, twenty-six men died when a northerly breeze backed around, became a southerly gale, and beat their brave little sailboats to pulp in a rising tide on Deadman Sands. Not long after, in 1951, engine power was made legal on the Bay, leaving only the elegant Chesapeake Bay oyster fleet under mandatory sail.

That remembrance is just a synaptic flash, a moment's pause, but it becomes a whole thought in that instant. I realize that the most vicious of uncertainties—once the companions of the fishermen of the sailing fleet—are now flying copilot in a new age. To be sure, the sea will always roar in dark, deadly patterns, but the airplane crash has become the modern incarnation of mortal risk there on Bristol Bay. Instead of talking about the DC–6, we sip our coffee, a simultaneous gesture like a nervous tic; the silence is not awkward. I ask her how many people died in the crash. Her shoulders rise and sag as the topic is acknowledged to be mortality.

"Oh, I hear two," she says. "But I don't know for sure. Poor things."

We don't mention the plane again, our conversation taking its usual turns through personal history, the size of the salmon run, money, boredom, and her philosophic vision of Bristol Bay as a home for lost boys and girls who refuse to grow up, who crave the single-minded pursuit of fishing out here because it brings a revitalizing kind of irresponsibility and freedom to life. Cooks on fishing boats and processing ships are like bass players in jazz bands; they keep the beat while everybody else improvises. The next day, another cook in another galley would tell me there were four aboard the DC–6 and that he didn't think there were any survivors.

At that point, an odd compulsion began to overtake me despite my reason for being on the Bay, which was to cover the fishing. It would eventually lead me to a scrap pile of wrecked airplane and smoking meat on a remote Arctic beach, after winding a twisted course through permanent truths that, somehow, would prove false. I had been to the Bay before, insulated in the protective wrapping of a journalist, but this time would be different.

TOWARD EGEGIK

I fled the processing barge and its inhabitants suffering under the lash of sixteen-hour shifts and bad coffee for a chance to get to the east side aboard the packer *Viking Queen*. I had met her skipper, Kari Toivolo, in the galley of the *Bering Star* while his crew was unloading. I learn that he is a twenty-six-year-old Finlander, that he's been running the *Viking Queen* for four years, that he put in his deck time aboard her during the glory days of king crab. The old-timers on the Bay tend to get more notice than the kids because fishing is a business that celebrates and rewards longevity, but king crab and the other high-bucks booms brought a fresh generation up through the ranks more quickly than usual. Many were very young when they went to sea to pick pots or run gear, tough kids in the new athletic fisheries that, more than ever before, paid well for youth's endurance and courage. Now, a man or woman of twenty-six can easily have ten years' experience as a fisherman or mariner, and many are running big boats or packing operations.

When Kari offers me a ride to the east side I accept without hesitation because I am drawn to the action and already in the tingling grip of curiosity about the DC–6 on Egegik Beach. And then there's the fact that a good salmon tender like the *Viking Queen* is almost a yacht, and I cannot turn down that kind of comfort on the water. The *Viking Queen* is a solid, ninety-two-foot, steel-hulled packer/crabber, one of ten built during the sixties at the Pacific Fishermen Yard in Seattle. She is a schooner, with an after-house, high whale-back bows, and plenty of room in between for three tanked holds chilled by a refrigerated seawater system.

Under way, the view from the bridge over the planked expanse of her deck is a visual mantra as we roll in waltz time across Bristol Bay, a pure example of the calming embrace of a gentle sea. Thought becomes a matter of harmony rather than details, a collection of images much too big to be carried by a fellow like me under ordinary circumstances. It happens to be Kari's wheelwatch as we pull away from the barge, and he sits silently across the bridge to my right. The constant conversation of meeting has fallen off now, and the only sound breaking the bubble of the grumbling engines comes when the young skipper reaches up every few minutes to adjust his autopilot. The Iron Mike responds with a series of ratchety clicks. I let my mind wander through the history of the Bay, with a piece of that history there under my boots and an heir to the tradition a few feet away in the captain's chair. Over the short span of a couple of generations, packing salmon from the Earth's most prolific run has been transformed from a primitive, feudalistic, food-gathering frenzy that was dependent on cheap labor to a breakneck dash featuring big money, fast boats, and airplanes.

LOOKING BACK

The *VQ*, as the *Viking Queen* is familiarly known, is owned by Icicle Seafoods, a company started thirty years ago by a few fishermen in Petersburg, Alaska, when the only processor in town closed its doors. They parlayed their instincts, energy, and a small packing plant into some good money. The money got very large in the late seventies when the Americans, with a stroke of the pen that signed the Magnuson Act, shut the Japanese out of the salmon, herring, and king crab grounds of the Bering Sea within two hundred miles of the coast. That meant they had to buy salmon, herring, and crab for their hungry markets, and guess who was selling?

Naturally, the Japanese wanted to ensure dependable supplies, so they invested heavily in American processing companies and triggered a nauseating wave of xenophobia. Japanese investments made for great debates in the bars and fishing trade papers, though. Some Americans, particularly Alaskans, who are very allergic to absentee ownership of anything, raved about Japanese control of their industry. Others pointed out that the Asian buyers were simply good customers, so what's the problem? The truth, as usual, is somewhere in between. In search of that truth, the state of Alaska commissioned a study on Japanese ownership that only confused things further because the researchers were never able to penetrate the veils of interlocking directorates that are common in Japanese industry. The charts in the report showing the flow of corporate investment looked about as meaningful as the stains left on the wrappings of a noodle lunch.

Nowhere was the Japanese outburst of investment of 1978 to 1981 felt more than on Bristol Bay, where, for almost a century, business as usual had meant tightly held, family fish-packing fiefdoms with highly dependent fleets of fishermen. For millennia, the salmon of the Bay had nourished the seasonally migrant Eskimos, Aleuts, and watershed Indians. The incursion into those ancient patterns and places by the American square-rigger fleets in the early part of this century established an order that remained essentially undisturbed until the Japanese buying frenzy arrived.

Of course, the technology and conditions changed over these years. During the square-rigger era, the ships would load lumber, cans, dories, fishermen, and Asian laborers in San Francisco and Seattle, sail north through Unimak Pass into the Bering Sea, and then head up into the funnel of Bristol Bay. There, the ships would anchor off their canneries, the captains would become superintendents, the fishermen fished, and the laborers canned the salmon. When they had a shipload, the laborers and fishermen would board up the canneries, pack the ships, and sail south with the goods. It was an efficient, though autocratic, proposition.

The square-riggers gave way to steam, and the sail-and-oar-powered dories went in 1951 when engines became legal. (Managers of the era believed that restricting fishermen to sail power was an effective tool to limit their catch.) That really was the beginning of the end for the old order. The engines made the fishermen far less dependent on the canneries, even though they remained employees and their boats were owned outright by the fish companies until the late 1950s. The harbinger of the next era of the independent fisherman was the *Judy Joyce,* a tidy thirty-two-foot gillnetter that, in 1985, was still fishing, though somewhat ceremonially. She was the first boat on the Bay ever owned by a fisherman, financed by Winn Brindle, patriarch of the powerful Red Salmon Company.

For another twenty-five years, through lean seasons while the Japanese fleets were slugging the salmon on the high seas and the inshore runs were weak, the fishermen remained little more than chattel of the packing companies. The canneries bought the fish but did very little negotiating on the price. (Virtually every fish went into a can.) They sold the fishermen food, fuel, and rooms in bunkhouses on shore and controlled the supply side of their marketing equation by placing their fishermen on limits when the runs were strong so as not to exceed demand. For canning companies such as Red Salmon, New England Fish, Whitney Fidalgo, and dozens of others, it was still Fat City.

In many cases, the arrangement between fishermen and packers was mutually benevolent, but abuses were common and the patterns of mistrust that took root remain today. After fishermen became "independent businessmen" in the late fifties, they formed a pair of hybrid unions: the Alaska Independent Fishermen's Marketing Association (AIFMA), based in Naknek on the east side of the Bay, and the Western Alaska Cooperative Marketing Association in Dillingham on the west side. The unions were technically hybrids because the courts had ruled that since each fisherman was essentially an independent business, they could only meet to discuss prices before negotiation with the canneries under special rules or they would be in violation of antitrust laws. Fishermen always complained that they were unfairly restrained while the canneries routinely colluded on the price.

AIFMA was the larger group, formed around a nucleus of fishermen of Portuguese, Italian, and Serbo-Croatian ancestry from California who were the heirs of the square-rigger tradition. Sometimes the bunkhouses sounded like a United Nations barbecue, and translators were necessary during negotiations. WACMA represented mostly local, native Alaskan fishermen, but they pretty much went along with the AIFMA line. Until 1980, the fishermen of the Bay wielded their power and independence in relatively straightforward ways. Every season, individual packers offered a price for reds, chums, kings, silvers, and pinks. Reds were the real money fish, and settlements for the others were always easy. The fishermen either accepted the red price or began a period of toe-to-toe negotiations prodded by the certain and imminent return of the run, which usually begins during the last week of June and peaks around July 10.

The fishermen's bargaining position gained considerable strength in 1974 when Alaska passed a law limiting the number of permits that would be issued to fish on the Bay to about 1,750. That meant the fishermen could enter negotiations with no fear at all that the canneries would hire scabs to take their places if they decided to strike.

CHANGES IN THE WIND

When the old order was finally displaced in 1980, Icicle Seafoods both literally and symbolically administered the coup de grâce. In 1978, the energetic little company from Petersburg slipped on a new set of financial pajamas and climbed in bed with Mitsubishi and Hoei Trading, major Japanese trading companies that approach their ventures like Godzilla devouring Yokohama. Icicle's main deal with Mitsubishi was a stroke of genius. Their Japanese partners and buyers financed two big, efficient processor-freezer barges—the *Bering Star* and *Arctic Star*—that Icicle could move among the herring, salmon, and crab fisheries. In return, Mitsubishi and its various subsidiaries got the rights of first refusal on the seafood. They could also tell Icicle just how they wanted it handled and packed and, with Icicle's several shore plants also going full steam, guarantee themselves a solid market share. Some canneries scrambled to install freezers in their shore plants. Floaters had been the coming thing, though, since the late fifties when Augie Mardesich came to the Bay with his primitive processor-freezer *North Star,* formerly Admiral Byrd's flagship. But nobody got it quite right until Icicle and the Star Fleet.

When the Icicle floaters arrived on the Bay, the old-line packers and fishermen regarded them as maritime incarnations of the Empire Death Star of *Star Wars* fame. What kind of services would these interlopers provide for fishermen, they scoffed. Where were the bunkhouses, showers, and mess halls that had turned the Bay into a kind of summer camp for fifty years? What kind of guarantees they'd be around next season? Who are these guys, anyway? Nothing but a front for the Japanese. They're nothing but glorified fly-by-night cash buyers. Who loves you, baby?

But the Icicle Deathbarges and another similar rig, Nelbro Packing Company's *Ultra Processor,* coincided with the arrival of a new kind of fishing boat on the Bay. Although the state limits Bristol Bay drift gillnet boats to thirty-two feet in length, the day boats of the old cannery regime were being replaced by glass or aluminum numbers featuring full galleys and berthing for round-the-clock crews. These big boats cost anywhere from sixty thousand to three hundred thousand dollars, but the money was there and with one of them, a Bristol Bay gillnetter was finally really independent. No longer did he need a shore plant to call home during the season. He could also run the coast for other fisheries, such as herring, if he had the permits, and his packing plant could go with him. Icicle, its partners, and emulators had it figured.

In 1980, the Deathbarges and their mobile, independent fleets of modern gillnetters, many of whom were highliners from Icicle's home grounds in Southeast Alaska, met head to head with the 48 Talls, as the packers of the old order were called. When the cannery fishermen tied up to wait for a better price and fired up their barbecues, the Icicle fishermen ignored the strike and went fishing. In the past, an AIFMA strike had been observed by virtually all fishermen on the Bay, either out of sympathy or in fear of reprisals (which were not unheard of) by striking fishermen. In 1980, the "scabs" of the Icicle fleet were joined by two to three hundred other fishermen who sold to other floaters and cash buyers anchored in the Bay. The docks at Naknek and

Dillingham rumbled with threats. Ugly, serious fights broke out at the Sea Inn, Hadfield's, Fishermen's, and the other bars. There had always been fights, but never like these.

With the clarity of hindsight, it's obvious that the Bay in 1980 was in the midst of cataclysmic change, that nothing would ever be "the same" again. High prices, enormous post-two-hundred-mile-limit red runs, and modern freezer technology combined to alter the entire character of the old soup. A lot of people didn't care for the flavor when the bankers, lawyers, and MBAs started doing the stirring, with recipes from the Asian joint-venture partners. It was a nasty time.

HIGH PRICES AND AIRPLANES

The 48 Talls had grown dominant in an era when getting experience extracted deadly costs in lives and money. Newcomers *had* to be wrong, they thought. But the high prices and vigorous Japanese competition meant there was still room for cleverness on one other potentially profitable front: transportation. If the wholesale price of red salmon jumps 400 percent in one year as it did in 1980, the fish can stand a lot of added value, but mainly in that one critical area. For the first time, the price was high enough to support shipping salmon by air to other freezer plants, canneries, and even directly to market.

Designer salmon struck another sour note for the 48 Talls who had built their companies and fortunes on canning. They steadfastly refused to believe that the sands were shifting. "Tin built the Bay," was the war cry during the strike of 1980, "and tin will keep it strong." But cans were invented for storing food for long periods. Some guy in the nineteenth century figured out how to can food for Napoléon so he could feed his armies. The emperor's field kitchens were not in line for any *prix de cuisine,* but that it was edible was enough, taste really didn't matter. To be sure, the canned salmon coming out of Alaska was probably the best canned fish you could buy anywhere in the world, and it had been a staple in many homes for years. But it's still canned fish, and it just isn't as good to eat as a well-frozen salmon. There was no way that the future of Bristol Bay would be built on tin, not if it was wrapped around salmon that cost a processor a dollar a pound at the dock.

". . . So, you falling asleep over there?" It's Kari Toivolo. "I guess I'm keeping you up." His bridge routine has brought him to consideration of the stranger, and now we talk again for a while. Soon, his wheelwatch ends and he retires for a nap, telling his relief to call him before we reach the anchorage at the mouth of the Ugashik River. I go below, too, to the galley, where I find the rest of the crew sleeping through the eight-hour run. When they're buying fish, sleep is rare, so now's the time. I decide to grab a few hours myself and twist into an upper bunk.

I grow restless in the tight confines and career from the peace of the *Viking Queen* under way to visions of the last moments of the DC–6 at Egegik. What did it look like? The version in my mind's eye is built with scraps of fear from other plane crashes I'd seen and heard of on the Bay. Like the midair over the beach on the west bank in 1981 that took Sumner Putman, Federico DeLaurentis, and one of the pilots from Texas who had come up with his family and seemed to be having such a good time out here. Then there was the C–119 at Egegik in 1981 that hit on the flats a mile from shore just at dusk, and nobody could get to the crew, who were crying out for help. Only after one of them fell into the water did they find out it was only shoulder-deep and they were in no danger of drowning, at least for a while. They were rescued.

Horizontal paradise overtakes me and I doze off.

IN THE UGASHIK

After what seems like only seconds, the cook wakes me and says we are in the Ugashik River. I stumble from the stateroom and, just as I reach the after-rail for a breath of air, a red-and-white Cessna 180 on floats taxies up to the *Viking Queen.*

"Can we get fuel?" the pilot shouts over the engine noise from his perch on his portside pontoon.

"Come alongside," Kari yells out the wheelhouse window, and the plane noses gingerly up to our starboard rail. The pilot is a spotter, hired by a syndicate of Icicle fishermen to fly over the Bay and look for hot spots, revealed by either swarms of salmon near the surface or other fishermen hauling back heavy nets. When he finds one, he radios his fishermen, who gain a competitive edge with such information. In the crowded skies over the Bering Sea, the spotter has one of the deadliest jobs in the world, short of combat in war. Some die every year.

"The problem," the pilot says, ignoring the obvious, "is that pretty soon everybody's going to be watching everybody else, and it'll be like a big dog chasing its own tail out there."

I ask him what he knows about the Egegik crash, and he tells me everybody was saved. He's not sure how many people were aboard, but the Moonies from their fish camp and some old guy with a chain saw were the heroes. The wreckage burned hot and is still smoking, he says, a black scar against the bluff.

For forty-eight hours, the *VQ* is in the Ugashik buying salmon. The familiar rhythms of fish tendering destroy time as the deckhands work 'round the clock and the gillnetters filter into the river from the flats with the news that the fishing is just okay. The protocol on the salmon grounds calls for the boat crews to unload the fish while the skippers come aboard the tender to check weights, sign fish tickets, place orders for food and parts, and gossip with the tender captain. Kari mans his station at a ledger desk in the forepeak.

Kari is the agent for the fish company, responsible for this first link in the chain of commerce that brings salmon to tables around the world.

As is also the custom, Kari and the company offer the fishing skipper a small gift with each delivery, a vestigial token acknowledging loyalty, usually a six-pack of beer.

At night, the scene intensifies under sharp halogen glow. Gillnetters appear suddenly alongside as they break into the ring of light, lurching apparitions festooned with orange and pink buoy balls, their crews in orange and yellow slickers rescued from comedy by the dead-tired expressions on their faces and the gunning of powerful engines. As the tender rolls, the light from the masthead is cast, farther away from us to illuminate other boats waiting in the shadows, bobbing violently in the choppy flow of the river. At night, the mortal danger of the Bay grows more apparent.

BOUND FOR EGEGIK

Finally, later on our second day in the Ugashik, Kari is ordered to sail and to deliver his salmon to the processing barge *Arctic Star,* sister to the *Bering Star,* anchored off the Naknek River to the east. It's about an eight-hour run from the Ugashik, and I'm elated. From Naknek, I can easily make my way to the King Salmon Airport, just ten miles away, and from there catch a plane to Egegik Beach. The certainty that I am going where I want to go is an anesthetic, and I sleep all the way to Naknek. There, I wake for thanks and good-byes to the crew of the *Viking Queen* and hitch a ride with a shore-bound tender.

Hitchhiking by sea, road, or air is an easy proposition on the Bay, and a day after reaching Naknek, I'm wedged into the tail cone of a single-engine Cessna 206 bound for Egegik Beach. The airport at King Salmon seemed calm compared with past years when the price of fish was so high that flying them out was a bargain. This season, there are fewer planes, and the activity on the ramps seems more organized than the circuses they became from 1980 to 1984. By the 1985 season, after four years of attrition due to economics and fatalities, the survivors of the air war on the Bay have the deal pretty well figured out. Most of the flying museum pieces—the C–119s, Boeing Stratoclippers, and C–124s—are gone, and the labor intensity that characterized the beginnings of the salmon-flying era has evolved into a coterie of veteran outfits such as Northern Air Cargo, Winky's Peninsula Seafoods, and Ball Brothers. Newcomers are less likely to take the plunge when faced with well-drilled competition that can accomplish such feats as picking up thirty thousand pounds of salmon from a beach and flying it five hundred miles, three times a day.

For freelance pilots and adventurous brokers, the end of the old order on the Bay, whatever its cause, was an opportunity to be seized. Speed is stock-in-trade if you're buying fresh fish, and that's what the airplanes brought to the Bay in the new age. When you're moving red salmon that wholesales for $3.50 a pound, you can just about buy the stuff a first-class seat and still make wicked good money. According to several sources who were in on the volatile early years of the Japanese frozen salmon action and collapse of the 48 Tall canners, all you had to do was get the fish away from the Bay and into cold storage and then hang on. In 1980, the price of red salmon went from $.50 a pound to $2.10 a pound in three months. If you didn't have to borrow money at runaway interest rates to keep control of your fish, you made a killing. That kind of situation presented itself over and over again.

And for that special tribe of people who live and breathe flight, Bristol Bay in the early eighties was a combination meal ticket and free pass to aviation-junkie heaven. The ramp at the King Salmon Airport was nothing short of a museum, with flying exhibits ranging from crop dusters to antique transports, such as those double-decker Stratoclippers that were essentially passenger versions of the B–29 and, of course, the crown jewel of the four-engine, piston airliners, the DC–6. And there was no shortage of modern equipment. Chartered jets with uniformed crews are routine on the ramp during the season. The DC–8 and 727 jets bear the colors of cargo lines you've never heard of unless you've been around a Third World war zone or read a lot of aviation mags.

PLAYING THE ODDS

The planes operate under the same rules out here on the edge of the world that apply everyplace else, but the amount of traffic and the vast areas of uncontrolled airspace make the Bay a statistical nightmare for pilots. Forget instrument approaches with virtually 100 percent certainty that you'll make it. Here, you roll the dice with maybe 80 percent certainty, or even 60 percent when you're taking off in soft sand, five hundred pounds over gross, and tail-heavy into zero wind except for the killer downdrafts from the bluff just thirty feet off your left wing tip. Another problem is congestion—just too many planes and choppers in the air at the same time. Generally, the pilots are okay, but you also have a bunch of hobbyists and flat-out flakes flying around up there, too. And that's the rub. Fatal crashes are not rare, with midair collisions leading the parade.

Nevertheless, the big flying fish packers are life symbols, dramatic evidence that commerce is under way, that food is getting to market, that the money is rolling in. The airplanes on the Bay are kin to the giant, near-mythic 747s and space shuttles. Like the magnificent square-riggers and steamships of the last age, they draw crowds to the spectacles of their comings and goings, somehow offering the people who come powerful reassurances that humankind is succeeding. A crash, particularly of a big airplane, is a serious threat to order, shredding those reassurances.

Our first approach to Egegik in the 206 that day is a failure. From my place on piles of gear in the windowless tail of the plane, I can see nothing without straining forward, and then my view outside is obscured anyway. Low fog blankets the beach, and though the ground winks up through a few sucker holes, none is large enough for landing. The pilot, a fellow from Arizona up for the season with his new wife, wisely decides to return to King Salmon. And there we wait for six hours, drinking coffee and watching the ground crew at Winky Crawford's Peninsula Seafoods, a.k.a. the Flying Circus. They are an odd assortment of characters, a cross between barnstormers and bikers. They're working on one of their DC–3s that crashed on approach the week before.

The plane, inbound from Soldotna, a little over an hour east, just ran out of fuel in bad weather. The pilot had 300 feet of altitude when the engines quit, and in the frightening silence, he aimed for a road to his left. At 100 feet, he saw he wasn't going to make the road and braced for a landing on the soft tundra. The wheels tore through the mossy ground cover right down to the ever-solid permafrost, and the plane slammed to a halt in just 150 feet, nosing over like a bird with its feet nailed to a board.

The trip over on the nose was a long split second, according to the pilot, because he thought the plane was probably going to tumble end over end for a while, probably killing the hell out of him. Miraculously, it settled back on its tail wheel, and Winky was able to tow it out of the ruts in the tundra with his surplus army truck. He towed it by the tail, back onto the road, and over to the airport, where the pilot and everybody Winky can spare is trying to get her flying again. The pilot walks around his plane with an energetic spring in his step and smiles easily, having shed some primal tension by walking away from that crash.

He explains, "I wake up every day and feel like I've gotten away with something." In the winter, he flies the DC–3 in the Bahamas. "You want to touch me?" he asks, just as my 206 pilot strolls over with the word that the skies over Egegik have cleared.

THE GROUNDS

The Egegik River flows north from a deep tundra pool called Becharof Lake and makes its way in loops and swirls for most of its fifty-mile length. The

Egegik carries a heavy load of silt and effluvia from the unstable terrain to the south and deposits it into Bristol Bay to form awesome tidal flats that defy imagination. On the high tide, the flats are awash, forming the favored channels for the spawning migrations of red salmon—productive but very risky grounds for drift gillnetters. The flats at Egegik, like those at the mouths of the other great rivers of the Bay, are perfect, though, for setnetters.

These fishermen set up camps along the bluffs, set their gillnets out below the high-water line, and let the wind and tide carry the salmon to them. On the ebb, they pick the nets and either fly their own fish to King Salmon or sell them to a buyer on the beach who consolidates the catches of several setnetters and flies bigger loads to Anchorage or fish plants on the Kenai.

Reaching Egegik, we land on a crude cargo strip in front of the International Seafoods of Alaska (ISA) beach plant, which is owned, lock, stock, and barrel, by the Reverend Sun Myung Moon and his Unification Church. The place was known as Hermie's until ISA bought it in 1982 during the church's colonial push into the Alaska seafood industry. (They also built a bottomfish plant in Kodiak.) New, tidy red-and-white buildings form a compound inland, back from the berm where the beach ends and the tundra begins. Highlighting the scene is a big sign facing the Bay: $2.10, the sign says, apparently the price they're paying for red salmon that day.

As I move my pack and tent off the runway, I watch a pair of forklifts hauling fish totes from the biggest of the ISA buildings to a staging area on the beach. In the painter's light of late afternoon, the yellows and silvers of the forklifts are snappy against the flat, gray-brown tones of the sand. In that light, the colors are so purely sensual that they edge over into the same realm as the sounds of the beach, the uneven snarling of the forklifts, the clatter of equipment against the cement floor in the building, and the distant whine of a Honda Big Red, one of those three-wheeled, all-terrain vehicles that now infest Alaska.

At odd moments, the more insistent sounds fade and give way to a kind of basso background hum that seems to come from every direction. I search for its source, finally looking offshore, where, for the first time, I see the fleet: hundreds of boats barely visible but shimmering in the rippling mirage between the sea and the sky beyond the mud flats, three miles away. As the picture of the place solidifies in my senses, it is shattered by an asynchronous murmur that grows quickly into a sound I know as heavy aircraft engines, big radials of the old sort turning high rpm.

And then it appears, maybe fifty feet off the deck, left wing down in a bank around the contour of the point where I am standing, its gear and flaps up, speed maybe two hundred miles per hour, buzzing the beach to clear it for a landing. The roar builds to earsplitting but exhilarating proportions. Though I have hung around airports all my life, I have never seen a four-engine transport at high speed so close to the ground. Usually, when they're that low, they're in landing configuration, with gear and flaps down, flying slowly in preparation for returning to Earth.

The plane flashes past, no more than one hundred feet from me, and I see the pilot nod as he sees me. "That's really something, isn't it?" says a man's voice behind me, as the noise level drops and the plane banks away over the sea for its approach to land. I turn to see an unlikely, shortish guy in wools and boots with a camera dangling from his neck and a red ISA baseball hat over a pair of bookish eyeglasses.

"Did you hear about the other one?" the guy asks, shifting his stance to face down the beach in the direction of the river. Perhaps because of the hazy afternoon light and shadows, I have failed to notice it until just now, a gray smudge against the bluff about a half-mile away. No, from this distance it looks like ordinary beach junk, and my eyes would not have lingered.

"Did you see it?" I ask the visitor.

"Oh, yeah," he says. "What are you doing here?"

At this point, I fall into what I can only describe as Moonie paranoia. Maybe it's that particular question put so bluntly; maybe it's the camera and the feeling I've been photographed without knowing it; maybe it's simple intolerance. My past experiences with the Unification Church have been positive, though I have had to temper my opinion of people who trade their responsibility for the major choices in their lives to remain blissfully childlike in the care and control of Reverend Moon.

And then there is the matter of Reverend Moon himself and his very real connections with Korean arms dealers and his perception of himself as the savior of the world—not *one* of the saviors, but *the* savior incarnate—and the fact that Father, as his followers call him, just this week has gotten out of a federal slammer on the East Coast after doing a little time on a tax rap. Most of all, though, I suppose it's the fear I can't suppress that arises from one of the tenets of their faith that permits any action or deception if it furthers the Reverend's goals for his church and his side action. They call it "divine deception," and it was explained to me by some pleasant church members in Kodiak a few years earlier when they were getting their bottomfish plant going there.

The people of Kodiak just about went berserk in 1979 when ISA bought the waterfront site and built the plant; it was one of only two in Kodiak at the time that could process bottomfish. There were anti-Moonie marches in the streets, outrageous harangues at city council meetings, and ugly threats. But ISA stayed and migrated to the Bay the next year. The church also owns fish plants and fleets on both the Gulf of Mexico and the Atlantic. "We're into food. It's just that simple," I was told in Kodiak by Joe Spiciani, the son of a New York brassiere manufacturer, who joined the church and became a fish plant manager. "We need businesses so our members can work and raise families, and what's better than food?"

"But why do you remain children all your lives?" I asked him. That was a long time ago in Kodiak. He was slated to be married soon in one of those mass weddings for which Reverend Moon is famous, but which have less than a 50 percent success rate.

"Who doesn't?" Joe answered.

People who have competed with ISA get a little hot about free labor and church subsidies and the like, but most who sell fish to the Moonies—many Egegik Beach setnetters, for instance—have few complaints. "They pay the highest price, they sell us food and fuel without gouging us, and they're good neighbors," says one woman whose family has been fishing at Egegik for several generations. "I think they're a little odd, and I wouldn't want to be one of them, but nobody's asking me to. And besides, this is Bristol Bay, and not much of anything out here is exactly what you'd call normal."

AN EYEWITNESS

Divine deception or not, I decide to talk to this guy on Egegik Beach. He is the first person I've run into who knows what happened for sure. I ask him if there were survivors, but his answer is lost in the roar of the arriving DC–6, which has now returned to land, kicking up tons of sand as its props howl in reverse thrust. "Everybody made it," he repeats. "There were three in the crew. It happened at night. We got there right away and pulled out the bottom of the cockpit with our tractor from up on the bluff. The guy you really want to talk to is down there, though." He points toward the wreckage. "He was in his cabin on the bluff when it hit. Let's go. I'll ride down there with you."

He walks back to the ISA camp and immediately returns with a Big Red. On the way, he shouts his version of the story over the noise of the engine. The plane was carrying thirty thousand pounds of salmon, a normal load for a DC–6, and was bound for Kenai. It was owned by Ball Brothers, a Dillingham company with a lot of experience on the Bay, and flown by a crew of three— pilot, copilot, and flight engineer. Darkness had fallen when the pilot attempted the take-off, and he apparently was unable to pick out a reference point in the blackness ahead to tell him he was drifting left on the beach, into the bluff. Just before pushing his throttles to take-off power, the pilot is reported to have said, "God, it's dark down that beach." And just as he rotated the nose gear to leave the ground, the entire, screaming mass of aluminum, steel, fuel, and fish started to come apart.

When it hit the bluff, the aviation gas fueled a fire so hot that the aluminum of the airframe melted into puddles on the beach. The flames were visible for thirty miles across the dark, hazy Bay, competing for brightness with the late-rising full moon that might have lulled the pilot into thinking he could make the night take-off. The salmon saved the crew, as it turned out, by piling up between the cockpit section and the wing roots, where the fire was most intense. And the weight of those fifteen tons of salmon moving forward when the plane stopped split the cockpit away from the flames.

People from camps along the beach arrived almost immediately, led by the ISA LARC, a big steel amphibious vehicle with a powerful winch. The rescuers maneuvered the LARC onto the bluff above the cockpit, and some unnamed hero skidded down the bank into the flames to throw the cable around the twisted metal. From inside, a terrified voice shouted over and over, "I've got men down here! I've got men down here! Help me! Help me!" Just that. And they were beating on the side of the plane.

The salmon started burning, too, the fleshy scent mixing with the sour odors of rubber, metal, and gasoline in flames. From the LARC on the bluff, the rescue crew took a strain on the winch cable, bringing anguished cries from the cockpit. The cable was wrapped around someone's leg, so down into the flames went the rescuers, this time with a chain saw that had materialized from someone's camp. Then one man was out, then another, and finally all were safe on the bluff.

DR. DEMI AND THE ANGEL

Even a week after the crash, the wreckage is terrifying, a reminder of transience and uncertainty of the highest order. We are just not accustomed to viewing an airplane of that size on its back, spindly landing gear pointing up, with shredded tires reaching for the sky. An airplane upright, poised to travel through the air, is a permanent truth, and images do not exist to prepare us for its opposite condition. Had the carnage been total, the sight might have been easier to bear, but as it is, the familiar shapes of the plane remain to remind me of what it once had been.

One huge engine is buried in the gravel of the bluff, driven into the primal till by the enormous force of impact. And the fish are everywhere, charred and discolored by the inferno and spread in a stinking glacier flowing from a big crack in the fuselage just behind the cockpit. My guide from ISA leaves me. He says he has to go to work.

I continue to prowl the alien scene, touching nothing and glad no one has died here, for then I would be guilty of gross irreverence. I walk up onto the bluff to look down on the plane. Miraculously, the setnetter's cabin, situated right over the wreck, is untouched. As I look it over, a man comes out and stands by my side. I notice the shadow of a wing burned into the tundra at my feet. We say nothing, exchange no greeting for maybe a minute, until I break the silence and say, "Hello."

"I was in the cabin, right here. I thought it was an angel's wing," the man says, glaring intently at me in a kind of stagy way. He looks a little like the actor Keenan Wynn. I ask him if he is, and he says no, he's Dr. John Demi, a newly retired chiropractor from Paradise, California, and he had never even been on a plane until he came to Alaska that year to visit a friend who owns the setnet site. His voice cracks with an anxious tension that I suspect has been there since the crash.

"We were asleep, in there," he says. "I heard the plane taking off, but that happens all the time, and I didn't think anything of it. Then it got real quiet until the crash and fire right outside the window, where the wing landed. I said. 'The hell with this,' and started running that way." He points across the tundra. "I thought the cabin was going to explode.

"I think I got about a half a mile and came back when I remembered that those guys in the plane needed help. We got them out," he says, smiling as though he's discovered a delight that has been missing from his life until then. "Have a drink," he says, passing me a bottle of cognac I hadn't noticed. Then he says, "I want to show you something." I take the cognac, and he disappears into the cabin.

Dr. Demi returns and edges around to stand between me and the bluff, forming a faintly lit silhouette in the evening light. Behind him are the lights of the fleet, just winking on, and the shimmering presence of the wrecked DC–6. He is cradling a twisted piece of aluminum, clearly molten once but now cooled in the shape of a running dog. It's a good three feet long.

"A greyhound, right?" says Dr. Demi, starting to laugh heartily. "I've got another one inside that looks just like a jockey. Can you believe it? I got to say this is one of the oddest places on Earth, but now I'll come back until I die.

"I really thought it was an angel's wing, come to take me to heaven, you know," and he hands me the greyhound. "Here. You want to hold this?"

The beach at Egegik is still a kind of garden spot for Bristol Bay setnetters, though the air show isn't what it was. International Seafoods of Alaska still buys fish and has kept its reputation as a good neighbor, and the tides continue to bring salmon and hours of backbreaking labor for the fishermen. I tried to find Dr. Demi, but no luck.

SECTION FOUR

THE WILDLIFE IS
REALLY WILD

As TOUGH AS the people of Alaska are, the real survivors are the animals. They and their ancestors have managed to eke out a living in one of nature's toughest proving grounds for thousands of years. Now they're dealing with the pressure of human incursion into their homes on top of all the other daily stresses that they face. But as humans watch animals, and animals watch humans, some wild encounters are bound to ensue. Here are some amazing tales of *really wild* wild animals in Alaska. . . .

ON THE HORNS OF A BULL

*M*ARK HEWKIN *and his hunting buddies had honed their archery skills as they eagerly anticipated the Alaskan moose season. And after it was over, he talked about the hunt that saw a moose turn the tables on his hunter.*

John Schneider put together our Alaska hunt in the fall of 1987. Our group included John's brother-in-law Jamie Lane, who had accompanied him on other big game hunts, and Mike Mitten, who asked me to be his partner. John is a carpenter, Jamie is an insurance salesman, Mike is a lab technician, and I am a laborer for a sewer and water company. We were all twenty-nine or thirty years old and married with children, except for John. All live in Illinois, except Jamie, who hails from South Dakota.

Bow hunters, we had a combined hunting experience of sixty-two years. Our kills included mule deer and elk as well as a number of animals recorded in the Pope and Young Record Book: twenty-seven white-tailed deer, two black bear, and three antelope.

John called several flying services in Alaska to determine whether we would book a guided trip or a drop camp where we would be on our own to float and hunt a stream. We favored a float-hunt but were told that the trophy animals we sought would be well back from the river because of hunting pressure. Ultimately we chose a drop-camp hunt where we would have the opportunity to hunt from a base camp without the hassle of constantly hiking off the river in pursuit of quality animals.

After much inquiry we settled on High Adventure Air Charter, a Soldotna-based flight service located on the Kenai Peninsula and only fifty air miles south of Anchorage.

The owner of High Adventure Air, Sandy Bell, assured us that we would have adventure during our hunt from August 28 through September 18. We planned to hunt caribou for six days and moose the rest of the time. A pilot would check on us one time in caribou camp and one time in moose camp.

Bright and early on the morning of August 28 we drove to the airstrip at Soldotna, stopping on the way to buy the licenses we needed. Sandy's son Greg, a twenty-four-year-old seasoned pilot, stowed our gear into a DeHavilland Beaver floatplane. The gear included two tents, one stove, sleeping bags, side arms, backup bear medicine (a 12-gauge shotgun and a .30-06), and compound bows and arrows.

Our first destination was the west side of Lake Clark, about a hundred miles west of Soldotna. We flew through Lake Clark Pass, bypassing several glaciers and snowpacked mountain peaks. Greg pointed out several caribou along the way before landing on a small lake nestled among three large lakes.

The surrounding area was rocky and looked lifeless. Rolling hills dappled with alder thickets pushed up to two thousand feet. Many small scattered ponds accentuated a moonlike landscape.

We eagerly set up camp, excited about the days ahead. We planned to seek caribou by hiking in a large circle that would get us high enough to see the area and yet bring us back to camp each day. Little did we realize that we would be covering fifteen to twenty miles a day.

On the second day, Mike stalked a bedded bull caribou near a sandy-beached pond. He sneaked within ten feet of the bull and arrowed him. The animal jumped to his feet and ran. Mike hit him again and dropped him. His first arrow hit the shoulder and the second penetrated the lungs. We headed back to camp, planning to retrieve the meat the next day. Back at camp, we saw signs that a grizzly had wandered through camp in our absence.

The next morning I spotted three bulls, and I got within twenty-five yards of one of them. As he quartered away from me, I placed an Easton 2219 arrow tipped with a Zwickey broadhead in his rib cage behind his left shoulder, the shaft stopping abruptly against the right shoulder blade. He went eighty yards before he piled up. I returned to camp for Mike's help, and we carried most of the meat to camp in our first trip.

Then Mike and I went to get his dead caribou. We found that a bear had picked him up and carried him about seventy-five yards over a hill and into the open. We mustered the courage to approach the kill with only knives for defense, but the bear was nowhere in sight. Mike's caribou looked like he had been hit by a truck. He was smashed flat and skinned. Every part of his body had been eaten on, and two-thirds was completely consumed. We salvaged only about sixty pounds of meat.

Meanwhile our buddies had sneaked to within eighty yards of a bull that would score very high for the size of his antlers, but they didn't connect. That turned out to be the last caribou we hunted, and we flew out of caribou camp September 2. Since we had not seen many caribou, we were a pretty disgusted group of hunters.

While flying to moose camp we spotted several of the big animals, two of them very impressive. We touched down on a shimmering, gray-blue lake at the base of snowclad mountains draped halfway up with alders, willows, and black spruce—truly the prettiest place I have ever seen.

While the rest of us set up camp, Mike ascended the hill behind our site, scouting for a suitable route the next morning. He saw three grizzlies, which didn't excite us. Their presence meant we'd probably see more of them and possibly have problems with them.

Next morning Mike and I headed south while John and Jamie went north. From the hilltop we saw six cow moose and several caribou. We stopped at a thousand-foot-deep gorge; it was the major obstacle to hunting the opposite side, which we planned to do the following day.

The next day, however, my partner left without me because I was sick; my hypoglycemia was acting up. My symptoms included blurred vision, headache, stomach sickness, and nausea.

Four and a half hours later, Mike reached the area beyond the gorge. His efforts were rewarded when he saw nine moose: seven cows and two bulls. Mike focused on a bull with an antler spread of some sixty-five inches. He crawled to within forty yards and got off an arrow, but it was high.

By this time Mike was so exhausted he just lay on the ground, wondering if he could make it back to camp. He looked up and saw a lone grizzly feeding on blueberries 150 yards away. It was one of seven grizzlies Mike saw that day. Sighting that bear gave Mike new motivation to get back to camp.

John and Jamie had seen some cows that day, and they also spotted a bull they had seen before, one they had nicknamed Hal. They determined to get Hal the following day. But we were learning that plans change. The following day we remained in camp to recuperate. John needed to rest his legs, which gave us an excuse to catch sockeye salmon and to watch Hal through our spotting scope.

Before daylight next morning Mike and I headed for the gorge. The first light we saw was at the top of the hill, and it was accompanied by a sea of fog. By noon the fog was so thick we could see only fifty yards. Wet and cold, we returned to camp to discover our partners had seen the fog roll in and stayed in camp all day.

It rained almost every day. The temperature was in the low thirties during the nights and the mid-fifties during the days.

Mike and I went to the gorge the next day. Mike saw two bull moose, one of which was below us on a near-vertical slope a half mile away. The other one was five hundred yards away. We focused on the closer one and began our stalk. Because of the steepness and our rapid descent, Mike hurt his ankle and I hurt my knee.

As we neared the bull, we slowed our pace and our senses intensified. We got into our stalking mode, silently creeping through the head-high willows and around the dead alder stumps. Then we spotted the bull. He was sweat-covered, standing over a scrape, simultaneously urinating and ejaculating into it and pawing the earth with a front hoof; this is the way bulls characteristically leave their scent for cows.

A small bull and a half dozen cows stood nearby. Whenever the young bull approached, the big bull became agitated. We watched for half an hour, unable to improve our position for fear of being spotted. Finally the big bull chased the little one away, giving Mike a chance to make his move.

Mike took a direct path through the alders to within thirty yards before drawing on the animal, which stood free of the brush in an opening. Mike released an arrow that took the bull in the neck. The animal ran ten yards before stopping, presenting Mike another shot. The second arrow entered behind the right shoulder and pierced the animal's lungs. The bull ambled off forty-five yards and dropped dead.

We took some pictures and then started off for the other bull, but we found only cows. So we returned to dress Mike's bull. He carried an antler spread of fifty-six inches, and we guessed he weighed sixteen hundred pounds. We quartered the bull in preparation for packing him out the next day.

We moved our base camp to a lake closer to the downed moose, thus reducing packing time and effort. (We discovered later that the downed moose was thirteen miles from our original camp.) We now had only five days left to hunt. Mike said he would pack the moose out by himself to our new camp, leaving the rest of us free to hunt. But Mike discovered that bears had found his bull and buried him.

We saw moose every day, but we were showing the efforts of our hunting. John's legs hurt badly enough that he had trouble getting around, which was contrary to his contagious spirit of adventure.

Soon we had only two days left before the plane would be coming to pick us up. I spotted and stalked a respectable bull, only to miss him three times from twenty yards.

The day after my miserable performance, we saw lots of bulls, but other than one Jamie stalked and lost, none interested us. Up to now we'd seen twenty-one grizzlies, three black bear, more than thirty cow moose, and twelve bulls, four of which had racks bigger than fifty inches.

Our scheduled pickup date arrived with strong winds; the lake we had landed on had four-foot waves. There was no way the pilot would be able to land and find the note telling him of our move to the new camp.

Sixty-mile-an-hour winds pounded us the following day. We saw our plane go over. At three o'clock I decided to go hunting.

I had two arrows—one of my own and one I'd borrowed from Mike. After I reached the knob of land that gave a good view, I looked through the scope for several minutes. I walked the eighth of a mile to the far end of the knob and sat down.

As I thought about our hunt and about going home, two bulls and a cow appeared from a big draw. I quickly headed for them, dropping my pack as I drew near. I eased into a streambed to help silence any noise and to enable me to speed my approach through alders.

I couldn't detect the animals till I suddenly heard a bull grunting. Fifty yards away, opposite an alder patch, a bull was slapping a tree with his antlers—not rubbing it but actually dismantling it.

I stalked within twenty yards of the grunting bull moose. All I could see was hindquarters. His head and half his body were hidden in the alders. Imitating a big bull, I scraped the brush with my bow and broke off as many branches as possible, trying to "call" him to me. Then I learned I'd stalked the smaller of the two bulls.

Now where is his big brother? I asked myself, starting in the direction I expected to find the larger bull. I spotted him and stopped behind a spruce tree. His rack stood out above an alder patch forty yards away.

I began breaking limbs and rubbing the tree with my bow, working the tree and grunting. The bull would have none of it. I recalled a sound Mike's bull had made when approaching a cow, and I imitated it. The bull instantly acknowledged me and walked straight toward me.

When he was five yards away, I tried to draw my bow string. I was so excited I couldn't pull it back. The bull turned and trotted toward the alders. I finally got the string to the corner of my mouth and launched the arrow. A 2219 Easton aluminum arrow thwacked into the back of his rib cage, striking bone.

Half the shaft stuck out his side as he vanished into the brush. *I'll give the bull half an hour to die before tracking him,* I thought.

Now the waiting game, the suspense. As time passed, I decided to play some games with the little bull. Standing behind a tree, I rubbed it with my bow, breaking limbs and trying to sound big. I was making one low-volume grunt. Then I made the sound Mike's bull had made when approaching a cow, and the bull came right to me.

I grunted and put my bow on my head, trying to imitate him, but he would neither give ground nor advance on me. He just stood there drooling, never more than twenty yards from me. His rack measured forty-five to fifty inches. I'm sure he would have made the record books. But still he was small compared with the bull I had just shot.

I started after my prize, the wounded bull. There was no blood, but his tracks were easy to follow. I crawled through the alders until I spotted him forty yards away, standing and slowly twisting his head from side to side. I drilled him through the neck with another arrow. Blood poured down his neck as he charged into some spruce trees and disappeared.

A couple of minutes later I went to the spot where I'd last seen him. My arrow had gone through him: I found it sticking out of the moss. I picked it up and continued pursuing him.

I hadn't taken two steps when the bull jumped up fifteen yards away and ran directly in front of me. I shot again, striking him behind the shoulder. Half the arrow was showing as the bull vanished into the brush.

Since the bull wasn't far away and it would be easy to come back with help the next day to find his body, I started back to camp. When I reached the top of the hill, I took a look and saw the bull lying on the ground, immobile. I was elated that he was dead and decided to examine my trophy. It was only five o'clock, so I still had plenty of daylight left. Back down the hill I went.

As I approached the bull, I noticed a hind leg begin to contract. The bull started to get up. With only twenty feet separating us, I turned and ran.

My feet outran my body and I fell down. I started to get up just as the bull's entire weight rammed into my back.

He hit me high in my left buttock, his horn piercing the cheek. He pushed me ten feet across the ground, then flung his head upward. I flew off his antlers into the air and came down astraddle his forehead. My arms shot out and around either side of his antlers, and I wrapped my legs around his nose.

I'm going to die! I thought. *I'm going to die!*

I hung on for dear life.

My next thought was, *If I get off his horns, he'll gore me to death.*

He kept ramming his head into the ground until my weight proved too much. He knelt down to rest and then tried again to gore me or shake me off. He continued to smash me into the ground.

Because I was between his antler palms, he could not get his tines into me. He was so weak that his forelegs were nearly buckling.

I was exhausted. My arms and back ached, and it required total concentration to hang on. I was looking into the bull's eyes. I will never forget his eyes or the smell of his wet hair or the cooing-type sound he was making.

The last time he lunged forward to stand up, he stepped on my left foot. The combination of his weight on my foot and his pulling back knocked me from his horns. I turned to get out from under him but actually turned into him. He trampled my body from one end to the other, producing the most pain of the entire experience.

I got up and ran. I looked back after thirty or forty yards. The bull had fallen to the ground.

I turned toward camp and started walking. My head and shoulders were covered with blood, much of which was from the moose. My nose was bleeding. I felt a hole in my buttock cheek and gauged its size by inserting three fingers. I pressed my left hand against it to apply pressure as I walked. Blood kept running down my leg. I was afraid of bleeding to death. I had cuts from sticks and tree limbs where the bull had slammed me around.

Although I didn't think I was going to live, I never gave up or gave in. I just wanted to get back to camp and help. I stopped at three different creeks to drink water and kept moving toward camp. Walking wasn't too difficult, but the bleeding and the thought of dying plagued me.

I was worried about encountering a grizzly. I smelled like a fresh moose steak.

Twenty minutes from camp I saw Mike and Jamie. I told them what had happened and asked them not to touch me because I wasn't sure what injuries I had. At camp, Mike got out the first-aid kit, and the guys worked on me. They found an entry hole and an exit hole in my left buttock cheek. The bull's horn had entered the center and exited the upper left side of the cheek.

They stuffed gauze into the two holes, packed them to stop the bleeding, and taped up the wound. My nosebleed had stopped. I had a couple of small cuts and bruises around my eyes. My arms and back were bruised pretty bad. They gave me Tylenol with codeine, and that night they periodically replaced the gauze as blood saturated it.

The following morning I was hurting all over. To lie in one position for more than a couple of minutes caused excruciating pain. My bruises hurt a lot more than the holes in my buttock. While I lay in agony awaiting our pilot's return, Mike and Jamie retraced my steps to find my gear and the moose.

Our pilot, Greg, flew over that day on his way to our original drop-off site. He flew over our former camp for five or ten minutes, but returned to Soldotna because it was too windy to land.

Four hours later Mike and Jamie returned with my backpack. They found nothing else.

Several planes flew over on the following day, and my partners tried to flag them down. Finally in late afternoon, Larry Van Slyke, a pilot and officer for the National Park Service, saw them waving, and he landed to help.

Larry and his partner helped me into their Skywagon and flew me to Port Alsworth on Lake Clark while my partners waited back in camp. Larry's wife made me some dinner while Larry arranged to have me flown to Soldotna.

Finally, back in Soldotna, I was picked up at the airport by another of Sandy's sons, Dave. He took me to their home, got me some clean clothes, and took me to the hospital. The hospital staff cleaned my wounds—the puncture in my buttock was two inches deep and an inch and a half in circumference—and then sent me on my way.

Meanwhile Greg had landed his plane and spent that night on a small lake not far from our camp. He found our note telling that we had changed camps. He found my partners and flew them back to Soldotna the next day, where we were all reunited after a hunting trip that I'll never forget.

Excerpt from *Jim Rearden's Alaska*

JIM REARDEN

HOLLYWOOD IN ALASKA

M W. "SLIM" Moore (the M. stood for Morris, which Slim never used) was one of Alaska's finest and most respected registered and master hunting guides. I met him in 1950 when I arrived at Fairbanks to teach at the University of Alaska. He was big (six feet two), bluff, hearty, and full of solid information about Alaska's wildlife. His sense of humor constantly bubbled to the surface. He was also a philosopher and a master storyteller, with a legion of friends.

Slim arrived in Alaska from Texas in 1926 and soon immersed himself in the wilderness as a hunter, a trapper, and a packer, eventually becoming a registered guide. He was a remarkable observer of wildlife. Many professional wildlife biologists, including me, listened carefully when Slim expounded on wildlife, their problems, and how they could be better managed.

For many years Slim and his wife, Margaret, owned and operated Summit Lake Lodge on the Richardson Highway. In December 1956, I took my tape recorder to the lodge and spent a week with the Moores. During the short, cold days, Slim, Margaret, and I hunted ptarmigan and tended Slim's beaver traps and snares. Evenings, Slim yarned and recorded his stories, told in a slow, humorous Texas drawl.

It was then that I recorded Slim's story of "Hollywood in Alaska." Here is the yarn Slim related to me, told in his voice.

I want you to get us some live wolverines," the director said. He wore knickers. A golf cap drooped over one ear. A long cigarette holder, sometimes with a cigarette in it, grew from his chubby face.

"Wolverines?" I repeated foolishly, stalling for time to think. I scratched my head like I wasn't sure what a wolverine was.

"Yes. Half a dozen or so will do I guess," the little fellow allowed. "Tell your trapper friends we'll pay two hundred and fifty dollars for the first one, and two hundred dollars each for the others."

Those were my first orders on the wackiest job I've ever had. I had just signed as animal man for a Hollywood movie outfit that had come to Alaska to shoot, as they say, on location.

It was 1933. For seven years I had guided sportsmen on big game hunts, run a trapline winters, and during summers had wrangled knot-headed horses packing supplies to mines in the Alaska Range. I thought I was qualified for the animal man job. If I had known a little about lion taming, and was a trapeze artist to boot, I'd have been better suited for the job.

The fine movie *Eskimo,* written by Peter Freuchen, had appeared a couple of years earlier. *Tundra,* the low-budget picture for which I was animal man, was made on the peculiar theory that the success of *Eskimo* ensured success of any far-North type movie that followed. They even used a single-word title.

My guiding season was over. I had just returned from a fine season with Fred Hollander, the famed naturalist-photographer-sportsman, when this funny little Hollywood gink offered me twenty bucks a day plus expenses to work for him. It was good money then.

"We're making a gen-u-wine Alaska movie. There'll be nothing phony about it," he swore, looking me right in the eye.

I had just agreed to take the job and had shaken hands with him on it when he ordered the wolverines.

We worked in Anchorage, at the time a little railroad town surrounded by good moose, sheep, and bear country.

Carpenters started building cages and pens for all the animals we planned to acquire. While they worked, I decided to pick up a wolverine or two myself if I could. In the meantime, we spread word to backcountry trappers that we wanted live wolverines.

I took a small outfit and backpacked up the old Crow Creek Trail on the Kenai Peninsula, not far from Anchorage. Early snow had covered the high ridges and mountains, and I prowled for several days on snowshoes, hunting for wolverine sign. I finally found where one had passed and followed his wallowing trail in new snow for a few miles and found a place that looked good for a trap. I had padded a bunch of number 4 Newhouse double spring traps, and with them I made several blind sets.

Next day I packed in a fresh moose head someone had left near the old trail. This I wired a couple of feet off the ground to a tree, and set a couple of my padded traps under it, beneath the snow, with waxed paper over the pans. I expected the wolverine to find the head and start tugging at it. It wouldn't move, and the more he pulled, the angrier and more frustrated he would become, until he'd forget caution and step into a trap.

Four days later I snowshoed to the head and found an angry beady-eyed wolverine there, caught by a front foot. The bandy-legged little devil growled, then crouched to leap at me when I neared.

I backed off.

A wolverine is an unfriendly cuss at best; when you're trying to pack him out of the hills and stuff him into a pen he's damn near impossible. I didn't dare tap him on the nose to knock him cold. I might have hit too hard.

"You won't buffalo me, you little so-and-so," I told him.

I fastened another padded trap to a pole and fished until I caught one of his rear paws, then I stretched him as tightly as I could. I figured I had him then. I walked up to tape his jaws shut, but every time I neared, he yanked and struggled and growled and turned his head toward me with those big popping ivories. A wolverine can bite through bone, a pole, and even wire. I sure didn't want him chewing on me.

I finally had to mush to camp for a big tarp, which I doubled until it had about six thicknesses, threw it over him, then lay on top of it. He couldn't bite through the canvas. But he roared. And he turned and twisted frantically under me.

I groped and found his head through the canvas and pinned it down. Then I peeled the edge of the tarp back one layer at a time so I could grab his snoot. I carefully wrapped a hand around his jaws, and with the other wrapped adhesive tape on him.

He hummed and growled, telling me what an ugly no-good two-legged buzzard I was. At the same time he snuffled noisily through his nose. I grinned and stood. He batted his nose against my leg as if he thought he was going to bite.

Next I slid my packboard under him and wrapped each paw, with its ivory claws, in adhesive tape. Next, with a stout cord, I lashed his feet to each corner of the packboard. I slipped into the shoulder straps, got into my snowshoes, and headed for camp. He weighed about twenty-five pounds, but I soon learned it was twenty-five pounds of whang-leather-toughness and coil-spring power.

He found he could pump himself up and down, which he did, with every ounce of strength he had.

I went weaving down the trail like a drunk. It was all I could do to keep my feet. As he pumped, he skidded his cold nose up and down the back of my neck, growling and mumbling and snuffling. When he did that the hair on the back of my neck came up like teeth on a comb, and the shivers chased each other down and up my spine, and down again.

I wondered how well I had taped his jaws. Finally, I stopped and wrapped another half spool of tape on them.

I packed him to Girdwood, which wasn't far, and put him in a barrel. I cut one foot loose at a time until he was free, and at the last instant I slipped my knife under the tape on one side of his head. He could claw the tape off then. Then I clapped a tin tub atop the barrel.

A few days later I caught another. I hog-tied him and shoved him into a sack. I lashed the sack to the packboard so he couldn't pump, and so he couldn't get his nose on my neck.

I took my pets back to Anchorage. The big money we had offered for live wolverines was starting to bring results. Wolverine skins were worth fifteen to twenty dollars. In 1933, the two hundred dollars being offered for a live wolverine was a lot of money. Soon we had eight live, growling, and cussing wolverines in our pens. A big black-whiskered guy brought one from Seward. He had firearms and knives strapped to himself until you'd think he was involved in a Mexican revolution. I swear, his whiskers reached clear to his belt. With his live wolverine he had two big buckets of porcupine meat.

"This here wolverine won't eat nothin' but porky meat," he declared loudly.

But what I remember most clearly, and the thing that has puzzled me for more than twenty years, is the cage his wolverine was in. It was a beautifully built miniature log cabin, barely big enough to hold the wolverine. The animal couldn't turn around, and there was no door. We had to tear the cage apart to let it out.

How did he get the wolverine into that thing? I wish I had asked.

A t first we kept the wolverines in bear cages, which were stout and lined inside with metal. But, after we had more wolverines than we had bear cages, the director, against my advice, decided wolverines weren't such fierce critters after all. He had plywood cages built for the wolverines, with three thicknesses of mink wire for doors.

These kept the wolverines fine for three or four days. But one morning as I started to open the door to the garage in which we had the wolverines caged, what sounded like a pack of loose wolverines slammed against the door crack, fighting each other and the door to get out. They had chewed through the mink wire doors of their cages. I nearly jerked the door off its hinges getting it closed.

I had a snare-pole for handling the bear cubs we had for the movie, and I decided to recapture the loose wolverines with the pole. But first I scouted around for someone to help me. The first guy I found was the cameraman.

"Say, uh, I wonder if you could come help me for a few minutes?" I asked.

"Sure, Slim. What's up?" the guy asked.

"Well, uh, some of the wolverines are loose in the garage and . . ."

He was silent for a long time, staring at me. Finally he said, nervous-like, "Gosh, Slim, I don't know anything about wolverines. Maybe you'd better get someone else."

It took all of my powers of persuasion to get him to help.

We found several empty oil drums and worked them through the door and into the garage, standing behind them for protection. The instant we cracked the door, all of them hit it again, but we were ready and braced. The noise they made was enough to curl your hair. The cameraman was pale, but he had guts and stayed with it.

When we yelled, the wolverines retreated. They growled and cussed and in general raised all kinds of hell. I was relieved to find only three of them were loose.

Once inside the garage we closed the door behind us and stood waiting behind the oil drums. A wolverine dashed toward us and came close enough for me to slip the loop over his head. I held the snare pretty tight. In fact that hot-tempered little cuss got pretty tame before I dropped him into one of the barrels and covered it.

One of the remaining two was completely wild. He charged and bounced off the barrels repeatedly, and dashed around so fast I couldn't get the snare on him. The third wolverine spent most of the time crouched under a bench, growling.

Finally the wild one dashed by and on impulse I dropped the snare and grabbed both his hind feet and picked him up. He started to double up and reach for me, and I automatically spun to keep him away.

By the time I had whirled around a couple of times, I wished I hadn't been so impulsive. It wasn't exactly like having a tiger by the tail, but it was close. I couldn't stop spinning long enough to drop him into a barrel. As the wolverine and I went around and around, I saw the cameraman's face peeking over a barrel. His eyes were like saucers. He ducked every time the wolverine swished by. I guess he was afraid I'd turn loose and dump the growling critter on him.

In about half a dozen spins I started to get dizzy. I was beginning to wonder how it would end when I staggered a bit, trying to keep my feet. As I staggered, I moved closer to a post in the garage, and the next time found I slammed the wolverine's head against it. That took most of the fight out of him, and it was easy to drop him into a barrel. I hadn't intended such rugged treatment, but it did take the "tiger" out of my hands, so to speak.

I tottered dizzily to get behind the barrels and waited until the garage quit spinning before going after the third animal. He was still under the bench and I reached in and got the snare around his neck and pulled him into the open. He braced his feet, growling, but I skidded him out anyway. I hated to lift him by the neck with the snare wire, so I asked the cameraman to lift his body while I kept the snare wire tight and controlled his head.

So help me it was accidental. I'll swear to it. The cameraman later accused me of turning the wolverine loose on purpose, but I didn't.

He grabbed the critter's tail and pulled, stretching the body tight. He intended to put one hand underneath and support most of the weight by the wolverine's belly while I lifted the head with the snare; we would drop it into a barrel together.

But, as he pulled on the tail, somehow the quick little devil pulled out of the noose. I honestly don't know how he managed it. One moment I had him, the next he was out. This put the cameraman in an awkward position; he had a wolverine by the tail.

I guess he remembered how I had handled the situation a few minutes earlier. Anyway, he lifted and started to whirl. At the same time he yelled, adding his excited voice to that of the angry wolverine.

With each spin the cameraman took a couple of steps toward the post where I had clonked my wolverine. His intent was obvious.

Now, I was responsible for those animals. I took my work seriously. I didn't want all my wolverines to end up with bashed-in heads. I hadn't bammed mine against the pole on purpose, though I suspect the cameraman thought I had.

Thinking quickly, I decided the only way out was to have the cameraman release the animal, so I yelled, "Turn him loose."

He took me at my word, but his timing was bad. That wolverine catapulted directly toward me. I flung myself down, and I swear he brushed me as he flew by. I heard him bounce off a wall of the garage and ricochet off one of the three barrels we had by the door.

I got to my feet and turned to see him staggering toward me. Automatically I held the snare-pole out, and he rammed his head into the noose as if on purpose. I jerked it tight, and without any more humane ideas of having the cameraman lift him into the barrel with me, heaved upward as if he were a big fish and dropped him into the last empty barrel.

The animals played an important role in the movie. The only human actor played the part of a doctor who was forced down while flying his small plane across arctic Alaska. He made his way south, afoot, looking for civilization. As if this weren't trouble enough, a plague had wiped out Natives in all the villages he came to. Of course, there had to be a huge tundra fire too, and that fire chased him across Alaska and practically to the state of Washington. The animals were there because they too were being driven ahead of the fire.

"A gen-u-wine Alaska movie," the director had said. I had to laugh when I learned the so-called plot.

The actor was a two-hundred-pound bruiser who didn't like any part of being in Alaska, and we had quite a time with him when it came to the wolverines. Getting him to go into a pen and act with them running around growling and fighting each other, and threatening him, was almost impossible. I guess he figured they were bad actors.

Every time one ran toward him with the apparent intent of sampling some raw Hollywood meat, he cringed and backed up. He was genuinely scared, and I didn't blame him.

"Magnificent acting. Did you get that?" the director would yell at the cameraman while the poor actor was dancing around defending himself. Acting was the last thought he had in mind when those feisty wolverines started for him.

Once I had the temerity to approach the director and point out, since we were filming a "gen-u-wine Alaska movie," that wolverines didn't generally run around in packs. His shrug, and explanation that we needed more action, didn't really satisfy me, but I let it go.

The wolverines got meaner and harder for me to catch every time we turned them into the pen to do some filming. I was almost as happy as the actor when the wolverine sequences were completed.

The director wanted it to appear that there were lots of animals being chased by the fire. At the time, the easiest animals to get in large numbers were porcupines. The Kenai Peninsula was loaded with them. Fox and mink ranchers fed them to their animals by the hundreds.

When we offered five dollars each for live porcupines, plus the cost of freighting them to Anchorage, we had three hundred porcupines before we could stop the flow. We had them in boxes, pens, barrels, cages, woodsheds, car trunks, and anything else we could stuff them into.

To simulate the huge tundra fire, we hired a gang in Anchorage to cut dry spruce, which we piled high. Then we threw on barrels of diesel oil and set the mass afire. Next we turned the porkies loose and started the camera.

Instead of running away from the fire, as often as not the porkies ran into it. Regardless of what we did, they wouldn't perform properly for the camera.

Someone came up with the idea of making tin chutes to slide the porkies down. Then, so the plan went, they would scuttle off past the camera, which was stationary. Smoke billowed past the camera and hid the chutes.

Of course the smoke nearly asphyxiated us. Our eyes watered so badly we couldn't see much. And have you ever tried to shove a live porcupine, head first, down a slick metal chute where it doesn't want to go?

We got the porkies to the bottom of the chutes all right by using snare poles, heavy gloves, and plenty of cussing. They dropped to the ground, but often they stupidly stood there, and the next porky to slide down the chute would drop atop them—and the one on top got a bunch of quills in its belly.

Porky feed was a problem. We spent a lot of time cutting boughs and brush for them to eat the bark from. Our outfit stayed at an old homestead belonging to H. P. Allen—we called him High Power—and old High Power had about three tons of rutabagas left from the previous summer's crop. His sales pitch convinced the director that they were just the thing to feed the porkies, and he sold him the entire lot.

As it happened the porkies liked the rutabagas. The trouble was, they were high power too; the resulting diarrhea killed porkies like flies.

In desperation, we hung dead and frozen porkies from piano wire and a guy back in the brush pulled a wire to yank them in front of the camera. They bumped and bounced across the snow and ice, their feet swinging back and forth. When the film was developed, I was astonished to see they looked more natural than the live porkies. They really seemed to trot across the screen.

Next, for some obscure reason, the director decided he needed some crows, and the little fish crows from Latouche Island, near Cordova, were exactly what he wanted. He bought several hundred of them that obliging Natives trapped. The fact that crows don't exist in the area the "doctor" was supposed to be struggling through made no difference.

We photographed the crows while they were in covered fox pens. Smoke blew past, upsetting the crows, and they hollered and fluttered and acted fine.

When we were through with them, the director, who was a softhearted guy, told me to turn them loose. Crows were not native to Anchorage.

At the same time, we were through with the porcupines, so he ordered they too be released.

The result was bedlam. For a few days there was a porcupine or three in about every tree in town (Anchorage was pretty small in 1933). And about every other dog in town had a sore face where quills had been pulled.

One old-timer with blood in his eye looked us up. He had a shotgun under his arm. He had been awakened before daylight that morning by a rattling and crunching on his front porch. He rolled out of a warm bed, poked a flashlight and shotgun out the front door, wondering what'n hell was out there, and found a porcupine busily gnawing down a post of his porch.

The director bought him off with a fistful of cash.

The little loudmouthed fish crows darted around Anchorage for quite a while. They were confused, and often went in gangs. Some of the rowdydow boys of Anchorage got out shotguns and had some pretty good wing shooting for a while. This burned up the more staid citizens. They blamed the film crew, including me, of course.

One of the more ardent shotgun artists went too far, though. He actually knocked a high-flying crow down amidst one of our filming operations. The dead crow tumbled through the air and landed with a loud *whump* not twenty feet from the actor, who was busily hamming up the scene in which he was supposed to be staggering through some knee-high brush. His startled look toward the dead crow made the director yell, "Cut."

I was standing there admiring the guy's magnificent shot when the director yelled at me, "Say, Slim, will you go see what you can do about the wise guy with the shotgun?"

He had faded by the time I got to the spot from which he had shot. But it did give me a chance to get away where I could laugh.

And then there were the bear cubs. According to the plot, there were two cubs, orphans, that the fleeing "doctor" had adopted. We had three cubs; one was spare.

They didn't know from one day to the next how to behave. One day we petted them, and the next, for the camera, we dropped trees on them, or maybe pushed them off a cliff, or dumped them into an icy stream.

One was bigger and meaner than the others. She weighed about a hundred pounds, and I think she was a yearling, whereas the others were in their first year. We called her Queen.

One day the actor was in a pen with a big fire burning outside. Smoke drifted across, concealing the wire, and to the camera I guess it looked fine. He was supposed to rush up and grab Queen and rescue her from the fire by carrying her away.

A few hours earlier we had felled a tree on the cub, for the camera, of course, and she was kind of on the peck. The actor ran over and reached for Queen, but he hesitated when she came up on her hind feet, snorted, chomped her teeth, and peeled her lips back. He went ahead and grabbed. Queen proceeded to chomp teeth up his arm like eating corn on the cob. She must have pinched a dozen big blood blisters. At the same time, her claws worked the actor over.

The actor had few clothes on because they had supposedly been torn off by the brush, so the claws went right through to skin.

Mr. Actor promptly dropped Queen.

"Pick that bear up and get it out of there," the director instructed the actor, taking his ever-present cigarette holder from his mouth.

But the actor had had all he wanted, with bites, scratches, and blisters where his "pet" cub had worked him over. "Ta hell with this," he growled and walked off.

The director's face became livid. He threw his golf cap on the ground and leaped on it. He dashed his long cigarette holder into a snowbank and screamed, "Get back in there."

His performance easily topped that of the actor, so the actor had no choice but to back down and return. I felt sorry for the guy, and substituted one of the other cubs for Queen, and that segment of the film was completed without a bear again trying to steal the scene.

Almost everything that happened on that job had a screwball twist to it. I happened to catch a couple of falcons in a trap, so we kept them, thinking they might fit into some scene. Someone had sent us a bald eagle. One day I turned the eagle into a pen with the two falcons. The falcons, on perches, screamed bloody murder, and so help me, one of them fainted and fell from his perch to the ground, out like Schmeling.

The eagle had a bad wing, but he could fly about a hundred yards. One day as the camera started to grind, he sat on a perch watching the actor trying to catch a rabbit. The poor two-hundred-pound guy was starving to death. As he stooped and started to sneak forward to one of the dozen or so rabbits I had turned into the pen, the eagle jumped from his perch, flopped his wings a few times, and landed on the actor's back.

He froze. "Get him off of me," he yelled. I knew if I picked the bird up his claws would tighten and really give the actor something to yell about.

"Lie down and roll over," I advised. When he did, the eagle stepped off onto the ground.

Later when the "doctor" caught a rabbit, we gave him some fried chicken, which he ate in front of the camera, hamming it up gruesomely.

Next, the director decided he had to have a lot of mink in the picture. I warned him that every trapper in Alaska would send them in if he advertised as he had for porcupines, so he made a deal with a mink rancher near Anchorage to use two hundred of his caged mink. Next, he got permission to use a big auditorium, which he had camouflaged to look like woods.

Lights were strung around the bottom of the auditorium to illuminate for the camera. At the last minute, the cameraman decided to use overhead lights only, so we unscrewed the bottom lightbulbs. Those mink, fresh from cages, frantically dashed around, and half a dozen of them jammed their wet noses into these light sockets and were knocked stiff. I skinned electrocuted mink all one day.

I worked for that outfit for four months. Sometimes I laughed, and then again I was ashamed to be mixed up with a thing like that. I got so I'd slink down the street and turn my head when I met a fellow guide or trapper.

The movie is still around. I have heard that it appears on late evening TV, and it even showed up at a Fairbanks movie theater near my home a few years ago.

I am often asked what I thought of the finished movie. I usually hedge, "Well, it was a 'gen-u-wine' filmed-in-Alaska movie."

If the questioner persists, I have to answer truthfully: "I don't know. I've never seen it."

*A*fter telling me this story, Slim Moore shook his head and said that, while there was plenty to laugh at about the making of the movie, he hated the pressures put on him and on the animal "actors."

"It was a helluva way to treat animals," he said. "We didn't have time to gentle them, facilities for caring for them were makeshift, and the treatment they received when on camera wasn't very nice. I made sure they had plenty of food and water, and once their part in the movie was over, I released those that could make it back into the wild."

Slim often testified at public hearings of the Board of Fish and Game and of the later Board of Game while I was a member. His comments were pointed, usually humorous, and they always reflected his concern for wildlife. During the 1960s some guides hunted brown bears with small planes, landing near when they located a bear, and leading clients to an easy but unsportsmanlike kill. Slim contemptuously referred to such guides as "crop dusters." Others had testified against aerial hunting, but the board remembered Slim's comments best. Crop dusters was the perfect term.

It was Slim who recommended that the world-famous McNeil River area on *lower Cook Inlet be closed to hunting and set aside for the viewing of brown bears. In the early 1950s he took a client to McNeil River for a hunt and realized what a marvelous place it could be for the public to view the big bears. The Territorial Game Commission acted positively on Slim's recommendation and in 1955 closed the area to hunting. At statehood, the Board of Fish and Game retained the hunting closure.*

Slim was named Alaska's Guide of the Year in 1973 by the Alaska Professional Hunters Association. In 1977 the Alaska Guide Licensing and Control Board recognized him as an honorary Master Guide for life—the only person ever so honored. In that same year Alaska's legislature congratulated him in a formal resolution for his almost half a century of ethical and active guiding. At his retirement at the age of eighty, he was the oldest active guide in Alaska.

Slim Moore died in Anchorage in April 1982 at the age of eighty-three.

Editor's Note: To read more about Jim Rearden and his books,
check out www.epicenterpress. com.

Excerpt from *The Hidden Coast*

JOEL W. ROGERS

❦ JOEL W. ROGERS is an internationally published outdoor photographer and writer. His work can be seen in such publications as *Outside, Audubon, Men's Journal,* and *Sierra Calendars.* Rogers's stunning photographs and his gift for observation and reflection vividly portray the wonders of the West Coast. *The Hidden Coast* is a magical journey experienced from the cockpit of a sea kayak. ❦

ORCA

JOHNSTONE STRAIT TO BLACKFISH SOUND

They come out of the North Pacific depths in a coordinated attack. Orcas, the killer whales, quietly encircle the sockeye returning to the rivers of British Columbia. The salmon mill in confusion as the orcas, one by one, charge the center of the school. Those salmon prudent enough to flee discover the ring of orcas, like a net holding them in, each predator patiently awaiting its turn to feed.

It is early summer off the northwestern tip of Vancouver Island. The scent of the Fraser, western Canada's largest river, draws the salmon on as they follow their spawning urge, seeking their ancestral stream. They gather and turn south into the increasingly confining waters of Queen Charlotte Strait. The orcas follow, feeding at will.

By June, families, or pods, of orcas begin arriving at their summer "village." This gathering site is at the western entrance to a great passage of saltwater that continually floods and ebbs between the massive northern flank of Vancouver Island and the myriad islets and inlets that buffer the mainland of British Columbia. Known as Johnstone Strait, this entrance is one to three miles wide, forty-seven miles long, and over one thousand feet deep. It is a natural gauntlet the salmon must run to find their spawning grounds. During the five months the salmon pass this way, up to 170 blackfish, as orcas are also known, will congregate in these waters, herding salmon, teaching their children, families reuniting with families.

So too in June the humans come, heading north from the universities and research centers, passing through Seattle and Vancouver up the fabled Inside Passage to Johnstone. They bring with them underwater microphones, cameras, and computers. They bring, as well, a curious reverence for the orca that separates them from their brethren. For they have a common conviction that the orcas are something greater than one more precious organism swimming in the sea. They study the behavior of a marine mammal that rules the world's oceans and has captured the hearts of all who study it. Paul Spong, who initially approached studying the orcas as you would a laboratory rat, described in 1974 after six years of research a far different understanding:

> [The orca is] an incredibly powerful and capable creature, exquisitely self-controlled and aware of the world around it, a being possessed of a zest for life and a healthy sense of humor, and moreover, a remarkable fondness for and an interest in humans.

This viewpoint was not easily accepted. The orcas had long been named killer whales—toothed whales that have no enemies and, in Dr. Spong's estimation, no fear. They have been witnessed by seafarers to be swift and effective hunters of all major fish and mammal stocks. The orcas themselves were hunted sporadically by the Japanese and the Norwegians, and shot at by every self-righteous fisherman out for the same catch. They were assumed to be ruthless, voracious killers. The assumption was wrong.

Into the 1970s, in both Canada and the United States, researchers' fascination with orcas and other whales resulted in a groping realization of these marine mammals' remarkable abilities. The first studies were conducted with captive dolphins, porpoises, and beginning in 1969 orcas, often in the circus atmosphere of the new marinelands. The first tests were simple nose-the-proper-button-and-receive-half-a-herring physiological studies. But in Paul Spong's visual acuity research, something went marvelously wrong: after twenty-four hundred half-herrings and a 90 percent success rate, Skana, the first captive orca to be studied, began giving the incorrect answer time after time—her only way to tell the researcher, "I want a new game."

Skana continued the education of Paul Spong, at one time seeming to correct him for leaving off a pectoral fin on her portrait by pointedly wheeling about her pool, the omitted fin splashing the artist. On another, Skana slashed her teeth across Paul's bare feet, only touching and causing no pain. He recoiled in instinctive fright but returned his foot to the original position. Skana repeated the movement, her head rising out of the quiet pool, her teeth sweeping over his extended toes. Again Paul flinched, but being a dedicated experimental psychologist, he repeatedly dangled his foot. Each time, Skana would lunge until he controlled his involuntary reaction. Skana then stopped and vocalized, staring back at Paul from the middle of the pool. He then realized that she was intentionally deconditioning his fear of her, establishing a bond of trust.

Through the 1970s, the studies of orcas evolved. No one doubted the whales' intelligence; their gentleness and family loyalty turned public opinion into a love affair, yet no one really knew the orca. Dr. Spong began studying free as opposed to captive orcas in 1974, by establishing a research station on uninhabited Hanson Island at the northern entrance to Johnstone Strait. Taping their voices and monitoring their daily patterns in the tidal wilderness, Paul's research turned personal and public. Together with a growing family of researchers, film teams, writers, and musicians, the clinician became an advocate and a voice for the orca, and Johnstone Strait rippled to the wakes of kayakers, researchers, and orcas interacting in open curiosity.

In 1981, David Arcese had caught wind of Dr. Spong's studies and asked me to join him on a kayak trip to Johnstone Strait. Quiet, soft-spoken, fascinated by whales, David's curiosity about orcas must have rivaled Spong's. We were well into September, late for seeing orcas, but going anyway, as we car-topped our kayaks along Highway One north through the clearcuts and gentle peaks of interior Vancouver Island.

Our put-in was Telegraph Cove, a tiny, protected bay rimmed by second-growth evergreens. Along the back bayshore lay an exhausted timber mill whose saws had been stilled for a decade, a general store and a boat launch for the new economy of sportfishing, and a boardwalk connecting an unplanned string of sturdy fir-framed houses. With one green exception, these houses were painted white, roofed with corrugated tin, and each was well kept and lived in. They were sited along the tideline wedged between outcrops of granite and the stumps of long-gone old growth. Spartan, clean, dotted with the passing of ravens, Telegraph Cove was as it once was, hedged in by the landform, overlooked, blessed to grow no bigger.

We paid the store owner a small sum for launching privileges, and paddled out into Johnstone and a rising southeasterly. Hoping to be with orcas and intent on making Robson Bight eleven miles distant, we headed east hugging the Vancouver Island shore, our paddles feathered to knife the wind.

This first paddle to Robson would be a stormy one. Much of our time was spent grounded beneath a rain tarp, as a strong southeasterly tore up the strait. We saw only two orcas pass on our third day. The following morning, wet and cold, we packed and paddled back to Telegraph Cove, promising to return.

Robson Bight is not quite a bay—it is a bend in the shoreline, an indentation deep enough to warrant a name but too exposed to give a vessel safe anchorage. In the years following our paddle to Robson, the bight would gain the attention of the world for its unique orca visitations. It would also narrowly miss becoming a timber booming yard, where the great log rafts would be created and towed to market. And its uplands, the climax forests of the Tsitika River valley—the last virgin watershed on the 285-mile-long island—would be slated for clearcutting. The government of British Columbia would designate the bight a marine ecological preserve in 1982, but in the end the timber industries have been allowed to cut the valley and only a two-hundred-foot coastal buffer has been saved.

There were other changes: new paths and new attitudes were bringing new people to the water's edge. Each year another massive ocean liner joined the popular cruise ships sailing the Inside Passage. Two or three ships a day passed the bight, immersing thousands of tourists into the magic of the forested islands, the eagles overhead, and, if they were lucky, the orcas. Telegraph Cove's old tug *Gikumi* had been converted to an orca-watching vessel, breathing new life into the Telegraph Cove economy. But one phenomenon stands out in the decade of growing interest over the orcas of Johnstone Strait: sea kayakers. These were newcomers with a relatively gentle impact, silently tracking to Robson Bight.

On a Sunday in July 1989, I returned to Johnstone Strait to meet up with David, who had founded Northern Lights Expeditions and was beginning his seventh season guiding sea kayakers into the strait. Amidst the salmon fishermen and whale watchers, we load and launch our group of twelve new kayakers into the little-changed harbor of Telegraph Cove. The weather is overcast and dry as we paddle out through the port entrance, the new seafarers bumping gunwales, hurtling this way and that as they learn to steer the fast, stable double kayaks. David and his assistant guide, Steffie Ackroyd, are moving like sheepdogs through the little flock, instructing and reassuring the neophyte kayakers, as we enter the open waters of Johnstone Strait.

As each pair of paddlers gets a rhythm going, we begin to speed up, relax, and take in our surroundings. Behind us hills of conifers rise up into the low clouds, hiding the steep three-thousand-foot almost-mountains that crowd the northern shore of Vancouver. Before us, two miles of open water sweep away to the east and west to form the strait. Beyond the crossing lies Paul Spong's Hanson Island, one of a hundred low-lying islands to explore.

With the chart and a firsthand look at this landscape, I can realize, almost see, the forces that have shaped the scene before us. Off our bows, miles inland, the islands turn to mainland and rise to mountains, like a mirror image of Vancouver Island. Between these two natural barriers a millennium of glaciers has come and gone, rounding the islands' edges, mining channels as deep as fifteen hundred feet along the strait.

As we approach Hanson Island, David steers us toward Weynton Passage and the entrance to Blackfish Sound. We cheat as only a kayaker can, and paddle behind the tiny islets that rim the west end of the island, avoiding the main channel and the beginning of the opposing flood tide surging in from the Pacific.

Once through the pass, we stretch out into the open waters of Blackfish Sound, moving at a beginner's pace. This is a casual exploration; all of us are watching for orcas, some more impatient than others. David is in no hurry. After all his summers running trips along the strait, he knows the people in his charge will settle into enjoying all there is to see and do here—and see orcas.

David is good at this business, in part because he respects the spirit of the land as well as the orcas. He knows the locals and works with the Kwakiutl people of the region to protect their heritage sites. He is respected by the long-term researchers who help him set self-imposed guidelines on kayaking in the presence of whales. And he knows the orcas from his reading, attending conferences, and simply being here in contact.

In a few days, we'll move back across Johnstone to the camps north of Robson Bight where whale sightings are routine. For now, we get to know our kayaks and our partners as we paddle our way to camp.

We beach on a small pocket bay that faces south and set to unloading the boats and putting up tents. I wander through the kitchen and discover it is possible to snitch a fresh piece of cornbread. As our dinner of fresh salad and grilled cod, salmon, and crab disappears, we idly watch the evening go by. On the far side of our vista, the last of the salmon fishermen power back to Telegraph, the whine of their outboards fading toward the setting sun. A bald eagle soars off to the left, over a perfect little island. For many of the people on this expedition, this is their first day in company with eagles. Conversation stills as we watch the great scavenger wheel away.

One of our group asks David about the small minke whale we'd seen earlier in the afternoon, when suddenly the ground begins to vibrate, strongly enough to stop the conversation. An ocean liner, massive and at speed, enters Blackney Pass southbound, passing our camp about a half mile out. The light shines from the ship's cabins with the color of a campfire. I can almost imagine the disco music over the sound of the engines. Although we're close enough to see people, the decks are empty. The ship swings to ride the centerline of the thousand-yard channel, comes around to port, steadies up on a course down Johnstone, and is gone. We stay quiet for a bit, to ruminate over this remarkable visitor. Elegant to some, an extravagance to others? No one says. We are undeniably on a different cruise.

The following days we explore Blackfish Sound, trailed by shy yet curious seals. Our real intent shows in our scanning of the way ahead for telltale dorsal fins, our ears tuned to the distant whoosh of orca breath. On the morning of our fourth day, we move our camp five and a half miles to the Vancouver Island side of Johnstone Strait for some serious orca watching. No sooner have we established camp than David spots a pod well out in the channel. We assist each other with our boats, and one by one we paddle from shore to intercept.

Whale watching is not unlike the behavior of a professional sports photographer on the sidelines of a football game. With every play, he moves farther downfield in an attempt to predict the advance of the team. The key to this analogy is that he cannot enter the field. Neither can we. Placing boats across the oncoming path of an orca pod might disrupt their activity—feeding, sleeping, playing—causing an unknown amount of stress to an already too popular mammal.

We paddle fast and hard, angling to approach the whales' course well ahead of them. David calls a halt and we gather into a group, staying still and hoping for the best. We wait. David had said that orcas have a distinctive cruising pattern of deep diving for three or four minutes at a time, then a series of shallow dives of ten to fifteen seconds duration. If we're in the right place, the pod should begin a shallow diving sequence about two hundred yards off our bows. We wait and watch, necks swiveling left-right-left, fingers focusing lenses from thirty feet to infinity and back.

"They're behind us!" someone shouts, as the sudden sound of exhaling air reaches us across the water. We turn to face the pod. The whales surface again, and we do a sort of sotto-voce mutual squeal because they have turned, coming straight at us. At a hundred yards, the orcas dive again and we go quiet, darting glances at each other. David says, "Just stay put."

One by one, their dorsal fins rise into the air right in front of us—so close it looks like a sure collision. At less than thirty feet, the largest bull aims right for me. I know from my reading and David's assurances that orcas do not intentionally attack or even bump kayakers in such a nonthreatening situation. I'm just trying to focus my camera. They dive, the male's six-foot dorsal fin sinking with a subtle side-to-side movement, and I realize it's flexible, not knifelike, not a weapon. I look into the depths of mid-channel for the passing of the twenty-five-foot-long submarine shape, its dorsal fin faint in the watery darkness—five tons of *Orcinus orca* beneath my fifty-five-pound kayak.

We watch transfixed as the pod swims beneath us, their white-to-gray "saddles" across their backs marking their progress. The orcas make one final surface, each exhaling followed by a sharp intake of air, and then they deep dive, tails rising from the water with an unhurried, fluid motion.

The water surrounding our kayaks ripples from sudden displacement. No one lifts a paddle. David suggests a course we can follow and we begin to move north toward Weynton Passage, keeping to the right of the pod's probable path.

In David's opinion, this pod is asleep. "Orcas sleep on the move, the adults taking turns on watch. See how they all breathe in unison." The pod surfaces well to our right, in easy rhythm, exhaling in the same uncanny synchronism; their high, jet-black dorsal fins rise and fall, parting the clear, jade-green water in mid-nap.

We learn that these four whales are called the C-5 subpod, a part of C pod, one of the larger resident families that summer in Johnstone Strait. The leader is C-5, the matriarch, the fifty-eight-year-old mother of C-2, a big dorsal-finned thirty-two-year-old male; C-10, an eighteen-year-old female; and C-13, a five-year-old toddler with the characteristic hook-shaped baby fin. These whales will stay together for life, a life that nearly matches ours in longevity.

Their colorless titles are disturbing—we would name them differently. David tells us that the numeric designations are a necessity for scientists. Whales in early studies were identified by more distinctive monikers—Wavy, Saddle, Nicola—with each name identifying a particular physical feature of the individual whale. But that became unworkable with the discovery of so many more whales at Johnstone.

Our own "pod" of fourteen kayakers looks pretty professional, paddling easily. Mirrored in the reflective greens and grays of the strait, our paddles rise and fall in unison, bow and stern sailors intent on the whales. Though David rarely shows it, he is pleased with the trip. We have achieved the skills to safely travel these waters, the people have warmed to the land's character, we all have been doing our dishes, and now we are in the company of orcas.

Suddenly the orcas' cruising pattern changes. They have doubled their speed, coming farther out of the water, awake and excited. The orcas have picked up echolocations from H pod, infrequent visitors to this area, moving through Weynton Passage and headed our way.

We paddle hard to keep up, but fall far behind as the giant mammals surge up the strait to greet their friends. The first orca breaches, his full body leaving the water, a ten-thousand-pound silhouette on the horizon, then a mammoth splash. Other orcas are "spyhopping" or swimming in place, propelling their upper torso clear of the water to see around them. Still others below are most likely curling around neighbors in physical touch. The sounds they are no doubt making underwater—clicks, whistles, and screeches—are identifications and greetings. Another whale breaches, this time close enough for us to see the distinctive markings of the whale's white and black stomach.

David brings us to a halt well short of the melee, at a two-hundred-yard distance, grouped, watching. Gradually the hubbub dies, and we lower our cameras. The pods deep dive, showing their tail flukes, and minutes later they surface separated. The H pod continues with the tide along the east side of the strait, and C-5 subpod crosses back toward our camp.

We have had our close encounter. In the gathering dusk, C-5 and her family swim away, and we slow to a stop to watch them go. Clustered together, our paddles resting across our neighbors' boats, we try to verbalize the sensation of paddling with orcas, David every bit as animated as the rest. But words are insufficient. One by one, our paddles bite the still waters of Johnstone Strait for the Vancouver shore.

Excerpt from *Shadows on the Koyukuk*

SIDNEY HUNTINGTON and JIM REARDEN

Half Athapaskan, SIDNEY HUNTINGTON, born in 1915, grew up in the Koyukuk River country of northern Alaska, a region that most Americans consider frontier wilderness. In his early years, birchbark canoes, dog teams, and paddle-wheel steamers were the primary mode of transportation. His Koyukon Athapaskan mother died when he was five, after which he lived at a Yukon River mission. Later, he attended the Bureau of Indian Affairs School at Eklutna, Alaska. When he was twelve, he joined his father on a trapline. Home was a log cabin, and the Huntingtons lived mostly off the land. He was on his own at sixteen, trapping and selling furs, hunting and fishing for food, and annually growing a vegetable garden. During his adventurous life, Huntington has learned the habits of wolves, moose, caribou, and other Koyukuk wildlife. Living in the wilds, he has had many narrow escapes, including a close call from a charging bear. He used his knowledge of wildlife when he served for twenty years as a member of the Alaska Board of Fish and Game and the Alaska Board of Game. Wild game and Yukon River salmon still make up most of his food. He observes many of the old Athapaskan customs and enjoys traditional stories that reveal the history and character of the Koyukon people. Huntington lives with his wife, Angela, in the Yukon River village of Galena, Alaska.

A few years ago my son Gilbert, trapping on the Big Portage just below Coffee Can Lake along the lower Koyukuk River, caught a wolf in a trap. Gilbert had never seen a wolf in a trap.

"He looked like a beautiful gray dog," he told me. And because he didn't want to kill a fine sled dog, he approached the animal to release him. He planned to put a rope around the wolf 's neck, so he could handle him and examine the foot for injury. As Gilbert neared, the wolf lay down and made no attempt to bite, nor did he fight the trap. As Gilbert worked to open the trap, the wolf pulled as far from him as he could and turned his head away.

"I could have petted him," Gilbert said.

Once released, the wolf stood up, looked at Gilbert (probably in amazement), and swiftly ran off. Only then did Gilbert realize that the animal was a wolf.

Gilbert's mistake is common; wolves do look like and to a degree behave like dogs, and many people unfamiliar with wolves and their habits think of the wolf and man's best friend in the same terms.

The wolf is Alaska's most efficient predator. He lives by killing other animals. His senses of smell, hearing, and sight are acute. He is intelligent, and hunts cooperatively in small groups or occasionally in large packs. Koyukon hunters have great respect for the wolf, and consider only the bear and perhaps the wolverine to have greater spiritual power.

Mature wolves weigh from 75 to 150 pounds. Black wolves are common and other colors include gray, white, and a brownish shade. Some wolves have a dark mask. Although wolves and dogs belong to the same family, wolves commonly kill and eat dogs that stray from camps or settlements; occasionally a dog chained near a cabin or at the edge of a village is killed by wolves. In the late 1970s, many Fairbanks residents became upset one winter when wolves killed many chained dogs at homes on the outskirts of that city. Once in a great while a female dog in heat may breed with a wild wolf.

One quiet evening in the fall of 1939, while hunting moose, I sat on a log at Hog River, looking over a little clearing. It was the time for moose to come out to feed. Then, for the first time in my life, I heard a wolf howl.

I turned toward the sound, listening. Again came the long, low, quavering howl. It had a nice tone. To some people, the howl of a wolf is spine-tingling or "chilling." But I enjoy hearing it, for it is a natural sound in the wildlands of Alaska.

When I was a boy, no wolves lived in the Koyukuk Valley, or they were so few that we were unaware of them. We never heard one and we never saw a track. With none of their major prey—moose and caribou—living in the Koyukuk, they had no reason to be there. Throughout most of Alaska, besides moose and caribou, wolves also kill and eat Dall sheep and Sitka deer. Snowshoe hares are an important food in some years. In summer, moose and caribou calves are a common food.

When moose became established in the Koyukuk in the late 1930s and then wolves arrived, as trappers we were pleased to be able to catch the animals for their valuable fur, although we quickly learned that wolves are smart and difficult to trap. At first, most of the furs were kept and used by Koyukon women in making winter clothing. Wolves continued to increase, for moose were abundant. An adult wolf eats six to seven pounds of meat each day, and a pack of ten wolves eats sixty to seventy pounds of meat daily. This is about fifty adult moose a year, or about 120 caribou. By the mid-1950s, wolves had increased enough to be a threat to the Koyukuk moose population.

In 1972 Governor William A. Egan appointed me to the Alaska Board of Fish and Game. This board developed all hunting, fishing, and trapping regulations for the state, and established policies for fish and game. At our long meetings, we studied reams of scientific information on various populations of fish and game, heard reports from fisheries and game biologists, and held public hearings. When the board was split in 1975, Governor Jay Hammond appointed me to the Board of Game, where I served until early 1992. As a member of these boards, I learned much about wolves from scientists who provided us with basic biological information on Alaska's wildlife.

Millions of dollars have been spent on studies of Alaska's wolves and their way of life.

The availability of food—primarily moose, caribou, deer, sheep—is the primary determinant of wolf densities in Alaska. When these prey species are abundant and easily taken, wolves fare well and have larger litters, and more pups survive their first year.

When food is scarce smaller litters are produced, and mortality of pups increases because of starvation and cannibalism. Under these conditions, 50 to 60 percent of pups born each spring usually die within eight months.

A number of studies in Alaska have shown that when the ratios of wolves to moose drop below about one wolf per twenty moose, the moose population is unlikely to maintain itself, and it will probably decline. In some cases moose have been entirely killed off from an area by wolves, at which time the wolves had nothing to eat and they themselves either starved, or left that area, leaving the land with no moose or wolves.

Many people believe that wolves take only sick and misfit prey. Several Alaskan studies have shown that usually wolves take moose or caribou in almost exactly the same proportion as found in the prey population. A cow moose heavy with calf is the most valuable moose, from the standpoint of the moose population, yet such a cow is most vulnerable to wolves. Moose and caribou calves are especially vulnerable, and they too are valuable from the standpoint of the moose population.

The Koyukons respect the wolf as an intelligent animal and an efficient killer of big game. Elders say that early Koyukon people viewed the wolf as powerful and important, and in the days before rifles they feared the animal. Until rifles, steel traps, and steel snares were available, it was not possible for the Koyukon people to take wolves in numbers. Rarely, wolves were killed with bow and arrow.

Throughout Alaska, wolf skins are prized for making parkas, boots, and mittens. Among the Koyukon people, only men were supposed to wear wolf-skin garments, but this tradition is not strictly observed today. The most important use of wolf fur is for a parka ruff. It is used in conjunction with wolverine fur; the wolverine fur lies immediately next to the face where the bulk of frost forms from the breath on cold days. Long, stiff wolf fur protects the face from wind, and the coarse hairs shed frost easily. A good wolf parka ruff can extend a foot or more beyond the wearer's face.

Wolves don't attack humans, although I am aware of one wolf attack on a child. Many years ago in the Bettles-Wiseman area of the Upper Koyukuk, toddler David Tobuk was playing on a beach along the river. Suddenly a wolf ran out of the brush, grabbed him by the head with powerful jaws, and carried him off.

A nearby Koyukon Indian named Napoleon, who saw the wolf steal the child, ran after the wolf with a rifle and shot it. I knew Napoleon, who told me the story.

David Tobuk survived. He was captain of the *Teddy H.,* trader Sam Dubin's steamboat, which rescued us after our mother's death. David carried a large scar on his face from the wolf attack. Occasionally the scar became raw, and it bothered him all his life. Photos of David I've seen always show him with his head turned to conceal the scar.

Eskimos tell interesting stories about the wolf. A few years ago I hunted in the Kobuk Valley in Eskimo country and killed four caribou from a herd. While dressing them, I was careful to save the legs for the skin, which makes fine winter boots. Two Eskimos, both about my age, arrived while I was working on the caribou.

"Sidney, you're doing a good job, but you're doing one thing wrong," one said. I remained silent, knowing that these Eskimos were probably going to share a belief that they wanted me to observe.

"You aren't taking the hooves off. You should do that," one suggested.

"OK. I'll do that," I agreed.

They showed me how to cut all the hooves off—a simple job. Then they put all sixteen hooves on a string. As I continued to work on the caribou, one of the Eskimos said, "This practice comes from an old story. We know the story is true, so we always cut the hooves off like that."

Then the Eskimos told me their story:

A long time ago there were more caribou than now. Our people could kill caribou year-round. The animals never left. There were really too many caribou in the Kobuk Valley. Soon wolves became thick, and they, like the caribou, were all over the place. Our people had no way of killing them except with bow and arrow. They managed this difficult feat once in a while. So many wolves roamed the area that the Eskimos' lives were in danger, for the wolves were fearless.

The wolves killed many caribou, and dead caribou lay everywhere. Day after day the wolves killed, and in about two years few caribou remained. Then the wolves started to kill and eat each other. Soon they were so hungry they started to attack the people. The Eskimos had no safe place to flee to, but old legends told them what to do.

The legends told the Eskimos to go into their underground igloos, where they could keep fires going to keep warm. Since they couldn't leave their igloos because of danger from wolves, they began to run low on food. They knew that if they stayed inside their igloos long enough, the wolves would kill each other off; then the people would be safe.

Soon the Eskimos had nothing to eat, so they began boiling caribou hooves, which keep for a long time hanging in a cache. The hooves, of course, have some dried tendons and meat attached. They supply some nutritional needs. The hooves must be boiled and boiled before the broth is ready to drink.

The Eskimos kept alive by boiling the caribou hooves and drinking the broth while they waited and watched. When the wolves no longer appeared, they ventured out of the igloos to resume life. They traveled to lakes and rivers to catch fish. By then the caribou were all gone, having been killed by wolves. The wolves were also all gone, for they had eaten one another or starved to death.

This story fascinates me for several reasons. It may be based on a time when wolves with rabies attacked Eskimos, or when healthy but very hungry wolves attacked these people. This traditional story also parallels the findings of Alaska's wildlife scientists—that wolves in Alaska can and do sometimes wipe out their prey and then starve or depart the area. This may be why there were no wolves or moose in the Koyukuk in the late 1800s and the first three decades of the 1900s. And the Eskimos' story of wolves eating wolves is supported by findings of modern scientists; wolf cannibalism is a trait well known to wildlife scientists, as well as to the Koyukon people.

SECTION FIVE

CONSERVATION

CONSERVATION IS A difficult topic in the state of Alaska, one that's been hard to handle since humans first settled here and one that will become more difficult as human populations in the state grow. Clearly, the state's people, and particularly the state's Native population, have a right to make a living off the state's land and seas. In addition, all the people of Alaska need the jobs that come from exploiting the land—whether it's through oil production, mining, hunting, or tourism. But if they exploit Alaska's bounty too much, they run the risk of destroying the very beauty and pristine wilderness that drew them to Alaska in the first place. Somewhere there's an appropriate balance between conservation and exploitation, between destruction and development. But that balancing point falls at a different place for just about every Alaskan resident. The following pieces aren't the views of the editors of this book—it really is true that everybody has a different take—but they do give some idea of the scope and size of the issue. And it's an issue that's going to be at the core of Alaskan politics and Alaskan life for the foreseeable future.

Excerpt from *North to Wolf Country*

JAMES W. BROOKS

⊱ JAMES W. BROOKS left his boyhood home in Michigan and made his way to Alaska as a seventeen-year-old in 1940. Here he found a new world that offered occupations suited to an adventurous young man: fisherman, railroad worker, Caterpillar operator, trapper, musher, wartime flier, walrus researcher, bush pilot, whale biologist. He led the Territory of Alaska's wildlife management program into the era of statehood and later served as commissioner of the state Department of Fish and Game. Brooks has published numerous scientific and popular articles on Alaska's living resources. He received an honorary Doctor of Science degree from his alma mater, the University of Alaska, in 1989. With his Cessna 185 amphibian airplane, Brooks and his wife, Christa, continue to visit friends and range widely over the state. More information about the author and this book can be found at www.epicenterpress.com. ⊱

Fish and game can lead to fightin' words in Alaska. When it comes to the salmon and bears and wolves and other creatures of this great land, everyone has a strong opinion. So it's no surprise I ended up in the middle of a few controversies during my time as commissioner of fish and game: it comes with the job.

Take the summer of 1972, for example, when over thirty dead caribou were found closely clustered on Donnelly Dome south of Fort Greely. The *Fairbanks Daily News-Miner* reported speculation that the animals died as a result of secret military activities. Public concern grew out of the known presence of a small nuclear power plant at Fort Greely, as well as suspicions about experiments related to biological and chemical warfare. Governor Egan was alarmed and asked me to look into it.

I felt queasy about the situation. I remembered back to a period before 1967 when I had top-secret security clearance to act as liaison between the governor and military people at Fort Greely. Periodically a uniformed Army general accompanied by civilian scientists would come to my office to brief me on experiments involving aerosols, pathogen simulants, dispersal projections, and other ominous aspects of biological and chemical warfare—along with their assurances that there was no danger to public safety. Neither the governor nor I knew whether such tests had continued beyond 1967—but if they had, was it possible now that something had gone wrong?

The mystery deepened when my department's biologists examined these caribou and autopsied some of them, finding nothing abnormal. Then one biologist noticed the hair between the animals' hooves appeared to be burned. They returned to Donnelly Dome to check the site of the deaths and discovered streaks and veins of charred soil and duff not obvious in the overlying vegetation. The caribou mystery was solved: the animals had been killed by lightning.

If you want to see a furor erupt, just try withdrawing what some Alaskans consider a God-given right. In late 1972 I concluded that aerial shooting of wolves should be stopped. I directed that no more permits be issued for shooting wolves from aircraft unless we knew that wolves were killing excessive numbers of big game. This action was the first significant legal restraint ever on killing Alaska's wolves.

I stopped this type of hunting for a number of reasons. From 1960 until 1967 I had worked to bring changes in the management of wolves, and now I felt a keen interest in reviewing how our treatment of the animals fit the contemporary scene. Segments of the public had begun to question the rightness of aerial hunting, prompted by abuses such as poaching in Denali National Park. Aerial hunters sometimes wounded wolves without being able to complete the kill, leaving injured animals. And there was nothing sporting about instances in which wolves were killed but the carcasses were then just left on the ground. Unfortunately, Alaska's free-for-the-asking permits for aerial shooting of wolves seemed to bear out official recognition of the wolf as a harmful, unwanted animal. In contrast, federal law already prohibited aerial shooting on federal lands except as part of an animal control program.

As soon as word got out that the state had also banned the practice, aerial hunters screamed about this outrageous protection of wolves. And of course people who favored the ban got into the act. The uproar drew wide, even national, attention in the media. In defense of wolves, petition-style letters arrived signed by whole classrooms of children who argued that the wicked nature of wolves was nothing but nursery-rhyme fiction. Governor Egan's correspondence secretary, Reva LaFavour, was near panic trying to cope with the deluge of mail, and I helped her compose replies.

Even though we stood our ground, I soon learned that denying permits for aerial shooting lacked any real effect. It didn't change the behavior of hunters and it didn't reduce the number of wolves killed. The hunters simply began landing on the ground and shooting the wolves they had spotted from the air. Or they claimed that is what they did, if they were accused of aerial shooting. In other words, the hunters exploited a loophole in the rules.

The Board of Fish and Game quickly found the wolf to be a lively agenda topic, particularly on the question of whether wolf control was needed in some areas. Most board members were careful in their judgments, but one unabashed wolf hater, Ivan Thorall from Fairbanks and Chisana, tried to quell debate by citing the Bible's book of Genesis as a testament to man's dominance over all living things. No one at the table had an audible response to Ivan.

In 1975 an aerial survey of the western arctic caribou herd indicated an astounding collapse in numbers from 240,000 to 50,000 animals within the preceding five years. There were a lot of possible causes—too much hunting, predation by wolves and bears, bad weather, disease. But in any case, it looked like a situation where wolves were at least partly responsible for killing caribou that could have been used for food by people living in the herd's range. So we issued permits for aerial hunting of wolves in the range. Forty-eight wolves were taken by aerial hunters and three times that number by hunters and trappers on snow machines (snowmobiles).

These efforts were thought to have removed about 20 percent of the wolves present at the beginning. The caribou herd then appeared to stage an extraordinary recovery. Killing of the wolves generally got the credit, and at the time I was happy enough to entertain this notion. On reflection, however, it seems highly dubious that minor jiggling of predation levels—getting rid of 20 percent of the wolves—could trigger such a quick and extreme response. By the year 2001, the herd had grown to a half million animals and expanded its range southward through the Seward Peninsula and beyond. The humbling conclusion may simply be that a wildlife population can sometimes take its own course, confounding our best assessments and remedies.

We also issued permits for aerial shooting of wolves in 1975 in a large area south of Fairbanks because there were indications that wolves were killing too many moose. After that the number of moose increased modestly. Drastic thinning of wolf numbers in the Nelchina River basin brought little or no enduring change in the moose population. These results, not at all spectacular, probably typify the uncertain effects of wolf predation.

Without human interference, wolves and moose likely trend toward sparser numbers. Early explorers in Alaska and the Yukon reported a scarcity of moose as the common condition, evidently the consequence of a freely operating predator-prey system with no tinkering by man. The relatively great abundance of moose in more recent times suggests they somehow escaped the bonds of predation. I believe this began to happen soon after the arrival of non-Native hunters and trappers with their guns, steel traps and snares, and especially strychnine to kill the natural predators such as wolves. With a greater density of moose, and probably sheep and caribou as well, other agencies of population control accordingly came into play.

I have to say that in my years of trying to manage predation by wolves, about the only clear results is that it prompts a terrific amount of public debate.

It sometimes felt like walking a tightrope as we tried to balance competing interests in the fish and other sea life of Alaska. The salmon failures in

1972 and 1973 were unprecedented. In all regions except the Yukon and Kuskokwim Rivers, salmon failed to return in anything like expected numbers (the result of earlier harsh winters that killed many juvenile salmon). We set severe restrictions on fishermen to assure that fish could escape to spawning areas. Imagine the frustration of the fishermen who reported fish in never-before-seen abundance, the water surface allegedly silver with jumpers as far as the eye could see. It turned out this was nearly the case in the Noyes Island district, but the fish were sockeyes (red salmon) bound for Canada. Alaska fishermen had no legal right to these fish.

Another tricky issue involved the sale of roe taken from salmon that were caught for subsistence use (for the personal use of the people doing the fishing). The law said that fish caught for subsistence could not be sold. This included the roe, which wasn't traditionally used by subsistence fishermen but was in great demand as caviar by Japanese buyers. Natives appealed for permission to sell this otherwise wasted by-product. My sympathies were with them. I ignored the advice of Carl Rosier, the director of commercial fisheries, and persuaded myself that the Natives would benefit and not abuse the right to sell roe.

Then came the flack. Senator Bob Palmer alleged that the move was politically motivated, an attempt to curry favor with the Natives. I was further embarrassed when fishermen betrayed my trust by catching more salmon than they needed for subsistence, discarding the surplus fish after stripping the roe. I had to reverse my original decision, incurring the wrath of all sides.

This disagreement was nothing compared with the battles over the state's rules on catching king crabs. During the 1960s the Alaska king crab industry had developed into perhaps the most economically rewarding fishery in the world. These giant crabs, looking like spiders that measured three feet across outstretched legs, were coveted by seafood dealers and consumers. By 1972 the fishery faced trouble from excessive harvests and competition. Regulations were aimed at conservation and at sharing the fishing opportunities, but of course not everyone was satisfied.

In August 1973 a group of king crab vessel owners in Seattle complained in a letter to U.S. Senator Warren G. Magnuson of Washington state that some Alaska crab regulations are "aimed solely at excluding us from competing with their [Alaskan] small fleets, and also with our Japanese, Korean, and Russian counterparts." In turn, Governor Egan called the Seattle group "a classical example of nonresidents who still feel they can come to Alaska, exploit our resources wantonly and get out without contributing anything. . . ."

After more jostling back and forth, the situation turned serious. Shortly before the scheduled July 1, 1974, opening of the Bering Sea king crab fishery, owners of the Seattle fleet announced they would not recognize the regulations or the jurisdiction of the state beyond three miles offshore. They declared their own fishing season, with an opening date of June 24. We quickly learned that many king crab pots were indeed already set and fishing in the Bering Sea. I promptly sent telegrams to the Seattle group, making it clear that the season in the Bering Sea would be delayed until the illegal crab fishing stopped and all crab pots were removed. Alaska had unquestioned authority to regulate within three miles, and because the crabs had to be delivered in live condition to shore plants for processing we held a strong hand.

With their huge fleet now mostly at anchor in Dutch Harbor, the Seattle owners retreated to a more conciliatory position. Their spokesman, Ron Jensen, appeared in Juneau to discuss the stalemate with me, offering assurances that the fleet would comply with state regulations. I knew Ron as a sophisticated, honest person and an astute businessman whose word was as good as gold, but the situation was aggravated by the illegal pots in the Bering Sea. There could be no compromise on the need to move all pots to designated storage areas, with gates open, and then to inspect the holding tanks of the vessels.

We didn't have an easy time verifying removal of the crab pots. We were limited to using chartered aircraft and two vessels. The immensity of the area to be searched coupled with bad weather made the task agonizingly slow, and fishermen's tempers frayed. But when I was finally satisfied that no significant illegal fishing was possible, I opened the king crab season. For the time being, at least in this case, the authority of the State of Alaska was affirmed.

The musk ox on Nunivak Island became quite an issue, prompting a showdown between state and federal authorities, with the Soviet Union also in on the tussle. An environmental agreement between the U.S. and the Soviets in 1972 led to a deal for relocating some musk ox from Nunivak, which is part of a federal wildlife refuge, to Wrangell Island and northeast Siberia. Originally roaming Siberia, musk ox had long ago been wiped out by humans for food. Alaskans would be happy to sample some of their own musk ox meat from Nunivak, so we asked the U.S. Fish and Wildlife Service to allow limited hunting. The agency said no.

I decided that if Americans couldn't enjoy the benefits of harvesting musk ox, we shouldn't give them away either. I notified the U.S. Fish and Wildlife Service of my opposition to the relocation. Despite this objection, the plan went ahead; the musk ox were caught on Nunivak and transported to Bethel on the Alaska mainland in preparation for the move to Russia. But Governor Jay Hammond agreed that the musk ox belonged to Alaska. State troopers halted the move, pending my issuance of a state export permit. The stalemate was broken when the Fish and Wildlife Service gave the go-ahead for limited musk ox hunting on Nunivak Island. The crated musk ox were then whisked away by a Soviet transport plane.

I didn't have a lot of time to enjoy the resolution of this crisis before a few people in Fairbanks, who had it in for me because I banned aerial shooting of wolves, saw the musk ox controversy as an opportunity to take me down. Independent journalist Joe La Rocca, whose writing appeared mainly in the *Fairbanks Daily News-Miner,* filed suit, alleging I had no authority to permit export of the musk ox and claiming it amounted to unlawfully giving away state property. I was subpoenaed to appear in Fairbanks district court, where I gave the judge a statutory citation authorizing my action. He promptly dismissed the case.

As commissioner of fish and game, I inevitably was pulled into the dispute over subsistence hunting and fishing rights. It's an issue that's not yet settled, and I would simply describe my limited involvement with it as unrewarding.

The Alaska Native Claims Settlement Act of 1971 compensated Alaska's indigenous Natives for land rights mostly ignored by the federal government since the purchase of Alaska. The act conveyed 44 million acres of land and $942 million to Natives, but it gave no protection to aboriginal hunting and fishing rights. From the perspective of the Natives, Alaska's rapid population growth and advances in transportation and in hunting and fishing technology gave plenty of reason to ring the alarm bell.

In 1973, members of a delegation representing the Alaska Federation of Natives asked me to meet with them on the subject of subsistence. I had some vague anxiety about what was in store for me. These were Native leaders with an entourage of non-Natives bent on a cause: hunting and fishing by Natives must have priority over other uses such as sporting, commercial, or even personal use by urban dwellers.

The Board of Fish and Game had adopted a subsistence policy that took account of the bush population's dependence on fish and game, but did not allocate among Alaskans because the Alaska Constitution declares that fish and wildlife are reserved to all the people for common use. So the board's regulations, applicable to everyone, were especially considerate of rural residents. Now, Native leaders were dissatisfied. They wanted statutory guarantees for preservation of cultural and lifestyle traditions that were changing or being abandoned. Indeed, the aboriginal way of life had already vanished in its pure form.

When I finished reciting the board's past actions and its policy to the delegation, the response was immediate, boisterous, and disapproving, conspicuously led by non-Natives. There was no doubt that I had been set up. Activists within the Rural Alaska Community Action Program, professional counselors to the Natives, had staged this encounter to ventilate and intensify claims for an assured Native subsistence priority. They clearly were also testing their powers of intimidation. The community action people accused the department of racism and genocide, demanding that I, as commissioner, apologize.

Whatever hope I had that we could talk about specific complaints was dashed: these folks were on a political mission. While they were laying the hickory on me, I thought how interesting it would be to put these proxy-Natives, identifying so passionately with subsistence, on a diet of beluga meat and seal oil for a while, even allowing a little pilot bread and Labrador tea.

However unpalatable it would be to them, they would not dare grumble for fear of drawing a stark distinction between themselves and the Natives.

The subsistence issue found political resolution, or at least mutation, in federal law in 1980, when the Alaska National Interest and Lands Conservation Act defined *subsistence uses* to mean "customary and traditional uses by rural Alaskan residents of wild renewable resources . . . for personal or family consumption or barter." The act gave a priority to subsistence users over other users. The state failed to approve conforming legislation, so the federal government later took control of fish and wildlife jurisdiction on federal lands and waters in Alaska.

The process of allocating priority hunting and fishing opportunities to a class of people, identified as rural by place of domicile, continues to move forward. There is disagreement on whether the process should be a state or federal function. State involvement would first require Alaskans to vote on amending their Constitution, an action the legislature has so far refused to initiate. Rural folks seem comfortable with the status quo, trusting federal officials to tilt more favorably toward them. Ever greater tilt may be needed because the unprecedented rural birth rate means ever more rural people will have to share finite resources.

Meanwhile, Native leaders seem determined to see that a rural priority is principally viewed as a priority for Natives. A prominent Native leader, Byron Mallott, told the 2001 Alaska Federation of Natives convention: "Rural means Native, and if people don't understand that they are either incredibly stupid or naive."

M y five-year term as commissioner of fish and game was up in 1977, and I decided to retire from state government and find other work. Department employees staged an overwhelming retirement party. I got to hear a lot of folks, including Governor Hammond, offer words of praise that I knew were overstated, yet they made me realize I must have done a few things right.

I think little decisions were responsible for this showing of kindness and regard from the people I had worked with. I remembered how I occasionally called for a "sun break" when the sun came out after weeks of Juneau rain: it meant that employees could go home after lunch. And I welcomed dogs in the Fish and Game building—the only state building that permitted this kind of trespass. As fast as the Buildings and Grounds officials posted their No Dogs Allowed signs, I had them removed. Then there were the Christmas gatherings, and every birthday among staff members was good reason for coffee and cake. I managed to help a few employees overcome alcohol problems, and I dealt fairly with another who resisted help. During my years as commissioner, I found real pleasure in seeing the good spirit that grew among employees and hearing that Fish and Game was a great place to work.

By this time I had accepted a job offer from the National Marine Fisheries Service, and was given an intimidating title: Alaska region chief of management and enforcement. Marine mammals as well as commercial fisheries fell within my purview. I would be dealing with the momentous new federal law that extended U.S. fishery jurisdiction out two hundred miles from the coastline, in a fishery conservation zone. This law came into being after foreign fleets had virtually destroyed many fish stocks close to our shores. Canada and the USSR, with expansive adjacent waters of their own, quickly declared similar zones.

DEBBIE S. MILLER

 Midnight Wilderness is a passionate and vivid account of one of Alaska's greatest natural treasures, the Arctic National Wildlife Refuge. Author DEBBIE S. MILLER draws on her thirteen years of exploring this unique, magical, and expansive territory, weaving chilling adventures, personal anecdotes, wildlife observations, and Native issues. Miller's work has been published in a variety of newspapers and magazines, including *Alaska* magazine and *Alaska Geographic*. She is the author of several award-winning books for children, including *The Flight of the Golden Plover*. She lives in Fairbanks. *Midnight Wilderness* can be found at fine bookstores everywhere and at www.gacpc.com.

Beaufort Lagoon is separated from the Beaufort Sea by narrow islands of coarse sand and gravel, about ten to twenty-five yards wide, that parallel the coast for several miles. Shorefast sea ice hems the barrier islands on the north side, with only a few open leads visible. Large mantles of sea ice, several feet thick, have gnawed at the exposed islands, and shoveled their leading edges beneath the sand and gravel. Within the half-mile-wide lagoon the ice is breaking up, and there is much open water. Some of the thin, melting floes are almost transparent.

As we fly along Beaufort Lagoon, I picture Sir John Franklin with his British expedition party in their two open boats dodging ice floes in this very lagoon, dragging their boats across shoals, and visiting Inupiat groups that were scattered along the coast in clusters of sod houses. Franklin was the first white explorer to visit this part of Alaska's arctic coast, during July and August of 1826. He named Beaufort Lagoon (Franklin referred to it as a bay) and Beaufort Sea after a friend and naval hydrographer, Captain Francis Beaufort. Traveling from Canada's Mackenzie River delta, Franklin ventured west along the arctic coast to Point Beechey. Today the Prudhoe Bay oil fields envelop the Point Beechey area, about 175 miles west of Beaufort Lagoon.

We follow the lagoon's shoreline for a few miles west until we reach an abandoned Distant Early Warning (DEW) line site. This small military radar station and a chain of other stations along the arctic coast were built back in the early 1950s during the cold war era. A few metal, windowless buildings still remain and are occasionally used by the USFWS staff as a base for summer fieldwork. The buildings and scattered rusted military equipment at Beaufort Lagoon will eventually be removed by the Army Corps of Engineers as part of a cleanup project. The site is an eyesore on the open tundra.

We land on a short gravel airstrip next to the DEW station, on a small point jutting into the lagoon. For now, Dennis is based at the lagoon with several USFWS and Alaska Department of Fish and Game (ADF&G) biologists. They are here to conduct an aerial census of the Porcupine caribou herd and to study the movements of more than one hundred radio-collared animals. I am here as a volunteer to assist with the census work, and to visit Dennis, who spends a large portion of each summer flying wildlife surveys within the refuge.

These biological studies are a result of a congressional mandate under Section 1002 of the 1980 Alaska National Interest Lands Conservation Act (ANILCA), directing that 1.5 million acres of the Arctic Refuge coastal plain be assessed for its biological importance and potential oil and gas reserves. This same landmark act added 97 million acres to Alaska's National Park and National Wildlife Refuge systems. ANILCA more than doubled the size of the original Arctic National Wildlife Range, to about 19 million acres, reclassified the range as a refuge, and designated 8 million of those acres as wilderness.

However, as part of the 1980 legislative compromise between oil industry and environmental factions, 1.5 million acres of the arctic coastal plain were put in an "undecided" category. Congress authorized the Department of Interior to study, assess, and ultimately recommend whether the "1002 area" (referred to as ten-oh-two) should be opened for oil and gas leasing, left as it is now—de facto wilderness—or legally protected as wilderness under the National Wilderness Preservation System. In 1983, we were in the middle of those mandated studies. Within a few years the Department of Interior would tragically recommend to Congress that the entire 1002 area be opened to oil and gas leasing.

At Beaufort Lagoon it's warm and buggy, with temperatures in the sixties—a heat wave for this arctic coast. The wildlife spectacle continues. Thousands of caribou mass together near the coastline, grunting and bleating, seeking relief from the thick swarms of mosquitoes. On this unusually warm and breezeless day the mosquitoes are at their worst. Many caribou pour off the ragged edge of tundra known to the Inupiat as Navagapak, which means big point. They jump five or six feet down to a narrow stretch of sand wedged between the lagoon and the tundra. Some caribou walk out on the ice to escape the insects. A few caribou lie like sunbathers on floating ice cakes. If only the wind would pick up to help ground the pests.

"The bou are bunching up," says Fran Mauer, a longtime biologist on the Arctic Refuge staff. This phrase I would hear frequently during the next couple of days. Based on past studies, biologists believe that caribou form the largest, and most dense, postcalving aggregations when the mosquitoes harass them during warm, calm weather. The herd begins to bunch up in groups of tens of thousands of animals. Census photos have revealed as many as eighty thousand caribou tightly massed in one group. Occasionally the entire herd masses together before they leave the coastal plain on their southern migration. In 1980 the entire Porcupine herd, then numbering about 110,000, left the coastal plain in one enormous procession, covering a distance of about ten to fifteen miles in breadth and one to two miles long.

From a biologist's perspective this is the ideal time to census the herd. It is Dennis's job to locate the groups by tracking radio-collared animals with the antenna-and-receiver system carried on board his aircraft. Once he finds large "bunches," he radios the Beaver, an ADF&G single-engine plane equipped with a large army-surplus aerial-mapping camera mounted on its belly. Its nine-inch-by-nine-inch negative format makes it ideal for taking pictures of tightly grouped caribou. If all goes well, we should be able to census the herd over a period of several hours.

On this day the whole herd is clustered in about two dozen groups scattered along the Niguanak River on the coastal plain and in the Egaksrak Valley in the Brooks Range about fifty miles to the southeast. Biologists must locate and count the animals in an efficient, precise manner. Otherwise, they risk counting groups of animals twice. They also search the surrounding area for any groups that might not have radio collars.

"Let's go for it," says Ken Whitten, a caribou biologist with the ADF&G. Federal and state biologists frequently coordinate their efforts on biological research projects within the Arctic Refuge because the state division has many biologists who are experts in their respective fields and who have conducted many years of animal research. Until the passage of ANILCA, there were only a couple of biologists on the Arctic Refuge staff, and little biological work had been completed within the refuge. After ANILCA's enactment, several new biologists were added to the Arctic Refuge staff, and USFWS entered into cooperative study agreements with the state of Alaska so that the five-year coastal plain assessment could be completed utilizing the best resources available.

We wait at the airstrip while a segment of the caribou herd crosses the runway. Once they are well out of the way, Dennis takes off in the Cub with another biologist, while three other researchers and I pile into the Beaver. The Beaver, with its large condorlike wings, slowly lifts off the strip, with ADF&G biologist Pat Valkenburg at the controls. The 1950s vintage plane lumbers along the coastal plain, giving the sensation that we are in slow motion.

Within several minutes Dennis radios Pat that he has located a large bunch to the west. Ken and I are in the back of the plane, and we prepare to lower the camera, which is about the size of a small copy machine, through a hole in the belly of the plane. Soon we catch up with Dennis and spot a huge group of caribou milling around a large river bar, like a swarm of bees on their honeycomb.

"I'd guess about twenty thousand or so," Pat says as he circles the herd at an altitude high enough, about fifteen hundred feet, so that the animals are not alarmed.

"I'm going to open the hatch, so stand back and hang on," Ken warns as he begins to raise a two-foot-square section of the floor. As he carefully pulls open the hatch, I look through the gaping hole down to the tundra. It is large enough for me to jump through, a fact that momentarily brings my stomach into my throat.

Ken gingerly unpacks and checks the camera, then lowers it into the hatch, taking care not to lose his balance. The camera fits snugly in the hole, and its 50mm lens is capable of capturing thousands of animals in one photo. Once we reach the edge of the group, Ken starts pressing the camera button, following Pat's signals.

When we have completed the first series of photos, Ken pulls the camera out of the hatch, and I grab the paper towels. The Beaver is notorious for spitting oil onto the camera lens, so it's my job to wipe the glass clean after each series of photos. With the hatch open, Ken tilts the heavy camera back just enough so I can wipe off the oil. As I clean the lens, the tundra races below me, and I have visions of a big bump catapulting me through the opening toward some unsuspecting bull caribou. Headlines read: "Woman Falls from Beaver, Gored by Caribou."

Within several hours most of the aggregating groups have been located. Tens upon tens of thousands of animals are crowded so tightly together that we can't see the tundra beneath them. In the distance the groups look like huge dark shadows of clouds. All of the animals seek relief from the mosquitoes. Some congregate along the coast, others swarm over river bars, and some climb ridges in the foothills seeking cooler elevations and a breeze.

When we return to Beaufort Lagoon, thousands of caribou pepper the ice floes beneath our wing. Sometime this month the fragmented lagoon ice will melt completely, and the sea ice will move north from the sliver of islands, given the right wind and weather conditions. There are a few open leads forming paths through the sea ice. Most of the white, gleaming layer resembles a sheet of broken shatterproof glass. The pieces still hang together.

In a normal year the ice will move several miles offshore by August or September, allowing barges to reach Barter Island and deliver annual supplies for Kaktovik's two hundred residents. Kaktovik is the only settlement that lies within the boundaries of the Arctic Refuge, an area almost as large as the country of Austria.

Ice-free waters also provide passage for beluga whales, and for the endangered bowhead whales during their westward fall migration along the coast. Kaktovik residents take advantage of the open channels as boating routes for hunting, whaling, and fishing trips.

It is late in the day now, and I decide to take a tundra stroll along the coast, walking along that final fringe of the continent. The sun rolls along the northern horizon, partially obscured by a thick mass of clouds that billows above the ice. I guess, by the tundra's rich color, cooling temperatures, and northern sun, that it is close to midnight. There is no need for clocks here, where days never end. You can read a good book at midnight if you want, but you probably won't unless it's storming and you're stuck in a tent. There is too much to see.

In the midnight sun arctic colors are at their richest; the low-angling light paints the tundra shades of amber and gold, and the sky rose-petal pink, saffron, and salmon. The light is soft, stunningly clear, as if the sea ice has pulled each ray from the sky, filtered from it any impurities, and thrown it back to the sun. Colors on the tundra are vivid, sharp. Dwarfed wildflowers, snug within the sedges and grasses, seem to jump out at you in their lavenders, pinks, and whites.

The land on top of the world magically glows at midnight, like flushed faces next to a winter's fire. Yet the level of radiance is more diffused in the Arctic, reaching the innermost petal of the tiniest wildflower, casting two-foot shadows beyond emerald sedges, bringing out the snow-whiteness of an old caribou antler.

Beyond the edge of moss and lichens, an eroding bank of ground and protruding roots falls three to four feet to the narrow shoreline, then to the lagoon with its giant puzzle pieces of floating ice. I walk down the tundra bank onto the narrow stretch of beach, which is covered with caribou tracks. With cooler temperatures the caribou have moved inland, leaving white tufts of their bleached, winter's fur scattered amidst the tracks. I pass several places where the caribou have bedded down in the moist sand, leaving shallow depressions, some with shorebird tracks scurrying through them.

A few hundred yards offshore I spot a Pacific loon, formerly called the arctic loon, diving for fish in a large open stretch of water amidst the floating ice. I have always loved the way loons proudly hold their heads, with their beaks tilted upward slightly, as if they are gazing at clouds. Then there is the loon's ancient, mystical call that seems to echo within itself before resounding across the water. It is a call that makes you stop in your tracks and ponder. The haunting voice of the loon seems to ask some unknown, ageless question.

Four species of loons (Pacific, common, red-throated, and yellow-billed loon) utilize the coastal lagoons and tundra ponds within the Arctic Refuge. The coastal lagoon system offers rich habitat for the fish-eating loon. The lagoons are protected by the barrier islands and are regularly fed with fresh nutrients from the many rivers and creeks that flow from the Brooks Range. Such waters offer ideal habitat for the prolific arctic char and many other species of fish, including the arctic cisco, flounder, and cod.

The Pacific loon winters along the Pacific coast and in Mexico's lagoons and estuaries. Several years ago Dennis and I wintered in San Ignacio Lagoon, on the west coast of Baja California. We were there to study the gray whales in one of their major breeding and calving areas. During our stay we spotted many of Alaska's migratory birds, including loons, at their winter home in the milder Pacific waters. I marveled at these northern migrants who had flown so far, and wondered if I had seen any of them in the Arctic Refuge only a few months before. Those south-of-the-border winged friends were kindred spirits.

Continuing along the beach, I notice a set of fresh arctic fox tracks weaving through the caribou hoofprints. I follow them along the shore, then up a small ravine onto the tundra. I walk over to a small pingo, a mound with an ice core that is forced up by frost action. It has been used as a perch by a snowy owl, and scattered on it are a few digested hairy pellets and one small white wing feather. Owls, as well as other birds of prey, regurgitate the hair and bones of their prey rather than passing them through their digestive tracts. I unravel one of the pellets and find a vole's tooth wrapped in its own fur.

Snowy owls are one of the few birds who live on the coastal plain year-round, although some of them will migrate into more southerly areas within the refuge. Because of their year-round white plumage, and the fact that they are one of the larger owls, they appear enormously striking against the tundra. They can be spotted at great distances during summer, like bright white sails at sea.

I decide that the shoulder of the pingo is a good spot to glass for the fox, owl, and other birds. Sitting down, I'm surrounded by several round cushions of moss campion. Each round cushion of mosslike leaves has the color and texture of a putting green, as though someone has manicured it. Springing from these mounds, one to two feet in diameter, are scores of delicate pink flowers rising a breath above the bright green cushions.

It is never silent on the arctic tundra during summer. Perhaps still, but never completely silent. Yet you always sense there is a ubiquitous curtain of silence shadowing all of the Arctic's perpetual voices: the lilting song of the Lapland longspur, the peeping sandpipers, the jaeger's cry, the loon's mystical call, the grunting of thousands of caribou. The arctic music is as constant as the twenty-four-hour daylight.

Across the lagoon I spot a large raft of old-squaw ducks, their slender tail plumes backlit by the polar sun. Of the thirty-two species of birds that have been sighted within the Arctic Refuge's coastal lagoons, the gregarious old-squaw duck is the most frequent visitor. In late July and during August approximately thirty thousand of these white-faced, black-breasted ducks congregate in the lagoons while they molt their wing feathers and begin staging for their fall migration.

Scanning the tundra with binoculars, I see the elegant long necks of a pair of tundra swans, formerly called whistling swans. Their graceful white necks and heads are held high as they paddle slow timeless circles in a tundra pond. Their coal black beaks, level with the Beaufort Sea, look as though they are balancing something on them. By now they must have hatched their young, and I wonder if the chicks are still in the nest.

The tundra swan is the largest breeding bird that utilizes the coastal zone of the Arctic Refuge. They mate for life and build large nests that are often reused. They usually nest near tundra lakes or ponds, often near river deltas. In recent years an average of 360 adult swans have bred within the refuge. After two or three chicks are fledged, and the swans complete their wing molt, they fly east to Canada, joining other segments of the population along the Mackenzie River delta.

From the delta, the tundra swans follow the Mackenzie River south across Canada's interior, and they eventually arrive at their wintering grounds along the eastern seaboard. For many years the majority of the tundra swan population wintered in Chesapeake Bay, until the bay's pollution level and subsequent loss of feeding habitat drove them south to coastal waters along the Carolinas. The Atlantic population of tundra swans now numbers about eighty thousand birds.

I'm about to leave my comfortable seat on the pingo when I spot the arctic fox loping toward me along the edge of the tundra. I sit still so as not to alarm the fox, hoping it will continue past me so I can get a close look. The fox lopes to within ten yards of me, pausing on the opposite side of the shallow ravine, its paw resting on a tussock. It has lost its white winter coat, and sports a new healthy-looking coat that appears soft and golden, blowing slightly in the trace of breeze.

The fox stares at me for what seems like forever, although probably only a minute or two. Again there is the eye contact; with this wild fox, its eyes are less trusting, more territorial. I'm not as comfortable looking into the eyes of a fox as I was with the caribou calves. I get the distinct feeling that it doesn't want me here. Perhaps I'm near its den.

The fox starts barking and howling at me, more high pitched than a wolf, much like the tone of a coyote. In my mind I say I'm sorry, I mean no harm. I stand up and slowly start to walk away. The fox still howls at me. I take a few steps, then turn around. "I'm leaving now. It's okay," I softly speak to the fox. It stops barking and looks at me puzzled. Then it slowly walks away, down into the ravine.

I walk back to join the others, thinking about all I had seen in one day on the arctic tundra. This is truly the most extraordinary of ancient birthplaces. There is a sacred quality about this ground, this tundra that so exquisitely sweeps to the Brooks Range, where so many diverse species make their annual pilgrimage, traveling thousands of miles, to breed, to give birth, and to nurture their young. It is America's greatest wildlife mecca.

There is something inherently special about places where humans and all members of the animal kingdom bear their young. Such places are looked to with reverence, renewal of spirit, and celebration of life. In the human world we cherish the miracle of the birth of our children. We treasure our newborns, celebrate birthdays, and remember our roots as we grow old.

My grandmother once took me to a patch of ground, a part of her old Oregon homestead, where she and her father and her grandfather had all been born. They had begun their lives in the same farmhouse, which had long ago burned to the ground. Grandmother was flooded with memories and tremendous emotion as she walked in circles looking at the barren ground on a hot June day. The surrounding homestead lands had changed little, unlike other old places, which might be paved over or turned into shopping malls. She did not have to face that sort of sadness, as many others might have.

Many people celebrate the birth of Christ, and recite the nativity story to their children. Thousands of people make their annual pilgrimage to Bethlehem to worship and give special recognition to Christ's place of birth. We celebrate and pay tribute to our great presidents, usually by recognizing their birthdays and enjoying a day off work. Our spirits are always uplifted with the birth of spring, a time of rejoicing.

Within the animal kingdom, we marvel at the salmon who travel great distances upstream to deliver their eggs, complete their life cycle, and die; or at the gray whales who travel thousands of miles from the Arctic to breed and deliver their calves in Baja's lagoons. On the coastal plain hundreds of thousands of birds and caribou have conducted their exhaustive annual migrations for millions of years to breed and bear their young on this northernmost stretch of plain. We should treat this special place, and all animal birthplaces, with the same kind of reverence and recognition that we give to birthplaces of our own species. Should we consider allowing the oil industry to exploit this ancient birthplace within America's only Arctic Refuge?

I stumble upon an old rusted fifty-five-gallon oil drum, a 1950s discard from the DEW line site. It is partially smashed, crinkled, and embedded in the tundra. Although most of the old drums east of Beaufort Lagoon have been recovered and removed by USFWS, there are still thousands scattered along the coast to the west.

I stare at the old drum for some time, picturing how oil and gas development would irreversibly destroy the wilderness before me—hundreds of miles of roads and pipelines, scores of drilling pads and rigs, thousands of oil spills, as in the case of the Prudhoe Bay fields. There would be spillage of toxic drilling

muds into the wetlands, piles of abandoned industrial junk, and other pollu-
tants: garbage, traffic, and noise.

The Arctic Refuge contains the only sliver of arctic coastal plain habitat—
roughly 150 miles of coast, stretching an average of 25 to 30 miles inland—
that is protected within a conservation unit. The remainder of Alaska's arctic
coast, some 1,000 coastal miles, has already been dedicated for oil and gas
development.

In the coming years the oil industry will endlessly lobby Congress, with
promises that it will develop this coastal plain in an environmentally sound
matter: build pipelines and roads so that caribou can cross them, use less
toxic drilling muds, clean up their many oil spills, curtail development activities during the caribou calving season. Promises, promises.

In light of the March 1989 *Exxon Valdez* disaster—the largest oil spill in
U.S. history—where thousands of birds, otters, and other animals suffered
and perished because of gross negligence and inadequate contingency plans
on the part of the oil industry, it is unconscionable to accept industry's promises, particularly when the nation's premier wildlife refuge is at stake.

SECTION SIX

Alaska's Dogs

FROM THE TIMES of the earliest human inhabitants to those of the newest tourists getting off a cruise ship, Alaska's sled dogs have been a boon to travel and exerted an endless fascination. They can be fierce or friendly, rough or tame, but there is no denying the draw that they have on human imagination. From stories of the great winter cross-country races to the story of a woman who drove across the Arctic on a dogsled, the tales of Alaskans and their dog teams are always thrilling. Here's a selection of some of the best of them. . . .

DOGS ON ICE IN ALASKA

Lucky Wilson is on a first-name basis with most of the wildlife in Resurrection Bay, from George and Martha, eagles that have been nesting in a scrag across from Lucky's helicopter pad at the Seward Airport for twenty years, to Michael, an old goat of the four-legged kind who has chosen to live out his declining years in a tiny, green square of nearly vertical pasture between two snowfields on a fiercely steep mountain.

"We're about a thousand feet away from him," Lucky says. "You get any closer you'll scare them, and if you scare them you'll change their habits, and that's bad." He points out a hole that a grizzly bear has dug in the side of a mountain. "He was after a parka squirrel," Lucky says. "I could walk into that hole standing upright."

We are hovering two thousand feet above sea level, Lucky in the right seat of a Eurocopter AS350 helicopter, on our way to the top of Godwin Glacier, and it's one of those gorgeous Resurrection Bay days when, as Lucky says, pointing south, "Look. Look right there. See it? That's Hawaii."

Godwin Glacier Dogsled Tours is the brainchild of Lorraine Temple, who used to mush professionally and has helped train teams for the Iditarod. "For years I ran a B&B in Homer and people kept telling me they wished they could see mushing in the summer," Lorraine told me. "Then, six years ago, I hired on to run a glacier dogsled tour out of Juneau with Libby Riddles," the first woman to win the Iditarod Trail Sled Dog Race.

Lorraine came home to the Kenai Peninsula and began scouting for a location to do the same thing. "It isn't easy. Everything is a national park or a protected wilderness. The Godwin Glacier is really the only place on the Kenai available to do this kind of thing."

Godwin Glacier is in the Chugach National Forest and the business operates under a special use permit, which means that each summer it hauls dogs, cook tent, sleeping tents, dog houses, dog harnesses, dogsleds, dog food—everything—in and out again. Everything. Lucky tells us he hauled out eight barrels of dog poop the previous day.

There are five passengers on board. It's a full load, but Lorraine has scored big time by getting a pilot with eleven thousand hours in helicopters from Prudhoe Bay to Papua New Guinea, and he has done his homework for this job.

He points out the still-evident effects of the 1964, 9.4-magnitude Good Friday earthquake, and tells us, "The Resurrection Bay fjord is seventeen miles long, and after the tsunami it was forty-five feet deeper for forty-five minutes." We fly over a large collection of blue-roofed buildings. "Ladies," he says, "you've heard what women say about the men in Alaska—the odds are good, but the goods are odd? Well, right down there are some of the oddest goods you'll find. It's the only maximum-security facility in the state of Alaska."

As we climb, the Harding Ice Field comes into view in the west. This sheet of Pleistocene ice is, in places, a mile thick. It used to cover most of Alaska and now, at thirty miles wide by ninety miles long, is the largest ice field in North America.

"And there is Chocolate Drop," Lucky says, pointing to a mountain shaped like a Hershey's Kiss that I am more used to seeing from Kachemak Bay. Everyone except Lucky is speechless.

He hangs a left and there is Godwin Glacier, an immense river of ice calving at the foot, fissuring on the corners, and, on top, smoothing into a vast basin of snow, the rim of the bowl made up of sharp crags. A little over the top on the Prince William Sound side, two more peaks rise into view, and Lucky points out how clean the snow is on one peak and how dirty it is on the other. "That just happened," he tells us, "a volcanic vent has opened up on the peak on the right and is giving off some steam and ash." It's only seven miles from the base camp. The difference in the two peaks is striking enough that I wonder nervously if we are about to take a front-row seat at the next Mount St. Helens.

The dog lot is a tiny collection of tents on skids and eleven rows of dog-houses on the vast glacial expanse, and when we land, we are met by Francine Bennis, a musher who is gearing up for another run at the Iditarod in 2004, and who complains bitterly about the heat of the day. Sled dogs like cold—the slowest times posted in the Iditarod are consistently during years when the winter is the warmest—and while the dogs send up a chorus of anticipation as we approach the sleds, it is evident that no speed records will be broken today.

There are more than a hundred dogs ranging in age from seven and a half months to thirteen years, Francine says. There is one Iditarod veteran. "Kobuk," she says proudly. "He's mine." Francine gives us our pre-mush brief-ing, which consists mostly of "The musher has to stay with the sled. If you fall off, don't worry, he'll wait for you to catch up." Yeah, I've heard that before.

Ken, Chase, and I ride with handler Steve Zirwes, a bronzed young man from Michigan who, when asked how he got this job, replies simply, "I said yes." It's his second year on the glacier, and at our first stop on the circular trail he points out a mountain that he snowboarded down. It looks maybe half a mile away. "Distances are pretty deceptive up here; that's actually a couple of miles away, and that's a pretty steep hill," he says. "It took me about eight hours—seven up and one down. I wouldn't do it again without a snow ma-chine." It's obvious that he just hates this job, which seems to be pretty much the consensus of the eight people who rotate in and out of the base camp.

I sit in front of Steve and the dogs kick snow in my face as they trot up the slope. Well, mostly they trot. Max and Mink are being broken in as leaders, and Mink is constantly looking over his shoulder at Steve, tangling everyone in the traces and bringing us to a halt. Steve finally trades him out with Bruno who, despite a tendency to abandon the trail in favor of a more direct ap-proach back to camp, brings us safely home, where Lucky is just touching down.

Lucky, ever the showman, tells us as we lift off the glacier that he has a surprise for us, something we'll "never see again in your lives, and something you can only see for four or five weeks out of the year." He hangs a right into a steep valley full of hanging glaciers, a left over a shallow mountain tarn at 2,500 feet that he says the crew is going to swim in before they break camp in two weeks, and hangs another left to reveal a red, white, and blue lake. No, no one's been up there with a paintbrush. "The white is snow, of course," he tells us. "The blue comes from meltwater on snow or ice, and the red is algae—the algae that feed the iceworms that come out at night."

It's not even ten minutes from the Seward Airport to the camp, but this distance is counted more in time than in miles. It's a different world up on the glacier, where the hand of man is very lightly and only temporarily laid. You understand Robert Service's "alone in the great unknown" a little better after a trip like that. I would have liked to have stayed there a while, to have felt the ponderous movement of ice beneath my feet, reshaping the earth as it went.

Comments in the guest book range from an enthusiastic, "This is 1,000,000,000 times better than everything in the rest of Alaska!" to the always classic "Wow!"

Couldn't have said it better myself.

PAM FLOWERS with ANN DIXON

≋ PAM FLOWERS and her dogs have also run the Iditarod Trail Sled Dog Race and made two trips to the Magnetic North Pole, among other forays. Pam's passion for running dogs has been honored by *Outside* magazine and the Society of Woman Geographers. She and her team live in Talkeetna, Alaska. More information about Pam's adventures can be found at www.pamflowers.com. ≋

≋ ANN DIXON has written five books, including the popular *Blueberry Shoe* and *The Sleeping Lady*. She is a full-time writer who lives in Willow, Alaska. ≋

The expedition officially began on Valentine's Day, 1993, under a cloudless blue dome of sky. If we succeeded, our adventure would be entered in the record books. If we failed—well, who would care? Only I and a few disappointed friends.

No matter what, I told myself, we'd have an incredible experience few people can even imagine. It was the best Valentine's Day gift I could hope for.

The first leg of our trip would take us back to Prudhoe. But first we had to get out of town. I knew from experience that dog teams have a knack for embarrassing their drivers whenever other people are around. To reach the tundra, about one hundred yards away from my friend Craig George's house, we had to cross a road. If the dogs decided to goof around for the small crowd of well-wishers that had gathered, they might turn onto the road and drag me straight through downtown Barrow.

Craig came to the rescue. "Would you mind if Geoff and I ride over to the tundra with you?"

Would I mind? I wanted to hug him! Craig and his friend, Geoff Carroll, were both seasoned dog handlers. If the dogs misbehaved, Craig and Geoff could help me keep them under control.

I stood on the runners of the front sled; Craig and Geoff sat on the trailer sled. At 2:00 P.M. I lifted the snowhook and squeaked out a command: "All right, Douggie, let's go."

Without so much as a woof, Douggie led us across Craig's backyard, past a snowmobile, between two houses, around the neighbor's garage, down a driveway to the road, across the road, across a field, and around a telephone pole. Then he turned right and headed for Repulse Bay.

I felt foolish for having doubted him. Obviously, he knew exactly what he was doing and didn't need a bit of help, thank you very much! I made a mental note to make it up to him later.

Craig and Geoff jumped off and waved good-bye. With that, we were on our way.

FEBRUARY 14, 1993   −5°F   10 M.P.H. E   28 MILES

The sun was shining and it was a beautiful day. I thought I would feel excited, but for some reason I felt very subdued. Maybe because we'd already sledded so many miles.

As the miles rolled by, I started to relax and feel happy. A growing sense of excitement started to creep into my mind. We were actually beginning our trip! It was really happening.

I felt so happy that I wanted to sing "On the Road Again" (more famously sung by Willie Nelson) at the top of my lungs. Instead, I hummed quietly to myself. My dogs would bear almost any hardship—except my singing. If I sang, they refused to run!

For the first few miles the land was flat tundra, a treeless plain covered with ponds, lakes, and swamps. Gentle rolling hills, only a few feet high, reached over the horizon. As in most places in the Arctic, the snow cover was wind-packed and scant, with gravel, small boulders, and tufts of mossy plants poking through. To some people this part of the world is boring. But I love it. To me the Arctic has a stark, mesmerizing beauty.

We were lucky to have a smooth trail to follow that first day, which allowed us to cover twenty-eight miles in three-and-a-half hours. The second day we left the tundra, climbing over a bluff and then dropping down to the coastline. When I looked out over the frozen Arctic Ocean, I couldn't help thinking about the tremendous forces of nature at work here: the sun, with power to renew light and life, or in its absence, plunge the land into darkness; the cold, able to freeze an entire ocean; and the weather, covering the earth with snow. Yet all those substances were made of the same molecules as I was. I, too, was part of the nature all around me, and part of the energy that had made everything I was seeing. Just thinking about it filled me with a sense of power so overwhelming that I felt as if I could do anything.

Here was a world in which I felt at home. What other people thought of me didn't matter. Money problems didn't matter. There were no fences, no boundaries, no artificial rules to hold me back. If I paid attention to the environment and used common sense and my survival skills, I knew that we would be all right. No matter what.

By evening the next day, we reached Smith Bay, fifty-five miles from Barrow. The next day was spent sitting out a storm. For once, I didn't mind the delay. I'd picked up some cold germs in Barrow, which developed into a miserable chest cold. The forced rest helped me recover.

When we headed south to Teshekpuk Lake, I tried running Anna in lead with Douggie to see how she would do. The land grew progressively hillier until we reached a steep bluff at the edge of the lake.

FEBRUARY 17, 1993   +2°F   12 M.P.H.   36 MILES

As we dashed out onto the lake and started to turn left, Anna got mixed up and wanted to go right for some reason. Poor Douggie! He's had to run with her in lead most of the day. She doesn't know any commands yet, but she has to have a chance to learn. I think she has the most potential of any of the puppies. Her mistakes are exasperating to Douggie, who has to not only follow commands but correct her as well. But he is generally a patient teacher.

Some lead dogs might snarl or nip at the ear of a teammate if the teammate doesn't understand a command. Some lead dogs even refuse to run next to a beginner. But not Douggie. He would nudge Anna gently to the right on *gee* or tug her gently to the left on *haw* to teach her.

FEBRUARY 18, 1993   +10°F   LIGHT WINDS   38 MILES

The weather today was pleasant, but the heat is causing a whiteout. All day Douggie had to lead us through ice-fog. It was so white that, at one point, when I stepped off the sled during a rest break, I nearly fell over as I looked away and across the tundra. The sled gives me some reference to keep my balance. But when I look away, there is nothing, and I can't tell up from down. There is absolutely no horizon.

I walked to the front of the team and looked out at what Douggie had to head into, and I didn't see how he does it. In one respect Douggie is the most amazing dog I've ever had for a leader. Each morning before we leave, I take a compass heading. Then, with the rear snowhooks firmly in place, I walk backward away from Douggie in the direction I want him to go. As I walk away from him, I clap my hands and call his name. He knows he can't come to me and just woofs at me. Then, I get on the sled, lift the hooks, and tell him to go. He follows the course I set for him all day, until I tell him to change. It's an incredible ability.

Later that day I noticed something that turned my stomach upside down: wolf tracks. I bent down to inspect them. The edges of the tracks were still clearly defined and the little ridges of snow in the middle of the tracks still soft. These tracks were fresh.

I'd heard that a large, black wolf lived in the area. With a dog team I'm more afraid of wolves than polar bears. A bear will usually keep clear of a dog team, but a wolf may walk right into camp and try to kill a dog in an attempt to protect its territory.

We were traveling through an area of rolling hills. Tonight, rather than camp in a depression, out of the wind, I decided to follow advice given to me by an Inuit hunter: always camp in the open, where you can see as far as possible in all directions. That way a predator has a hard time sneaking up on you.

We made it through the night without any wolf problems, but the next day brought total whiteout again. I knew from my map that we were near the Eskimo Island cache. In that fog it would be easy to miss, even for Douggie. We needed those supplies to make it to the Colville River cache.

FEBRUARY 19, 1993   +20°F   15 M.P.H. SW   34 MILES

The terrain seemed hillier than I remembered it. After a while I became convinced that we were going too far south. I tried to correct Douggie's head-ing and get him moving more toward the north. Each time I called "Haw," he would swing north and then immediately swing back to the right. Over and over, I gave him the same command, and, over and over, he did the same thing. He simply ignored me and kept going his way. The longer he disobeyed me, the angrier I became.

I was determined to somehow get things back under control when we crested a high hill. There, about a hundred yards ahead, were all those posts sticking up out of the ground that marked our cache site.

I'll never understand how that dog can run through miles of mist and somehow take me exactly where I want to go. What is more baffling is that he often does it in spite of me! Sometimes I think, if I could just teach him how to melt snow into water, I could stay home and send Douggie out there to lead the team by himself.

We sledded up to the cache and I walked up to Douggie, who looked at me and wagged his tail. I kneeled down beside him, gave him a big hug, and apol-ogized for yelling at him. Douggie woofed and gave me a big, sloppy kiss over my entire face, which was powerful enough to knock me over. Anna thought that was funny and started barking and bouncing around. Soon everyone was barking excitedly and wagging their tails. Then they all started to sing; more correctly, they started to howl in unison. I stood up, threw my head back, and howled with them. We were a team again, and everyone was happy.

The dogs don't mind if I sing their way!

BIG, BLACK, FURRY WOLF

Two days later we reached the Colville River cache. I could see the lights of Prudhoe Bay reflected in the sky at night and noticed an acrid odor from the oil fields. Though the aroma of civilization was unpleasant, I couldn't wait to reach Prudhoe. I found myself thinking constantly about food: pancakes, syrup, bacon, apple pie. A steady diet of trail rations was getting to me. I promised myself a hearty meal as soon as we arrived.

In a thick fog we approached Beechey Point, the site of an old, abandoned trading post. As we approached the weather-beaten building, a slight motion caught my eye.

FEBRUARY 22, 1993   −10°F   10 M.P.H. SW   41 MILES

I saw a black, furry rump disappear behind the right front corner of the trading post. The dogs saw it, too, and started lunging and barking furiously.

I felt panicky as I jammed both rear snowhooks into the snow. I snatched the third hook out of the sled bag and raced up to the front of the team and anchored them. The dogs were suddenly and strangely quiet already, but every eye was straining for a glimpse of whatever it was that was hiding behind the cabin.

I pulled the shotgun out, pumped a slug into the chamber, and flipped off the safety. The last thing I wanted was to confront a wolf. I was scared to go along the front of the building and lose sight of the team because I thought the wolf might be circling around the other side so it could attack my dogs. I faced the building and moved quickly to my right twelve steps: Then I saw black fur sticking out from beside the other end.

Something was wrong. This wasn't how a wolf would behave. As I looked more closely, I could see the fur seemed bushier and coarser than that of a wolf.

I edged slowly toward the animal. Huddled up against the building stood a black-eyed, shaggy-headed, dark-furred baby musk ox. I lowered my gun and stood there looking at this shy, frightened creature.

What a relief! Suddenly, I felt foolish. The poor musk ox had probably become separated in the fog from one of the herds grazing in the area. It looked healthy, so we quickly moved out, leaving it in peace.

Later that afternoon, we reached the Sagavanirktok River (locally known as "the Sag") and turned south toward our old camping spot near Catco in Prudhoe Bay. The dogs knew they were in familiar territory and picked up their pace. They raced down the river and made a hard right turn into Catco's parking lot. Suddenly they were speeding out of control.

They charged across the parking lot, leaped over a steep snowbank, slogged through several feet of deep snow, and abruptly halted at the exact place where they'd slept during our training. Without giving me a chance to unharness them, they began turning in circles, packing down the snow, and then curled up for a snooze.

I could hardly believe my eyes! In less than a minute, my gang of eight had gone from being a well-disciplined, orderly dog team to a tangled jumble of legs and lines. Yet looking down at their tired, furry bodies, I thought about how hard they'd worked and how contented they looked.

I dropped to my knees and began crawling alongside the team. One by one, I unsnapped and removed each harness, rolling the dog on its back to do so. I rubbed the dog's tummy, gave a big hug, and said, "Thank you for all your hard work." Not one dog looked at me. They all kept their eyes closed and bodies limp, in a state of total bliss, completely enjoying a few moments of love and heartfelt attention.

Soon I was enjoying my own bliss—a hot shower and full meal. The first leg of our journey was complete! As I ate and chatted with Prudhoe Bay friends, everyone had a good laugh over our encounter with a big, black, furry "wolf."

GOOD-BYE, PRUDHOE

The dogs rested for four days while I thawed an inch-thick crust of ice from the inside of my tent, inspected my equipment, and made repairs. Because there hadn't been much snow this year, broad stretches of gravel on the frozen rivers and on the tundra had badly damaged my sled runners. I installed new half-inch-thick, ultra-high-density plastic sled runners, tough enough to last the remaining 2,280 miles. Everything had to be in perfect working order, because from here on, villages would be few and far between. We would be on our own more than ever.

When I left Prudhoe Bay this time, I wouldn't be back. It was quite likely that I'd never again see the people I'd come to know there. A number of people had been friendly, helpful, and encouraging. I knew I would miss them. When I thought about that, it made me feel lonely.

At the same time, another part of my mind began taking over. I knew that, except for my dogs, I'd be spending lots of time alone in the next few months. I started shutting down socially, withdrawing from the people around me. I made no effort to talk to anyone. I think that's how my mind begins to deal with solitude. It's hard for people to understand, but it's what I have to do.

I focused entirely on preparing for the miles ahead. Again and again I went over each piece of equipment. I took only what was absolutely necessary, so I became compulsive about being sure every item was there. Any piece of gear, if lost, would be very difficult, perhaps impossible, to replace.

The last night in Prudhoe I splurged with long-distance phone calls to a few of my best friends. Everyone wished me luck, but only one friend, Dottie, told me she was confident we would make it. I always felt encouraged after talking to Dottie.

Somehow, although I was nervous and a little scared, I thought she was right.

After some brief good-byes, we left Prudhoe Bay for good on February 27. For the next few days, the weather was perfect.

FEBRUARY 28, 1993   −36°F   5 M.P.H. SE   35 MILES

The dogs are still looking happy and raring to go. We set out at a fast clip, heading east under a beautiful clear blue sky. It's a good feeling to watch the dogs moving along and enjoying themselves. The puppies aren't puppies anymore, now. They're over a year old and have developed into everything I could've hoped for. They're all hard-working, strong, healthy, and good-natured.

The only problem I have is with Roald. Whenever he starts out in the morning running beside his sister, Sojo, he always looks over at her and barks in her ear. He does it because he is so excited about starting out and he knows she'll let him get away with it.

Sojo is sweetness personified. She will not stand up for herself against

Roald. I've decided to embark on a campaign to build her confidence. When-
ever we stop for a rest, I always walk up and pet everyone and talk a little to
each dog. Usually I start with the front of the team and work back to the sled.
Now, I've changed my pattern. I make a point of walking up to Sojo first and
giving her attention. Then I start as usual at the front of the team and work
back. This gives her twice as much attention as anyone else. Hopefully this
will make her feel special and build her confidence.

When we reached Bullen that afternoon, I parked the team in the sun. The
dogs could rest, but I had a big job ahead of me. The door to the room containing our cache was now almost completely buried behind a huge snowdrift.

After digging for about fifteen minutes, I finally managed to reach the door.
The inside of the room was drifted halfway full, so I grabbed the edge of the
door and started working it back and forth. Finally, the door would open far
enough that, if I took off my parka, I could squeeze inside.

It was about −30°F, and the idea of standing around without my parka on
was not very exciting. But I did it anyway. I shoveled and pushed and pulled
as hard as I could to stay warm and get the door open. Finally, I got it open
far enough to toss out the supplies and squeeze back outside, where I quickly
donned my heavy, warm parka.

The dogs were bummed a bit by the increase in sled weight as we pulled
out. They will have to get used to pulling a heavy load again. As we moved
along, the wind changed from the SE to the NE and clouds starting coming in
from the SW. All indications of a nasty storm.

We camped on the edge of the Arctic Ocean by the entrance to the Arctic
National Wildlife Refuge (ANWR), after covering thirty-five miles. Consid-
ering all that happened today, that's a very respectable mileage.

As we left camp the next day, we sledded over to a tall, lonely-looking black
pole on a small rise overlooking the tundra. It marked the boundary of the
Arctic National Wildlife Refuge.

We moved on to Point Brownlow and picked up the last cache from our training runs. Because we were making better time than I'd expected, we were getting ahead on supplies. That was better than being short on supplies, but tough on the dogs, who had to pull the extra weight. I noticed that the wind was blowing stronger and thought about setting up camp in the shelter of the buildings there. But it was only 2:00 P.M., too early to stop.

MARCH 1, 1993   −18°F   10–15 M.P.H. SW   20 MILES

As we left, I looked out over the Beaufort Sea and marveled at how different the ice looked from previous years. This stretch of ice had sometimes been a little rough, but usually there was enough flat ice to allow easy passage. This year the ice was pushed up in huge piles, well over twenty feet high. It was an awesome-looking sight. That nature has the power to hurl pieces of ice up like that, weighing thousands of pounds, is quite intimidating. Thank heavens there was a narrow stretch of beachfront that allowed us to pass through.

We'd only gone a little over seven miles when I realized I'd probably made a mistake. The storm I'd been watching for the last twenty-four hours was definitely coming and would overtake us soon. So, reluctantly, I stopped and pitched camp.

As I sit listening to the storm beating away at my tent wall, I really wish I'd stayed back at Point Brownlow.

MARCH 2, 1993   −20°F   10–15 M.P.H. SW   20 MILES

Amazingly, the storm died off during the night. But what a mess! Everything was drifted over. There was a small, snow-covered hump next to my tent, and I knew it hid my wonderful blue tarp. It took me two hours of digging to free up the tarp and remove the drifts from the back of the tent and dogsleds. But I didn't lose anything. The snow was so fine and powdery that it found its way into everything. Even the sled bag, which was lashed shut, was full of hard-packed snow. I finally got it cleaned out and repacked the sleds.

The dogs patiently watched me work and, as usual, started barking and jumping around when I brought out their harnesses. After they'd been harnessed, I lifted the hook and off we went.

As we slipped along over the hard-crusted snow, I watched my little gang of eight. Their furry ears turned backward to help keep the wind out. Their thick, bushy tails hung loosely, and their tough little padded feet moved lightly along. Even at twenty below, their coats kept them comfortably warm. Their tongues hung out just a tad to help them cool off. They were relaxed and happy, and watching them work was a beautiful sight.

By late afternoon we came to a camp of oil exploration workers. I headed straight for the kitchen and introduced myself. In the Arctic, it's considered rude to pass someone without stopping. Fortunately for me, it's also rude not to invite someone to stay for a meal!

Chicken, shrimp, peas, beans, potatoes, gravy, salad, and a table full of canned fruits and desserts—what a meal! As I ate, I visited with several of the workers.

They asked the usual questions and seemed genuinely enthusiastic about what I was doing. That was nice, because sometimes people will tell me they think I'm crazy, and they don't mean it as a compliment.

Here, one man said he hoped he would have the chance someday to do something like I was doing. I hear this a lot and always try to explain my belief that anyone can do whatever he or she wants, if the person is willing to make the necessary sacrifices.

MARCH 4, 1993   −10°F   15 M.P.H. SW   38 MILES

We headed around the shoreline of Camden Bay. The ice in the middle of the bay was very rough, and I hoped to stay on the shoreline. But as we moved along, the beach began to narrow. Douggie stopped and looked back at me, waiting for me to tell him what to do.

I walked up on top of the bluff and looked around. There was very little snow cover on the tundra. Pulling the sleds over it would be terribly hard on the dogs. From my vantage point I could see out over the ice for miles. It looked broken and rough as far as I could see. But at least there was some snow on it. The sea was our best choice.

I told Douggie to go left. At first he just looked back at me, as though he was certain I'd made a mistake. He patiently waited for me to come to my

senses. I called "Haw!" again, and he started left into the rubble ice. Then he
turned back and started to climb up the bluff.

I couldn't really blame him. From his low eye level, the rubble ice must
have looked impenetrable. So I set the hooks and walked ahead through the
ice for about a hundred feet. Then I walked back, got on the sled, and called,
"Douggie, haw!" He put his nose down, sniffed my tracks, and started moving
along my trail. When he reached the point where I'd stopped, he stopped
again and looked back at me.

Off the sled I got. I marched quickly through the ice for another hundred
feet and then back to the sled. Over and over, we repeated the same procedure.
Slowly, in hundred-foot increments, we moved forward.

After about three hours of struggle, we emerged next to Anderson Point at
the east entrance to Camden Bay. As we drew closer, I saw a large pole sticking
out of the ground atop a steep, ten-foot bluff.

I'd seen poles like that before in the Arctic. This one stood about twenty-
five feet high, with steps cut into it almost all the way to the top, where a small
platform rested. From there, people could have easily surveyed the land for
game, or to see if hunters were returning. The lookout pole also served as a
landmark. In a land that's almost totally flat, a tall, dark pole could be seen for
miles to guide a returning hunter or traveler. In a storm, it might even save
lives.

Beside the pole I found a drying rack made of thinner, shorter logs. Whoever once lived here would have hung caribou or polar bear hides to dry on
this rack.

On the treeless tundra, where did this wood come from? The evidence was
all around me. Every summer, trees float down the mighty Mackenzie River,
more than two hundred miles east in Canada, to the Beaufort Sea. Ocean currents carry everything west along the northern coast of Alaska, though only a
few trees make it this far west. Increasingly, as we moved east, the shore became cluttered with driftwood.

By six that evening we were in Kaktovik, a small Inuit village of about 250
people, located on Barter Island about seventy-five miles west of the Canadian border. It was the last village we would see in Alaska.

In spite of all the rough ice, we'd covered thirty-eight miles that day. I was enormously proud of the dogs. After taking care of them, I headed into the Waldo Arms Hotel for a shower. I'd contacted the hotel manager, Doug Barrette, several weeks earlier to ask about finding someone to take out some supplies. Doug quickly fixed me up with a chicken dinner on the house and made arrangements to transport my provisions.

The next stretch, between Kaktovik and the first Canadian village, Tuktoyaktuk, was 320 miles. Because of the frequent storms this winter, I doubted we could carry enough supplies to make it that far. It was decided that the cache would be placed about seventy-five miles east near Demarcation Bay. I made the agreed-upon payment.

The dogs and I rested up a couple days, during which I washed laundry, picked up the dog food I'd previously mailed to the post office, and spoke to the kids in grades four to ten at the Harold Kaveolook school. I told them what I was doing, and why, and tried to encourage them to believe that they, too, could do something hard if they really put their minds to it. Everyone, I told them, has a right to try to make his or her dreams come true.

GOOD-BYE, ALASKA

MARCH 7, 1993 −14°F 5 M.P.H. NE/SW 39 MILES

When we left this morning, we got into some rough ice on the Beaufort Sea right away, but I decided to run closer to shore and that helped a lot. There is a line of barrier islands along the coast here. As long as I stay inside them, the ice should be relatively smooth.

The dogs are slow but steady, even though the load is light. They've found their traveling pace and it looks like it's going to be slow. We spent a lot of time putting in caches during training and hauling heavy loads around. That made the dogs travel slowly, and once the pace is established for the season, it's very hard to change it. But we're doing well, and the dogs are happy and healthy, so I'm satisfied.

In the distance I can see the Brooks Range, which crosses much of the northern half of Alaska and comes almost down to the sea by the Alaska-Yukon border.

The border between the United States and Canada, marked so dramatically by the mountains, was less than forty miles away. Once we crossed that frontier, we would be sledding over land I'd never seen before. For weeks, during training, we'd been mushing back and forth across the North Slope of Alaska, often in areas I'd been to previously. The prospect of finally traveling over unknown terrain filled me with a new sense of exploration. When we camped that night, at the end of our first day out of Kaktovik, I stared off toward Canada feeling excited and happy, as if the expedition was now truly under way.

Then I noticed Roald was chewing on a tent stake and Matt had somehow managed to get hold of a food bowl and was trying to gnaw a hole in the bottom. It was time to feed the dogs.

MARCH 8, 1993   −2°F   20 M.P.H. SW   25 MILES
   This morning it was whiteout and blowing snow. Visibility was very limited.

After breakfast I loaded up the sled and headed down the beach in search of the cache. I was feeling pretty nervous. The weather was nasty, and visibility was deteriorating rapidly.

I wasn't certain exactly where our provisions had been cached, so I decided to sled along the beach where I could look out over the ice and across the tundra. This soon proved to be a mistake because the beach was clogged with driftwood. Dogs know what trees are for and so we kept stopping every few inches. I yelled at them to keep moving but no sooner did they advance than a sled would get stuck.

While I struggled to free the sled, the dogs discovered more trees. After about half an hour of this I was beside myself with frustration. To make matters worse, the dog lines kept getting snagged on upraised roots and branches and soon the dogs were bunched in a tight little knot. Robert didn't like having all the other dogs beside him, Matt kept trying to get acquainted with Sojo, Roald kept trying to straighten out Matt, and Lucy and Alice quit working altogether. Anna was wagging her tail and thoroughly enjoying all the excitement. Everyone was totally oblivious to my rantings. Poor Douggie stood looking stoically out over the tundra with a detached expression on his face that clearly asked, Why me?

Sometime later I found the cache at a spot where three cabins stood. I'd been there once before, on a trip I'd taken in 1986. I remembered thinking then that this was the most beautiful place on Earth. I wanted to camp here and soak up some more of that beauty. If only the weather would improve!

For once the weather favored me. The next day was perfect.

MARCH 9, 1993   0°F   LIGHT WINDS, NEARLY CLEAR SKY   0 MILES

What a wonderful gift nature gave us when it created this part of the world! To the people who once lived off the land, this must have been paradise. To the west are seemingly endless miles of open tundra that would have sustained abundant caribou and musk ox. To the south and southeast stand the magnificent mountains of the Brooks Range, with their jagged, snow-covered peaks. These mountains would have provided berries, greens, and small land mammals.

To the east is Demarcation Bay, providing fish and a large, protected harbor. Beyond lies the Arctic Ocean with its char, whitefish, seals, whales, and polar bears. The beach is strewn with hundreds of logs to provide building material and firewood.

To a people who lived off the land, this was all anyone could have asked for. Food, shelter, and beauty. With the exception of a few passing hunters or summer adventurers, no one ever comes here anymore. It's like a land stuck in time. The air is so pure it has no smell. The land is so silent it has no sound.

This area, so rich with resources for subsistence living, was as beautiful as I remembered. I spent the day exploring the area, imagining what life might have been like for the Native peoples and non-Native traders who once lived here. I found many of their abandoned log cabins and sod huts, as well as some old wooden grave markers. I stared at the inscriptions on the rough planks, trying to make out the names and dates: Annie, 1913, and Alonik, 1922.

It was impossible not to feel the history of the place. Who were Annie and Alonik? Were they young, or old, when they died? What was the story of their lives? I would never know, but I wished I could.

We easily covered the five miles across Demarcation Bay the following day, despite fully loaded sleds, now heavy with fresh provisions. On the other side, we stopped to investigate an abandoned whaling ship that must have been beached decades ago. A huge snowdrift reached almost up to the deck, so I was able to climb right on board.

MARCH 10, 1993   −10°F   10 M.P.H. NE/SW   25 MILES

On its deck stood huge, six-feet-wide and three-feet-deep pots that rested on steel stands about eight feet in the air. These must have been used to render the whale oil out of the blubber and placed high in the air to help keep the stench out of the sailors' faces.

The ship looked to be about a hundred and fifty feet long and was in excellent shape. I went below deck but found only empty rooms that appeared to serve as cargo holds, crew quarters, and galley.

The abandoned whaler was beached a few miles west of the Canadian border. As I stood in that beautiful place, I hoped that no type of tourism would ever be permitted there. No matter how carefully planned and executed, even eco-tourism would change the land forever. I wanted—and still want—some places on Earth to be left alone. We almost took all the bowhead whales. I hope we are smart enough not to take all the land.

Leaving the ship, I lifted the snowhooks and sledded over toward the Canadian border. After a little searching, I found a three-foot-high obelisk standing a few feet back from the shore. This was all that marked the boundary between the United States and Canada. It was covered with dozens of initials scratched in the white paint, so I carved "PF" on the American side. Then we slipped over an imaginary line into Canada.

❦ A native of Boston, LEW FREEDMAN was appointed sports editor of the *Anchorage Daily News* in May 1985 and spent seventeen years there before he moved off to the lower forty-eight to be a big-city sportswriter and reporter at the *Chicago Tribune*. Before moving to Alaska in 1984, he was a staff writer for the *Philadelphia Inquirer*. He has written prizewinning short fiction, has received dozens of journalism awards, and has been included three times in the *Best Sports Stories* anthology, published annually by *Sporting News*. In the spring of 1990, he taught in the journalism department at Colorado State University under a teaching fellowship from the Gannett Foundation. Freedman graduated from Boston University with a degree in journalism and earned a master's degree in international affairs from Alaska Pacific University. He has traveled extensively, visiting all fifty states and, in recent years, has traveled to China, the Soviet Union, and Africa, writing about those places for his newspaper. Freedman lives with his wife, Donna, a feature writer, and daughter, Abby. Please check out *Iditarod Classics* and other titles by him at www.epicenterpress.com. ❦

MARY SHIELDS

WOMEN COMPETING *in, and winning, the Iditarod Sled Dog Race are taken for granted today. But it wasn't always so.*
Mary Shields, forty-seven, of Fairbanks, was the first woman to finish the

Iditarod. She completed the 1974 race in twenty-third place, just ahead of Lolly Medley. Her time: 28 days, 18 hours, 56 minutes.

Shields never entered the Iditarod again. However, she has raced the one-thousand-mile Yukon Quest race between Fairbanks and Whitehorse, Yukon Territory, and in 1991 she competed in the Hope '91 International Sled Dog Race from Nome, Alaska, to Anadyr in the Soviet Far East.

Shields, originally from a suburb of Milwaukee, Wisconsin, is an author who gives sled-dog demonstrations on the banks of the Tanana River each summer for passengers from the sternwheeler Discovery. *She loves to mush her dogs on long winter camping trips.*

D uring the winter of 1973, my husband John and I went on a Christmas trip to Tanana with my dogs and we broke trail about every inch of the way. Coming home, a lot of trail was drifted and we did more snowshoeing. So when I heard of the Iditarod, a thousand miles of broken trail sounded like a wonderful opportunity to see more country.

In the late 1960s, I lived by myself in a little cabin about halfway between Anchorage and Fairbanks along the Alaska Railroad. I learned how to use an ax and a saw. Some friends from Fairbanks came down in October, 1969, to see if I was still alive. They suggested that I use a few sled dogs to help pull in the firewood and to haul the water. They went back to Fairbanks and sent down three old sled dogs and a sled and a pile of dog food. There was a little sign on the sled that said, "Dear Mary, there's nothing to it. Just put the dogs in front of the sled." It was a little harder than that, but eventually I got 'em harnessed up and learned how to do it.

That spring, I took them into McKinley Park and went fifteen miles out to the Sanctuary River. I felt like I was going to the North Pole. I thought that was adventuresome. I had a wonderful time.

I had gone on short trips, but when I look back now at the level of competency I had before the Iditarod, I realize I was pretty green. I think I wore blue jeans the whole way. And a sweater and corduroy kuspuk and shoepacks. It's incredible that I made it, looking back. But when you're young and foolish I guess you can get through anything.

I owned only six dogs, so I bought two more dogs because you needed a minimum of eight to start the race. I trained them around Fairbanks.

My neighborhood had a potluck dinner and kids brought their piggy-banks out and they raised money. I think it cost me $700 to run the race, total.

When I called the Iditarod to sign up they sounded skeptical. They asked what I'd done and I hadn't done much. They said, "Well, you can come and start if you want to." I got the feeling they didn't take me seriously.

At the start, I was nervous. Anchorage was a big city and I didn't like being in Anchorage. I didn't like having to go up in front of all those people and pull out a number.

I remember a few nervous tears welling up at the start. I wasn't scared, I was just overwhelmed. I was saying good-bye to John. That was part of it.

We started at the Tudor Track. I remember people standing along a fence and someone hollered, "You better turn around now, you'll never make it." That he would tell me I wouldn't make it meant for sure I was going to.

The first stretch wasn't bad. No big storms or anything. When we crossed Ptarmigan Pass we hit a bad storm. I remember going out and meeting seven teams that had turned around—it was too windy. We went back and spent twenty-four hours at Rainy Pass Lodge.

I was prepared for the weather. Most people weren't. They had emergency rations flown in and everyone was complaining, "The race committee has to come and rescue us and bring food!" I thought, *That's not what this race is about.* I thought we were supposed to be out here doing it on our own, not complaining that we want someone to break trail for us. I was carrying what I needed to take care of my dog team and I was disappointed that other people were traveling so light. It seemed they should know better than to think the weather was always going to be clear.

I got the impression that other mushers didn't take me seriously because I was a woman, and they didn't particularly want to be seen traveling with me because that meant they weren't doing so well. People were nice, but I got the impression they were embarrassed to be going at my speed.

At Shaktoolik, I remember pulling in and a bunch of teams taking off, and the checker saying, "Well, that's strange. They were going to spend the night here, and then you pulled in and they all took off."

The race was new and the villages were eager to have you. I remember coming into Nulato to cheering. I asked what was the big deal. They told me they were doing a lot of betting. I guess every time Lolly Medley and I got to a checkpoint the women would make money because the men had bet that we would drop out at the first or second checkpoint.

That was when I realized women were watching what I was doing. I remember leaving Nulato and thinking that some of those women were riding along in the sled with me, that I was not racing just for myself. That gave me encouragement during some hard times along the trail.

Near the end of the race I had made a little goal: I wanted to beat Lolly Medley. We both stopped in Safety, and I thought we said we'd stay for two hours, or four hours, or some length of time. We'd get some sleep. I remember waking up and realizing she'd left before whatever this agreed time was, and I didn't know how long she had been gone.

That made me mad, so I wanted to catch her if I could. I don't know what happened between Safety and Nome. I remember being on the trail, knowing she had left ahead of me, and then seeing cars up on the road. So I gee'd my dogs up there 'til I got up to the road and they thought I was Lolly. I said, "No, she's ahead of me somewhere." And they said, "Look, there's a headlamp." And there she was out on the ice behind me. I don't know how I got past her.

I got into Nome about three o'clock in the morning. The fire siren was on and four hundred to five hundred people—it looked like a lot for that time of day—cheered me in. And they had that banner across the finish line: "You've come a long way, baby!" They had quite a celebration. They had the mayor's wife welcome me instead of the mayor and the disc jockey's wife interviewed me instead of the disc jockey.

At the time it didn't seem like any big deal. I'm a little embarrassed that people make a fuss over it.

Excerpt from *Honest Dogs*

BRIAN PATRICK O'DONOGHUE

Journalism has taken forty-eight-year-old BRIAN PATRICK O'DONOGHUE from shooting photos atop the Great Pyramid to interviewing oil-field construction workers in 70-below conditions out on the Arctic Ocean's ice pack. He's reported, firsthand, on what it feels like to steer a soaring F-16, cruise Prince William Sound in a supertanker's wheelhouse, and mush a seventeen-dog team up the 1,150-mile Iditarod Trail. Such experiences color O'Donoghue's twenty-year career as a photographer, reporter, and editor for daily newspapers in Alaska and alternative weeklies in Baltimore, New York, and Washington, D.C. He's covered the Alaska legislature for television, and while most of his assignments involved politics, the oil industry, or military reporting, O'Donoghue is the author of two nonfiction books about sled dog racing: *Honest Dogs* and *My Lead Dog Was a Lesbian,* recounting his own last place runs in the Yukon Quest and the Iditarod, respectively. More recently, he edited photos and provided text for photographer Laurent Dick's *Yukon Quest.* In the fall of 2001, O'Donoghue left his post as editorial writer at the *Fairbanks Daily News-Miner* and joined the University of Alaska–Fairbanks journalism team. The assistant professor now teaches the department's main newswriting and reporting class, mass communications, and investigative reporting, emphasizing storytelling skills applicable to every media and discussions crafted to hone news judgment. O'Donoghue holds a B.A. in history from the University of California–Santa Cruz and a master's degree in journalism from New York University. *Honest Dogs* is available at www.epicenterpress.com.

Bruce Lee appeared invincible four days earlier in Central, where he beat Nadeau to town with eighty minutes to spare. More telling, the rookie stayed behind when the veteran struck out for Eagle Summit at 11:30 A.M. on February 18, after seven hours' rest.

Lee read the Ghost's restraint as a concession: *It looks like Nadeau's gracefully accepting second.* He applauded his rival's good judgment. *He's racing in unknown territory. Starting to drop a few dogs. All of the sudden he's realizing he's got to rest. That's being very realistic. He's protecting position.*

Conditions were calm and mild as Lee began the climb late that afternoon. The team was past the tree line, well into the first slope, when the musher noticed one of his leaders glancing down the mountain. *I ought to get whoever did that out of lead—right now.*

But the dogs were moving steadily. Stopping carried its own risk. Near the first tripod, both leaders veered off on a traversing path. Lee stopped and straightened the team out. Afterward, the front pair took a few steps and paused, facing slightly downhill. That decided it. Lee quickly changed leaders.

"OK, let's go," he called.

Nobody moved.

"I can't believe this," Lee muttered. Concealing his concern, he strolled the gang line, petting his dogs. When he again ordered them forward, the team took two, maybe three steps, then halted.

Lee tried bearing down, shouting "All right" in a stern voice. When that didn't work, he again changed leaders. It didn't help.

"Well," Lee told himself, "I'll just drag them up."

Shedding his heavy coat and gloves, Lee picked up his snow hook, figuring he could use the line to drag the sled upward, easing the teams load. The team advanced several steps. Encouraged, Lee tried it again, with the same results. He developed a system: dragging his sled about eight feet, setting the hook backward to hold it in place, then guiding his leaders forward until the slack was taken up.

I'm going to get soaking wet here, the musher realized after a time.

Stripping to his undershirt and pants, Lee considered giving the dogs a breather where they stood. Quest history argued against it. *A lot of teams have tried resting here and never got going again.*

He recalled passing Jerry Riley, the 1976 Iditarod champion, not far from where his own team was now stalled. Riley, who had finished the Quest in second place only the year before, had been leading the race when his team crashed on the mountain and the musher called it quits.

You not only may not win this race, Lee realized. *YOU MAY NOT FINISH.*

He squatted by his dogs, petting them as he assessed the situation. *This is the point you've got to take everything you've learned in twenty years of dogs, and figure out what it takes to get them over. What do they need? What can I do?*

He'd heard that climbers on the upper reaches of Denali pause to catch a breath between each step. The sled-pulling routine struck him as similar. "I'm not going to sit here and lose this race," Lee vowed. "If it's eight feet at a time, I'll take it eight feet at a time."

He resumed hauling his sled by hand. After a while, Lee took the heaviest items out of his sled, two armloads' worth, and piled it all some sixteen feet ahead. The musher walked back to young Clovis, who was again in lead by default, prepared to coax him. Before he knew it, the dog was hauling his teammates straight for the pile.

It gives him a target!

Lee moved the pile higher up the slope. The result was the same. The musher didn't even have to pull his sled at all. He merely gave the word and walked alongside Clovis, who made a beeline to the next cache.

Cresting the first of the summit's two pitches, Lee threw everything inside his sled bag and mushed into the bowl, which was cloaked in thick fog. The wind kicked up as Lee's team neared the base of the final wall. Clouds parted, revealing markers leading straight up.

Lee saw his front four dogs staring at those markers. *They know where we're headed.* He saw their heads turn back down the mountain. Again, he read their minds: *No way are we going up there!*

Lee stopped the team before his spooked leaders did any damage. He had ten strong dogs—more than enough to cruise over this summit. The barrier here was psychological. Clovis, Canvas, and his other young leaders had never faced a challenge of this magnitude. *This is where I could use Miles.* His old leader would have stormed over the ridge or died trying. Once more, Lee found himself cursing that hole in the ice approaching McCabe Creek, the bad-luck mishap that had knocked Miles out of the game.

"OK," Lee whispered, regaining control. "We'll do this one the same way."

The musher unloaded his sled and, with several trips, carried the gear about a third of the way up the slope. Returning to the sled, he ordered Clovis and Canvas forward. The leaders went right up the mountain, continuing on past Lee's pile. Pushing his sled from below, Lee's lungs burned. He wanted to hurl. *They're NOT going to stop because of me.*

Nearing the top of the rise, the musher cried: "OK!" The team dashed up onto the summit's exposed crest.

Fierce winds buffeted dogs and man. Lee's face stung from bombardment with coarse chunks of ice and sand. He was soaking wet and stripped to his inner clothes—his parka and mitts both heaped with the gear stashed near the bottom of the last slope. Flipping the sled on its side, Lee stomped his snow hook into the hard pack, praying the combination might anchor his scared puppies. Soaking wet and gasping, he staggered back down the slope.

By the time he reached the pile, Lee's nose felt solid; both nostrils were plugged with ice. *My face is freezing!* Scooping up gear in his stiffening hands, he flung himself at the climb.

Regaining the summit, Bruce Lee felt the wind sucking his life away. The threat was no abstraction. He'd been with Jeff King the night his neighbor from Denali Park froze a hand on Rosebud, forcing him to scratch from the 1988 Quest.

Lee knew that his own nose was probably frozen, along with parts of his ears and who knows what other body parts. *You've got to do something right, like right now.*

He was tempted to flee; a wild charge would put him at the bottom of the valley in a matter of minutes. But his hands were barely functional now. *If you wait, you may not even be able to get your mittens on.*

Deal with it now, Lee told himself. *Right now, in these few minutes, even if everything gets soaking wet. At least you'll be warm enough to get out of here.*

Ignoring the cruel wind, Bruce Lee methodically redressed himself. It was an act of faith in the power of reason, because the frosty gear initially chilled him further.

The descent was rough. Then Clovis and Canvas kept losing the trail down in the valley. The musher repeatedly scouted the Quest markers on foot, then dragged his team back to them across ice and gravel. The frontrunner was spent and hugely relieved when he finally mushed into the Quest's Mile 101 Steese camp.

Accommodations were sparse at the closed gas station, which now functioned as a storage yard for trucks and industrial equipment. Quest volunteers had opened the bunkhouse cabin for mushers, and the handful of officials, handlers, reporters, and others motivated to make the four-hour drive from Fairbanks. Lee made short work of his dog chores and headed inside, where he hung his wet gear over the stove and began gulping water.

The latest timesheet showed Nadeau out of Central two hours behind him. *At least I knew where I was going,* Lee thought, reflecting on his summit ordeal. He did some quick calculations, then turned to an official. "If Andre isn't here in four or five hours," he said, "I'd think about taking a look to see if he's OK."

With that, the battered race leader sought the bunkroom.

W anting to keep it handy, I left the guide rope dangling from my waist. Nearing the last wall I saw it was futile. Given the sheer angle, I was needed pushing the sled from below. Kahn and Hobbes had to handle this. "Go ahead. Go ahead," I cried, offering the command like a prayer.

Though this climb was far steeper than the last, nobody showed even a hint of quitting. Though the trail was soft, the snow cover was deep enough to provide Khan and Hobbes with a defined groove, which made all the difference.

We climbed and climbed, attaining what I reckoned to be the quarter mark, then the halfway point. Ever onward and upward.

I noticed a bright red shape ahead on the right. A Fulda parka. The coat was dangling from what I took to be a marker, roughly two-thirds of the way up the mountain. The flare of color on the blue-white landscape struck me as funny.

For all I knew, some poor bastard was missing that coat right now. Or, and this was even better: Had somebody tackled the climb wearing it, sweated up a storm, and simply cast the parka off rather than risk stopping on this infernal hill? *I can see that happening. Oh yeah.*

The parka came alive, revealing a bearded man clutching what appeared to be a large-format camera. The discovery excited Khan and Hobbes, who suddenly dashed off on a soft diagonal path toward the photographer.

"No. No. No!"

Hesitant to offend me, Hobbes and Khan froze. The two leaders looked up at the summit ridge, still distant. Then they looked down.

Once, in the process of colliding with a station wagon while riding a motorcycle, I reached out in what felt like slow motion and grabbed the lip of a half-open side window, snatching myself clear as the bike crumpled under me. Seconds stretched as I stared through the window at a screaming young passenger. "He's hanging on!" the kid cried. "He's hanging on!"

The wagon traveled at least another block before the driver finally pulled over. "Please, don't tell my Dad," the kid whimpered afterward. His license showed he was sixteen years old.

On another occasion, flying through the air for what seemed like an eternity, I turned my shoulder and neatly caught the impact with a backpack, saving my hide. I'm not bragging. These weren't thought-out escapes. I'd compare them to a bug's mad scramble when a rock is overturned.

Roughly forty feet of gang line separated the sled from my lead dogs. Time slowed as Hobbes rose on her hind legs and twisted downward, drawing Khan with her. I found my hand on a snow hook, saw myself leaping, incredibly slowly, mind you, and stabbing the hill above the sled.

Life resumed its frantic pace as the entire team gleefully joined the leaders' rebellion. All nine of my dogs cascaded through the deep powdery snow, passing in a disorganized rabble on the far side of my sled. Below me, the group sorted themselves out under the pressure of the tightening gang line, which abruptly snapped the sled around.

Perched atop the hook, I braced, gripping the anchor line with both gloves. Everything rested on what happened next.

The line sprung taut.

The hook held, arresting the team's plunge.

Now what? The dogs and sled faced straight down the Quest's steepest goddamn mountain. I was scared to move. *If this hook pops. . . .*

A motion from the photographer converted my paralysis into rage. *He's responsible for this,* I decided, forgetting our troubles on the lower slope.

Feeling righteous, I screamed at him: "*The caption on that photo ought to read 'Photographer Fucks Up Ascent.'*"

He came rushing over. "Can I do anytink?" the German asked.

"Just stay the hell out of the way," I snapped.

I was already feeling embarrassed by my outburst. "Listen," I said, "I'm a photographer myself. I admire your hustle reaching this spot, but that's *not* the place to be standing. The dogs are distracted, you understand? Take photos from above. Understand?"

He didn't argue.

I rose, stomped the hook more firmly into the snow, and then boldly strode/slipped down the mountain, leaving the German cowering by my sled. Taking Khan and Hobbes by the neck line, I turned the leaders around and, scrambling to stay ahead, guided them back up the hillside until the gang line again stretched taut.

The brief climb left me gasping. Far above us I could see the first evening stars peeking over the summit's black rim. *Still got a nasty hill to climb here.*

I hauled on the gang line behind Khan and Hobbes until their comrades pulled the sled back around, facing uphill. All of this was done with artificial confidence owing to the silent witness and his camera. In truth, I remained wary. Disaster had been averted, but barely.

I retrieved the snow hook and shoved the sled forward. "All right, Khan. All right," I barked, giving my best imitation of a Marine drill sergeant. The dogs cooperated. We resumed the climb, but haltingly this time.

Pausing was dangerous, but I couldn't help it. I'd push for three steps, then I had to gather myself for another faint charge. Three steps, then stop. Three steps, then stop. *The Mowth would enjoy this,* I thought, smiling at Mowry's likely reaction to my miserable physical state. I could hear him crowing: "The Machine isn't just red-lining, it's shot, O'Donoghue—sucking valves, blowing oil. Face it, you're getting old!"

I couldn't let Mowry have the last word. "Go ahead, go ahead," I gasped. My voice was hardly authoritative at this point, but the dogs needed to know I was still watching them, still driving this outfit, fragile though I might feel. And I was scrutinizing Khan and Hobbes every step. My eyes never left their heels.

Our goal, the top tripod, was within reach when the trail vanished under the sand-blasting effects of the winds. The little snow that did remain here was crosshatched with snowmachine tracks. Khan and Hobbes battled each other, pulling us right, then left, then right. "Straight ahead! Straight ahead!" I shouted, reinvigorated by terror.

Onward the dogs came. Charging back down the mountain we'd so nearly conquered.

Between the big, frosty parka and his icy mustache, Nadeau towered over his dogs like a weathered statue of Joseph Stalin, at 9:30 P.M. on February 18, when his sled glided to a stop, just past the front-runner's resting team.

The statue sprung to life, revealing a snow-caked rookie, who had been far more worried about his team's condition than he let on. That was the reason he called off the chase in Central, all but conceding the race. But Andre Nadeau's seasoned soldiers proved even tougher than their master dared hope, marching straight up and over Eagle Summit. He'd reached Mile 101 only two and a half hours behind Lee.

Nadeau's arrival caused a furor, of course, but the penetrating wind, combined with the musher's reluctance to speak English, soon tempered the excitement of the media and other race spectators. They retreated to the cabin, leaving the second-place musher huddled over his cooker. Lee awoke from his nap parched; he remained a bit dehydrated from his ordeal atop the summit. Emerging from the bunkroom in search of something to drink, he was hit with a question: "So, is Andre sleeping in there with you?"

"I didn't even know he was here," the veteran blurted. His was more surprised to learn that Nadeau had pulled in more than an hour ago. "Is he still here?"

"Oh, he's out fooling with his dogs," responded one of Nadeau's handlers.

An alarm wailed inside Bruce Lee's brain.

He got in and I didn't know it. It doesn't make sense that he's still out fooling with his dogs in this windy place. There's no way this adds up.

The musher slipped on his boots and went to see for himself.

Outside the trailer a single dog team was resting under the glaring yard lights.

You dropped your guard! He hasn't given up. He saw a window of hope and stepped right into it, Lee realized. *This won't be over until you cross the finish line.*

Nadeau's stealth put him back on the trail roughly seventy-five minutes ahead of Lee. There was an inch of fresh snow on the ground. The rookie's dogs were working hard—even before they hit Rosebud, the Quest's last mountain.

Trailing the Ghost out of Mile 101, Lee had a hunch Nadeau's move might actually backfire; those Siberians were putting down a scent for his own leaders to follow and that couldn't hurt mushing across Rosebud's long, bare ridge. But his better-rested team overtook Nadeau's near the top of the first rolling hill. The veteran ordered his leaders on by and reclaimed the Quest lead.

The other team quickly fell behind. But one of Lee's leaders balked climbing the next rise. "Oh no," he gasped. "Not again."

He was changing leaders when Nadeau mushed up from behind. The rookie executed a neat pass and continued up the mountain, giving Lee's excitable dogs something to chase. As soon the ridge leveled off, Lee's team shot ahead, reaffirming the musher's belief that fatigue wasn't the issue. *It's just a mental thing,* he observed. *You don't have that hardened leader.*

At the base of the next pitch, Lee's young leaders staged another strike. This time Nadeau hung back, electing to snack his dogs.

He's waiting to see if I can get them over, Lee realized, reading the implied challenge. *He's not going to give me a free ride.*

Lee walked forward and petted his leaders. "C'mon, guys, let's go," he said, walking on ahead. Showing off their lessons from Eagle Summit, his dogs picked themselves right up and paced their master up the slope.

It was dead calm and clear at 2:30 A.M. on February 19, when the Quest veteran mushed onto Rosebud's top ridge. The moon, entering its last quarter, cast its silvery glow across a grand expanse of surrounding valleys. But Lee's eyes were glued to his lead dogs. They were the weak point. He coaxed and praised them, using every trick, every cue he could think of to instill confidence.

Descending the mountain, Lee felt a lightness of being, an abrupt easing after nine hundred miles of mounting tension. And why not? His swift dogs had only to pad their lead on this downhill dash through the woods, then it was clear sailing to Fairbanks.

No one had briefed mushers on the glaciation unleashed by several days of wild temperature swings. Patches of ice and overflow turned the woodsy, winding trail into a careening nightmare. Small willows and alders repeatedly smacked the sides of his sled, flipping it once, twice, six times.

Picking himself off the ground after one of the latter crashes, the leader of the Quest found himself laughing at the cumulative pain. "This just isn't going to be easy, is it?"

While Lee sensed his young dogs were mentally fragile, their speed remained supreme. He hadn't even seen Nadeau since coming off the summit.

Spreading straw for his dogs behind Angel Creek Lodge, where the rules of the race mandated an eight-hour stay, the veteran ticked off the passing minutes with barely suppressed joy. *I'd like to have an hour on him,* Lee thought, reckoning that a lead of that magnitude would allow him the liberty of giving his dogs a break or two during the final hundred-and-ten-mile sprint for the finish.

But Nadeau dashed that hope, trailing him into the checkpoint by twenty-nine minutes.

"Well, that's probably enough," Lee said. "But we won't be stopping on the way in."

A gain, I flung down the hook. Stomped on it. Squatted on the twin blades. And watched the dice roll.

The bottom of the summit basin was no longer even visible. *If this breakaway succeeds,* I thought, staring into the darkness, *if we have to do this over— even if no dogs are crippled, even if this weather holds—I won't make it.*

"I flat won't make it," I repeated out loud, suddenly as tired as I was energized a moment earlier.

Dumbly, I realized the hook was holding.

The German was at my side. "Can I halp?"

My anger was exhausted, along with all pride. "Yes," I said, "you could stand on this hook. Understand? Put your foot here."

"Yes, I know," he said, "I, too, am a musher."

The comment revived my fury. *If you're a musher,* I thought, *what the hell were you doing distracting dogs halfway up a mountain?* I let it go. Leaving him by the sled, I trudged down to fetch the dogs.

This time I guided Khan and Hobbes all the way to the tripod, where we took a delicious pause. It was about 8:00 P.M. It had taken us more than five hours to go, perhaps, twenty-five miles. But I didn't care if they were slowest on the trail, my dogs stood on top of a world populated by stars dancing over a wavy black horizon. Scratching Khan behind the ears I reveled in a breeze sweeping this narrow plateau, ruffling fur on Danger and my other long-haired dogs. To my eye, they all had the bearing of champions. "All hail, the conquerors of Eagle Summit!" I shouted.

It was too dark to make out the distant valley floor, but the descent to it appeared alarmingly steep. I considered rough-locking my runners, the equivalent of putting chains on tires for traction, to slow our upcoming descent. But I hadn't seen the chain Freshwaters helped me make since Dawson, and didn't want to waste time looking for it. *Don't sweat it. These dogs are as tired as you are.*

My headlamp caught a distant marker. Pulling Khan to a likely connecting trail, I took position behind the sled and ordered the team over the edge.

The thin snow was peppered with loose rocks and patches of dirt churned by the brakes of prior teams, making for a thrilling ride. I restrained the dogs as best I could, but I had to keep laying off the brake or risk tearing it off on the rocks. Khan and Hobbes took advantage of the freedom and soon had the whole team loping down the slope.

Several lights were creeping along on a distant ridge. *Folks must be following us on the highway.* One light, particularly bright, was aimed in my direction. I waved, wondering if it was a video crew. Had Fulda's army stuck around for the finish? "Nah," I said, amused at my own apparent craving for coverage.

Kate was wearing that shining light. Her doubts remained strong when the second headlamp first peeked over the ridge. "It's probably a snowmachine," she whined to Erica, who had remained behind to share Kate's lonely vigil. But the time for gloom was past. "Of course, it's Brian," Gwen's mom said, laughing and hugging my wife.

The light was certainly dimmer than the first. And the musher's descent was much, much slower this time. Then Kate actually heard my voice: "Go ahead. Go ahead, Khan," carrying across the canyon.

"Oh, Babe," she yelled. "Babe, I'm here."

The canyon acoustics didn't offer two-way communications. I saw the light tracking the team's progress from afar. That was comfort enough.

As it was, controlling the sled demanded full attention. With the runners skipping between high sides of hard-packed snow and the deep powdery trough cut by earlier teams, it wobbled crazily. I found myself gingerly straddling those runners, using my weight to counterbalance the sled's ever-changing plane of descent. It was a strenuous task. My arms soon turned to lead. On the verge of losing control, I intentionally rolled the sled, then dragged, belly down, for about ten feet while it plowed a new trench.

"Whooa!" I grunted stupidly late, as if my dogs were likely to rip loose the anchor provided by the overturned sled. "I am seriously freaking thrashed," I muttered, grinning like an imbecile as I lay there in the snow.

Watching from the highway, Kate saw what she now accepted as my light blink out. She combed the dark hillside through Jim Crabb's binoculars, but couldn't penetrate the darkness. *Brian must be having trouble with his headlamp,* she decided.

The dogs, refreshed by the pause, took off the instant I righted the sled. My dance on the runners began anew. "Rock and roll," I said, enjoying the dipping, tipping ride.

My control, tenuous from the start of our descent, steadily worsened. I wasn't the least bit sleepy, but the events of the previous hours left me utterly drained. Just before the slope flattened out, the sled again rolled, slamming me down hard on the icy turf.

Glancing up, I saw Search watching me with concern. "Don't worry, girl," I said, dusting myself off. "Takes more than that to kill the boss."

Nearing the valley floor, the trail became icy fast and fragmented into a broad band of parallel side-hill threads. Judging from the paw prints and runner tracks, there was no single preferred route. A sweep of my headlamp beam turned up markers affixed to nearly every scrub tree. Some were left from years past. I took comfort in the confusion: Mile 101 was definitely straight ahead.

A glare of ice stretched before us. Khan and Hobbes trotted straight across, making for the double-lined funnel ablaze with reflective markers heralding the entrance to Mile 101. Gwen's team was parked just beyond a long trailer. I stopped my dogs alongside the rusty unit, hoping it might cut down on the wind whipping through the camp.

Kate greeted me with a dazzling smile.

"How did it go?" she asked, brightly.

"Babe, I was at my limit. My absolute limit," I blurted, feeling my knees sag under weight of the passage. "Dogs turned around on me *twice* up there. I had serious doubts about making it."

My wife looked perplexed. "Gwen said it wasn't that bad."

The end game had begun.

Lee, for the second time in his life, led the Yukon Quest approaching Valley Center.

He had been thirty-five years old in 1991, a man in his prime, mushing dogs that appeared unstoppable as early as Dawson. Neither Lee, nor Schandelmeier, who was then thirty-seven, regarded the third member of the Quest's front pack as a serious threat. In his patched parka and graying pig tails, Charlie Boulding looked so much older and frailer than his forty-eight years.

Coming off his eleventh- and then tenth-place finishes in the two previous Quests, the cackling trapper with the Carolina drawl had joked that he was racing because he "enjoyed pain." His dogs were so thin they looked played out from the start, particularly Lilly Mae, the lead dog named for Boulding's first wife. "She's so ugly, I was looking forward to shooting her," he'd say, a gleam in his eye. "But Lilly Mae ended up being the best dog I ever owned—because I was so hard on it, wanting it to fail."

Ol' Charlie was good company, but a threat to win? Yeah, right.

Moving up the Yukon River that year, though he possessed the fastest-trotting team, Lee played conservative. He thought he was being so crafty letting Schandelmeier's powerful young crew set the pace. As for Boulding's raggedy outfit, well, it was amazing they even managed to keep up.

Schandelmeier remained in first place leaving Angel Creek, then the last checkpoint before the finish. Lee trailed him out, reasonably confident the young dogs ahead were overdue for a fall. He was right about that. Schandelmeier was never a factor. The real adversary rose up from behind on that night already electrified by the Aurora. Ol' Charlie had set him up: He'd trained that mangy Lilly Mae and her companion Charlotte to lope.

They couldn't rock and roll the entire seventy-five miles. No dog team could sustain such abandon that close to the end of a thousand-mile race. But dropping his artful concealment of the team's true forte, Boulding called them up for short bursts, repeatedly chasing down Lee's team, then melting back into the night as he gave those hellhounds another break. All the while, edging ever closer to the finish. Stalking the prey.

Boulding bided his time until they were past Valley Center. On the next surge, he sent Lilly Mae and Charlotte charging ahead. Bruce Lee retained hope, even then. Twenty miles from the finish line, only forty-five seconds separated the pair. But then spectators spooked Lee's leaders at a road crossing and the cackling trapper stole away for good.

Of course, Boulding's legend was just getting started. He went on to become the Quest's first two-time winner and a top contender in that richer race to Nome. None of which sweetened the taste of Bruce Lee's crushing five-minute loss. *I should have been racing Charlie way back on the Yukon,* he reminded himself yet again.

His present lead over Nadeau provided no assurance. The race route had changed in the seven years since Lee's last Quest. Instead of the straight shot from Angel Creek, the trail now dipped into North Pole, paying homage to a refinery serving as a major Quest sponsor. The detour added some thirty-five miles to the home stretch, a fearsome development for a competitor nursing Lee's memories.

As far back as Circle, Nadeau had worn a confident smile talking about his plans for the punishing final run. "I will march straight through, because I can do one hundred miles."

Lee, on the other hand, knew that was farther in one shot than his young dogs had ever been in their entire lives. On two occasions during training, he had trucked his team to North Pole and run them through to the finish line. He was hoping the memory would kick in when his dogs reached the same stretch tonight.

Many sled dogs possess a remarkable ability for recalling trails. But Lee's young leaders were unproven in that regard. Fatigue and stress might overshadow those fleeting training experiences. In addition, the musher knew, none of his dogs were going to be pleased at North Pole, where he intended to blow through an apparent checkpoint, ignoring the rituals practiced over the past thousand miles.

The trail didn't enter the actual city of North Pole. The new route took Quest teams over a dam and past a park pavilion on the outskirts of town, where mushers were expected to don their numbered bibs before continuing to the finish line in Fairbanks.

"Who's got my bib?" Lee shouted, nearing the pavilion.

A woman stepped forward from the crowd.

Lee spied the bib in her hand. He paused only long enough to grab it. "Let's go," he cried, leaving race officials and cameramen staring at his back.

A few hundred yards past the pavilion. Lee noticed his leaders were glancing backward, acting puzzled. *That's not good.*

Approaching a marked turn, Lee delayed giving the usual command, testing to see if his leaders remembered the trail. They nearly missed the turn before the musher broke his silence. *That tells me you guys don't really know where you are.*

The team's attitude seemed to improve after the trail dropped back onto the Chena River. Passing the first houses outside town, however, his leaders were distracted by the residential lights, the bonfires, and the shouts from spectators on the riverbank. Suddenly, Lee's leaders left the trail, hauling for one of those exciting houses.

The musher had to stop and pull his dogs back to the trail. The incident was repeated several times, causing Lee to change and re-change his leaders. The musher tried nearly every dog in the team before he noticed that Tiger, a young female, far from discouraged, was impatiently hitting her line, pulling toward the trail. Lee had seldom used Tiger in lead, but her behavior suggested the move was overdue: *She's the one who remembers where we are.*

With young Tiger paired in lead with Hawk, a four-year-old male, Lee's team took off, flying down the river toward Fairbanks. The Ghost's threat faded with each joyous ripple in the chain stretching ahead of the musher's sled.

"No one can take this from us now. We're going to win," whispered Lee, uttering the forbidden words at last.

Another musher approaching his first-ever victory might have looked ahead, reveling in to the celebration to come. Lee's state of mind was closer to reluctance. Any minute now, he knew, all hell was going to explode.

Bruce Lee switched off his headlamp and focused on the present—willing himself to remember this moonlit moment on the frozen Chena, shared with these fine dogs, his pups all, bounding forward as one.

You'll never be here with these dogs in this place again.

DICK MACKEY

IDITAROD FANS *were astonished in 1978 when Dick Mackey won the closest race in Iditarod history, winning the title in a photo finish with Rick Swenson after the two mushers raced across Alaska for two weeks. At forty-five, Mackey was the oldest race champion.*

Mackey's winning time of 14 days, 18 hours, 52 minutes, 24 seconds was one second faster than the time given Swenson for second place. The race was so close that it caused a dispute over the rules. Did the whole team have to cross the finish line? Or just the nose of the lead dog? Officials ruled that only the lead dog must cross.

Mackey was one of the organizers of the first Iditarod in 1973 after a career as a sprint racer. He has homes in Nenana, Alaska, and in Branson, Missouri. Dick and his son, Rick, the 1983 winner, are the only father-son combination to win Iditarod championships.

Mackey, who came to Alaska after graduating from high school in Concord, New Hampshire, has lived in many parts of the state, including Anchorage, Wasilla, Nenana, and Coldfoot, where he operated a last-chance gas

station and lodge for trucks driving north to the Prudhoe Bay oil fields. One
winter he says the temperature fell to eighty-two degrees below zero there.

I remember before the Iditarod got started Joe Redington called me and said, "What do you think?" I said, "Well, hell, I'm the second one to sign up." He said, "What do you mean?" I said, "Ain't you signed up yet?" Well, that was in November, 1972, and we went from there.

This idea of a sled-dog race from Anchorage to Nome was a far-fetched scheme. It was an adventure that first year. We thought we were racing. But as you look back on it, certainly compared to now, it was a big camping trip.

You never will be able to duplicate the feeling of the first one. Nobody knew what they were doing. Wives and sweethearts were down at the starting line in tears because here we were going off into the wilds, never to be seen again. It was that kind of attitude.

I had fifteen or sixteen dogs that first year. Oh boy, it was a learning process. Everybody went pretty much during the daylight hours. Maybe you'd stretch it a little to get to a certain place, and then you made camp.

Oh man, I was walking ten feet tall at the finish. First didn't make any difference. Everybody was a winner. Dick Wilmarth got there first, that's all. That was the attitude not only of the mushers, but the attitude of the public, too.

Of course there was no idea of doing it a second time. This was a one-time event. To be part of it was . . . hell's bells, I'd rather have done that than been president of the United States.

There's no doubt it was tough. And those of us that went the second year found out that in some respects the second year was worse.

The weather was atrocious. Hell, a half-dozen of us got trapped there going out of Puntilla Lake. The chill factor was 130 below.

I had a good team every year. I was into the organizational part of the race, though. The first year, I was in the office. I sent out all the information to potential mushers, did all the signing up, took all the money, made all the phone calls.

Finally, in 1978, it dawned on me that the core of my team was getting a little ancient. I had a damn good dog team and I told myself, "I'm going to back off from the organization this year and train dogs."

We went up to Eureka. We went to Talkeetna. We went to Cantwell. Wherever there was snow, we trained, as well as out of my home in Wasilla. I was thinking I had a team capable of winning it. I went into the race with that attitude—that I might not win, but I could keep up with anybody. The "anybody" turned out to be Rick Swenson. He was defending champion. Emmitt Peters, Rick Swenson, and I were the top contenders as the race progressed. And Rick and I were the leaders.

I let Rick lead. The only time that I was in the lead was where it was easy to be in the lead. When it was difficult to be in the lead I let him lead. Difficult in terms of trailbreaking. He was perfectly content to do that.

Now don't get me wrong. Rick and I are good friends, but at that time in his life he was pretty sure of himself—"I'm the defending champion and you're number two." I was willing to play that game until we got to Nome.

Swenson and I were probably never more than a hundred yards apart for the last eight hundred miles. We'd go to camp for the night, or however long we were going to camp. He'd get out his cooking stuff and I'd say, "Well, I'm going to go down the trail a little farther." And it would just blow his mind. I was the guy who never took the harness off my dogs. The dogs were always ready to go.

Anyway, this became a head game with Rick. Constantly. He made comments like, "I've never seen anybody who can get ready to go as fast as you can." Or, "I can't lose you for nothin'." And on and on. Well, we got about three miles from Nome and I got my lead dog right between his legs and he turned around to me and says, "We got it made. Just stay right where you are and we'll be first and second." I thought, *Yeah, sure.*

As we came up over the sea wall onto Front Street, I reached in my sled bag and pulled out a whip just as he glanced around and saw it. So he reached in and pulled out his. And that's the way we came down the street, just driving those dogs for all there was in us.

He was in front of me and I got in front of him, actually gained about three hundred feet on him. We both had troubles. I went off onto the sidewalk. He got tangled up with a school bus. He went into the crowd. It was chaotic. Everybody was jumping up and down. And then I got tangled in a camera tripod just as I entered the chute area, and I had to run up front, grab those dogs, and pull 'em out. We crossed the finish line just bang-bang, a second apart.

My leaders Skipper and Shrew crossed the finish line and it was a solid mass of people. When his leaders crossed the finish line, Swenson stopped.

I went to fall down in the sled and missed the damn sled. I had the heavy parka on and I couldn't get the darn thing off. I thought I was going to die from lack of air. Anyway, somebody said, "You gotta cross the line." And I said, "No, you don't." Well, every race you ever ran, you could be running alongside your team, doing anything, when any part of that crossed the finish line, that constituted a finish. You had to be equal to your sled or better. You could pull the sled backward and be holding onto it, that's OK. With one exception. Nome Kennel Club rules, from way back in the All-Alaska Sweepstakes Race, said team, driver, sled, all had to cross the finish line.

But we weren't running under the Nome Kennel Club rules. They were simply the host club at the finish line in Nome. An official asked Myron Gavin, who was the race marshal that year, "What's your decision?" And it was classic. Myron said, "You don't take a picture of the horse's ass."

Rick was on the back of his sled same as I was. When our leaders crossed, we both stopped. He sat down in his sled and I collapsed into mine.

Tom Bush of KNOM said, "You've got to cross the finish line." They congratulated Swenson, and he said, "For what, coming in second?" Then someone said, "You've got to cross the finish line." So Swenson got up and pushed his sled and himself through the crowd. In the meantime, the race marshal made the determination that as long as anything crosses the finish line, that constitutes a finish.

Swenson and I had equal dog teams and I just out-snookered him into thinking I was willing to be complacent enough to take second. And I wasn't. He learned a lesson.

You know, it was more of a thrill watching my son Rick win the Iditarod in 1983 than my winning. I absolutely went berserk. It is special to be able to say that we are the only father and son so far that have done it. It creates a bond there that you just can't duplicate.

SECTION SEVEN
NATIVE VOICES

No collection of true stories in Alaska would be complete without some selections from the works of Alaska's Native peoples or works about them. The pieces in this section of the book will make you laugh or cry—or even both, at the same time. This section also features a piece by Nick Jans, who is one of the best writers writing about anything anywhere ever. Don't miss it!

Excerpt from *Raising Ourselves*

VELMA WALLIS

❧ VELMA WALLIS, one of Alaska's best-known authors, was one of thirteen children. When she was thirteen, her father died and she left school to help her mother raise her younger siblings. Years later, she moved to her family's traditional hunting land, a twelve-mile walk from the village, and learned the traditional survival skills of hunting and trapping. An avid reader, she passed her high school literacy equivalency exam and began her first literary project—writing down a legend her mother had told her, about two abandoned old women and their struggle to survive. Wallis won the 1993 Western States Book Award and a 1994 Pacific Northwest Booksellers Award for her first book, *Two Old Women,* which has been translated into seventeen languages and is a bestseller in Germany, the Netherlands, and Spain. *Raising Ourselves* is available at www.epicenterpress.com. ❧

In those days, my parents worked hard. My father trapped in the winter. He would load up his toboggan with traps, his gun, and store-bought food, and he would disappear down the road with his team of dogs. My older brothers could not go with him, for they had to attend school. When my father returned home days or weeks later, we younger ones would fight over who pulled off his canvas boots, which were still frozen with ice from the overflow that he had crossed. In winter, even in fifty-below temperatures, sometimes the ice will crack on frozen lakes and rivers, and water will seep through.

After my father had warmed up, we children would take a flashlight and go out to his toboggan and unwrap the frozen string that tied everything down, to see what furs he had trapped. There were frozen lynx, marten, mink, and fox, but we were interested only in the weasels. My father let us have those, and we sold the skins to the store for fifty cents apiece, which equaled six candy bars.

After the animals thawed behind the woodstove on the floor, my parents would roll up their sleeves and sharpen their skinning knives. Wooden stretchers of all sizes would be brought into the house from the cache and every night for almost a week my mother and father carefully skinned each animal. They had to make sure each fur was well tended or the storekeeper would not buy them. These animal skins were the livelihood of our family. The money they brought in allowed us to buy food, electricity, and other items necessary to raise thirteen children.

Once my father took a candle and held its smoking end, slightly tilted, near the mink fur he was tending. He had a gleeful smile upon his face as he brushed the fur, watching the black smoke darken it. This was a way of fooling a buyer into thinking that the fur was more beautiful than it was. We knew this was cheating, but we smiled along with our father.

While my father trapped, my mother cared for our house. She was the jack of all trades within our two-room cabin. She cooked, cleaned, and cared for us all. The older siblings helped her when they could.

At night, after she put us younger ones down to sleep, she would dig out her sewing. She was always working on something. If she was not sewing our boots, parkas, and clothes, she worked on items to sell to the teachers, nurses, and Air Force men who lived temporarily in our village. Many nights my mother spent carefully sewing Indian dolls complete with fur parkas and boots. She used old socks to stuff the dolls, for she had nothing else. Today she laughs that somewhere out there in the world are handmade dolls filled with our old socks.

We helped our mother whenever she asked. We fought over who would scrape baby "dah" off the sodden diapers with a table knife. We also proved helpful when my mother prepared to sell her home-brew. We washed the green wine bottles in a big tub. As the stuff brewed in its yeasty scent behind the stove, we lined up and took turns dipping the ladle into the barrel for a taste. My mother was irate at the time, but later I heard her laughing about it with some adult. My mother and father tried bootlegging, but like others who tried they always ended up being their own best customers.

E very fall, my older brothers gathered dried goose grass from along the lake for bedding for the sled dogs. From August until mid-September, my parents cut and hung the dog salmon that they caught in the fish wheel for their winter supply of dog food. We helped by keeping out of the way and demanding little of their time.

With all this activity going on, the dogs lolled in the yard all summer. We hardly noticed them—they were workers, not pets. They seemed to know their status in life and treated us children with contempt, snapping their eyes at us, or yawning in boredom as they watched us play. Just before snowfall, the dogs would perk up, knowing their time in the harness was approaching.

My older brothers cooked the dog food in a huge blackened container on the fireplace outside. They put cut-up pieces of fish, water, and God knows what else into that pot. All through the afternoon, the food would cook and simmer. At night, long after supper and just before bedtime, we younger ones had to find a way to get the dog pots away from the dogs to feed them. The pots were whatever my father could get his hands on: coffee cans, basins, cooking pans. They were bent and beat up by the aggressive chewing, and with a long stick we managed to collect them. Then we would carefully dunk a coffee can into the dog food and scoop it out, evenly portioning it out to the more than a dozen barking, hungry dogs.

Whatever had been put into the dog pot, it smelled horrible. When one of us was unlucky enough to get it on our gloves, the stench was hard to get out.

I was afraid of the dogs. Some of my older brothers cuddled the dogs but I never had the nerve, for most were bigger than I was. I played with the puppies. The bigger dogs always seemed famished, and some had husky or wolf in them. When it was time to feed them, we practically threw their pots to them as they strained ferociously against their tethers. I had nightmares about wolf dogs trying to eat me.

Before winter set in, my father took his older sons out into the woods with his boat and they would gather more than seventeen cords of wood. My brothers cut, chopped, and stacked the wood, enough to heat two stoves all winter, with no shortage. The wood would cover one end of our yard right up to the front window. We younger ones loved playing on the woodpile. My mother warned us of the danger of falling off, but when she looked away we were climbing again.

In addition to tending the woodpile, the older boys had to keep our fifty-gallon galvanized water barrel filled. The rule was that the barrel had to be filled high enough that we little ones could dip out water. When the water level sank below our reach, the older brothers had to fill the barrel again.

Occasionally the water level would get down to the bottom. Once Barry and I felt we were dying of thirst as we stretched down trying to get some water. He heaved himself over the edge and tried to scoop water into the dipper. He lost control and found himself falling toward the foot of water at the bottom of the barrel. I screamed and tried to hold onto his feet. But he caught himself with his hands on the inner sides of the barrel and slowly inched himself back up. Our mother had to be dragged away from her work to help extract him.

To fill the water barrel, the older brother had to haul water from a hole chopped into the thick ice on the Yukon River. The water hole was chopped into the ice using an ax and a chisel. People from the village cooperated in keeping the hole open. Sometimes they kept it from freezing over by covering it with cardboard or canvas. Other times they tossed handfuls of clean snow into the water, and that kept the hole from freezing up. It was considered a minor crime to allow the water hole to freeze up.

We younger siblings sometimes helped the older boys push the sled laden with water buckets up the small hill to our house. The buckets were made out of square five-gallon Chevron gas cans. The gas smell was burnt out of the cans, which were then washed with soapy water, and carried by handles woven out of baling wire. The water jostled around and splashed us if we were not careful.

Every day or two, all year long, the water tank had to be filled if we wanted water to cook and clean with, and to drink. Villagers who packed water for wages made a good living, especially in the summer when the buckets of water had to be carted on a handmade wheelbarrow.

Our neighbor "Pa" Williams packed water for a living. People went to his house and let him know that they needed their barrels filled. It cost from three to five dollars, depending on how far he had to haul the water. When the men of our family were too busy, my mother would depend on Pa to pack our water. Others packed water, but most people preferred Pa because of his lively sense of humor. After filling the barrels, he would linger to fill his customers in on the village news.

In the spring, we looked forward to the returning sun and its heat that melted everything until the leaves let go of their fragrance and it filled the air. My siblings and I fought like dogs over the muskrat tails that we toasted on top of the woodstove until they were crisp and tasted like pork rinds, only better. Beaver meat was delicious, too, with its willowy flavor, and we devoured the boiled meat with relish. But there was no comparison to the singed duck soup that my mother made with dried vegetable flakes, adding rice and macaroni. We always ate our duck soup with Pilot Boy crackers spread with margarine. These foods were all we knew, and to this day, I can't say I know of a finer meal.

Summer arrived with its long, languid days. The mosquitoes came alive, and soon the flying ants landed. Then came the pincher bugs we called antennae bugs, followed by the horseflies that bit into our flesh. At the end of summer, the gnats came, as the days got cooler and the stars above could be seen even before it was truly dark. Our summers were heralded in and out by these bugs, who made their presence known in great numbers. Every now and again we would get our hands on some "bug dope" to repel them, but the rest of the time we tolerated them without giving it much thought.

At the end of June and in early July, my parents caught, cut, and dried the huge salmon that swam up the Yukon to their spawning grounds. My mother would be completely oblivious to the bees and flies that tried to get at the fish as she expertly cut them to hang in our cache behind the house.

The big salmon hung low from the high racks. We children would sneak into the cache when no one was around and eat off the bottom of the hanging fish. It mattered little whether the fish was raw or dry. We devoured the meat, and when my mother caught us she scowled, telling us we were no better than the camp-robbers, the gray jays that hung around caches to steal meat.

In these times of our village life, there were long periods of peace, but in between there was conflict and violence. I remember coming home from school one Christmas, all happy and filled with hope, but as I drew closer to our house I could smell the home-brew. I knew then that we children were in for one long holiday.

The adults of Fort Yukon always had good intentions. They wanted to take time off from all their hard work and from raising their many children, but they never seemed to resolve the issues in their lives when they were sober. When they drank, all those issues came out in the form of tears, blows, and harsh words.

Throughout the year people drank occasionally, but most of the drinking took place during Christmastime or the Fourth of July. We children expected the holiday drinking but we were promised a happy time.

My father would order new clothes for us and give us haircuts, while my mother made us brand-new canvas boots. The tree was put up, and the adults were heard whispering, filling us little ones with excitement. All the while the home-brew was slowly concocting in the wooden barrel. The scent filled our noses, vaguely warning us that the happiness would not come.

On Christmas Eve we were put to bed. None of us could sleep for the air was always filled with tension, exciting yet foreboding. Friends would arrive, and my father would generously pop open the first bottle of home-brew. Everyone would toast the season and take their first drink. We children would peek out from the back room. We watched our parents laughing and telling stories with their friends. We noted that the older siblings always disappeared during these times. We could not sleep as the noise got louder.

Before midnight, and with half a dozen empty green bottles littering the table, the happy adults began to cry. Then their tears would dry up into angry words, and before anyone could redirect the party, it would erupt into anger. My father would end up tossing people out of his house left and right.

About this time my parents would start fighting. Jimmy, Martha, the younger siblings, and I all witnessed my father beating my mother with his fists.

It was unfathomable to us why my mother would not back down. One moment she was lying in a heap on the floor, but as soon as she recovered she was like Muhammad Ali, bouncing back up and challenging my father all over again.

"Hit me again, Pete!" she taunted him over and over.

Then we children would try to intervene. We begged our father to stop hitting our mother, and we pleaded with our mother to stop telling him to hit her again. But they were in their own world and did not even notice us.

After days of drinking and fighting came the slow, painful task of sobering up. My mother's swollen face would gradually heal. My father's face would go blank as if nothing had happened. There was an emptiness about our cabin as in the aftermath of war—a war no one had won.

Slowly the stove became warm again, food smells filled the air, the older siblings trickled back to the cabin, and we began to cheer up. Life returned to normal. My father would pretend to forget that he had beaten the woman who had given him thirteen children, and she would pretend to forgive him. We had to pretend, too—pretend that we had not witnessed anything out of the ordinary. It was a neat little trick, one that we performed again and again.

Once, my mother looked out the window at us playing in the yard and saw us reenact their fights. No one wanted to be Mom, but everyone wanted to be Daddy. The rest of us played our parts, crying, "Daddy! Daddy! Don't hit Momma!"

My mother ran out of the house. She had an urgency about her, as if she did not want this rude reminder of those times she so desperately wanted to forget. We went running in different directions, for she had caught us playing the forbidden game of "Hit me again, Pete!"

In sobriety, my parents' relationship was strange. They were like business partners who happened to have children together and each intended to contribute a fair share to raising them. They worked well side by side, cutting fish or moose meat, or preparing other Native foods. While he trapped and worked outdoors, she kept everything in working order at home. But they rarely showed any sign of affection for each other.

At times, they would sit at the table and talk with each other laughingly. We played contentedly by their feet. Some part of us knew the other story to be real in its ugliness, but for the sake of our parents we played along with this fairy tale, knowing it would not last. We loved our parents when they were sober but detested them when they drank. The drinking patterns were so predictable that we automatically treated them with disrespect during those times.

This part of our life together was always there. As much as we hoped the drinking would go away, it was interwoven into our lives. When it wasn't our parents being disruptive, it was our neighbors or a friend's parents. We watched sadly from a distance as a man chased his wife down the road. My heart would cry for the woman when she was caught.

A painting by Andrew Wyeth appeared in one of my schoolbooks. This picture always stuck in my memory, showing a slender woman in a mustard-colored dress sitting in some dry, wheat-colored grass. She seemed to be hiding from a nearby house. I imagined her to be one of the abused wives. In my mind I hid with her and hoped for her safety.

I referred to the periods of drinking as the dark days and the periods of sobriety as the sunny days. Many times Barry and I sought solace from the violence of our drunken parents by pretending we were the children of a man and woman whose faces we had cut out of a wig advertisement. They were a handsome couple. Barry and I would lie in our beds holding the cut-outs as they smiled lovingly back at us. In the front room of our cabin, our parents drank. We never told anyone of our fantasy, for it would have seemed disloyal to our parents, who were good people when they were sober.

I did not know it then, but my mother had not started drinking until 1964, when my brother Grafton was killed in an accident with a truck.

Grafton was a born imp who loved to tease and play. The morning of the accident, he had teased his sisters relentlessly before school. He threw them in the snow and pulled their hair, so they ran back to the house to complain about him. Grafton kept running back into the house for dry gloves, for he kept getting his wet. Because he was teasing his sisters, my mother told him to get out and not to come back again as she handed him his third pair of gloves. Those words would ring in her head for years to come.

Completely unabashed by his mother's words, Grafton gleefully ran out of the house and off to school. On his way, he spotted the clinic's water tank being pulled by a truck. The driver, a responsible person, always kept an eye out for the mischievous kids who tried to grab the truck's back fender and get a free slide on the ice. That day he did not see Grafton behind him sliding along the ice. When the driver backed up the truck, my brother was crushed.

After Grafton died, my father was full of blame. He wanted to kill the driver. My mother sank into her own oblivion. Both parents slunk off into their dark little corners. They could find no relief from their grief over this special son.

My mother sought refuge in liquor. My father, who always drank, found one more reason to do so as he sat for hours crying. When they sobered, the pain was still there, but they faced the daily drudgery of their lives stoically until the next alcoholic episode.

I was too young to remember Grafton. But when my parents drank they cried unceasingly over his memory, and this made me sad. To this day when I am around those who drink into the night when the tears and sorrow come, I feel an indescribable pain.

In the late sixties, my father was diagnosed with diabetes. He was forced to quit drinking. When he quit drinking, so did my mother. But Itchoo still drank.

On the first of the month when the welfare checks came in the mail, people would scurry to pay their bills at the store and at the utilities company, and then they sought out the bootleggers. After she had consumed the bootleggers' wares, Itchoo would come stumbling into our yard wearing her long dress and a scarf wrapped around her head like a turban, with a cane in one hand, either singing a song or cussing up a storm. A dark cloud of rage would come over my father's face and he would send my mother out to contend with taking Grandma home to bed.

Itchoo and my father understood each other too well. Many times we saw the tightening of his lips when she summoned him, and we heard his complaints about "those people uptown" who made her drink.

For many years, Itchoo lived in a small house by the river near Aunt Nina. I visited that house once when my brother Brady was born. Midwives had piled into the front room of our cabin. There was Nina Flitt, the local midwife, and Olive Solomon, the trained nurse, and a couple other women who would aid my mother in the birthing of her twelfth child.

My younger siblings and I littered about nervously, not understanding what all the whispering and the preparations were about. In the nine months that my mother had been pregnant, we had not noticed. She had not altered her chore routine at all, nor did her weight seem to change. She was always round. She once said that it was years before she could see her feet again.

The midwives puttered about silently in the sacred ceremony of childbirth. We became frantic as they pinned a couple of bedsheets around the big white bed from the Hudson Stuck Memorial Hospital, one of which could be found in just about every cabin in Fort Yukon after the auction years before.

The midwives commanded my older siblings to take us down to our grandmother's house by the river. We were hesitant, for we feared our mother's life was in danger. Nonetheless, we were taken almost by force to Itchoo's.

In the gray daylight of the February day, we sat by the table next to the window, watching Itchoo placidly cooking biscuits in her skillet pan atop a potbellied aluminum stove that blazed hot and even. From her homemade hutch Itchoo took down porcelain cups, placed them on rose-bordered saucers, and poured into them mahogany-colored tea. As we sat chewing on buttered biscuits and drinking hot, sugared tea from delicate cups, our wide eyes took in the many mysteries of our grandmother's domain.

Her small cabin had no back door, only a screened front door and three windows, two long ones on the side and one small one on the front. Inside, colorful fabric hung along ropes to serve as walls for her bedroom. The chamber pot, typically kept behind the front door in the winter, was hidden in her bedroom.

That would be the last time we had a privileged glimpse into the life of the woman who would remain forever a mystery to us.

Itchoo was the cause of recurrent arguments between Aunt Nina and my father over who should take care of her. In her old age, she could hardly move around. She was partially blind, for she had contracted a virus that had resulted in the loss of one eye. In its place she wore a blue glass eye, and she could hardly see out of the remaining eye.

Given the choice, my grandmother chose the offspring who offered her the best treatment at the time. After living near my Aunt Nina, Itchoo one day moved into a cabin next to ours.

Itchoo seemed close to our older siblings. Despite the fact that the older ones did not speak Gwich'in any more than we could, they had a rapport with Itchoo that we younger ones were not able to establish. We never knew that Itchoo had lived in a different culture before the coming of the Western culture, and no one thought to explain this to us.

While my grandmother doted on my older siblings, she was a harsh stranger to us. In general we kept our distance. As children we tried hard to please her, sometimes being brave enough to approach her for treats or some token of her love. Sometimes she surprised us by giving us money, candy, or a friendly smile. More often we were perplexed by this woman and her blue glass eye, and we would peek at her only to be shooed away when she caught us.

At times when my older siblings were off doing their own thing, my mother would ask one of us younger ones to spend the night with Itchoo. Sometimes Martha and Jimmy would do it, but occasionally I was selected, and my heart would do little frightened flip-flops at the thought of spending a night alone with my strange grandmother. I would beg Barry to accompany me, and he would do so reluctantly.

Aside from being taught how to be devout by the Episcopal Church, Itchoo was very superstitious. She said Barry would one day be a medicine man, and for some reason she was never comfortable in his presence. But I would be there and she did not fear me.

Before Itchoo went to sleep, she would take out her blue glass eye and set it on her bedside table. Then she would perform various other bedtime rituals, fluffing up her pillow and rearranging her bedclothes. Finally she began to pray.

Barry and I peeked at her from under our covers. We could hear the word *Nagwathut,* which means God. Just when it sounded as if she had finished her prayers and we would be able to go to sleep, she would remember one more person she had forgotten. Eventually, her prayers would end and then we would lie awake, listening to her snore and dream out loud.

Excerpt from *Through Yup'ik Eyes*

COLIN CHISHOLM

☙ Born in 1967, COLIN CHISHOLM grew up in California's Sierra Nevada. He received an M.F.A. in creative writing from the University of Montana, has published stories and essays in numerous magazines and journals, and was a finalist for the National Magazine Award in 1995. *Through Yup'ik Eyes* is his first book. He lives in Missoula, Montana. This title can be found at fine bookstores everywhere and at www.gacpc.com. ☙

Tired from all the visiting, our father goes to bed while Brad and I join our cousin Natalia in the upper row of the community center bleachers in St. Marys, a village about a hundred miles upriver from Kotlik. Many of our relatives moved here from Kotlik when the Catholic mission school was established. Children of all ages scamper around the open floor of the community center, dressed in clothes of popular culture: Raiders' jerseys, Nike Air Jordans, backward baseball caps, sweatshirts hanging to their knees. In contrast the old women wear babushkas over their heads and colorful, shin-length Yup'ik dresses, or *qaspeq*. The older men wear blue jeans, wool shirts, and baseball caps declaring CAT: DIESEL POWER, or SKOAL, or ANDREAFSKY EAGLES, the name of the local high school's athletic teams. Despite the chaotic wrestling of children everywhere, a sense of calm prevails. The dancing is about to begin.

The children scatter as our cousin Fred Mike begins the first dance. Short and thickly muscled, broad in the shoulders, he kneels in the center of the room. He has short black hair, deep eyes, and a wide, sharp jaw. The young women watch him, one giggling as she whispers into another's ear. In each hand Fred holds dancing fans, circles of wood from which six long eagle feathers protrude. He breathes deeply, stares at the floor in concentration; he is "Waiting for the Drums." He waits for the story to begin.

A younger man, maybe sixteen years old, kneels to Fred's right and follows Fred's motions. Pimpled, he wears a White Sox T-shirt and 501 Levi's. He stares, like Fred, at the floor.

With the first beat my ears tense, then settle into the rhythm of five drummers beating their walrus-stomach drums. They hold the drums away from their bodies, above their heads, and beat them with long, thin wooden drumsticks. On the third beat Fred begins his dance, his hands flowing with the beat of the drums and the singing drummers. He sways from the waist, but the dance emanates primarily from his arms and hands as he moves the dancing fans with and against the motions of his body. As the rhythm increases, the feathers seem rooted in his hands, and his arms slice the air like wings.

The beat quickens, the drums boom louder, and, one by one, women join Fred on the floor, each with her own reed dancing fan, woven by grandmothers and passed from one generation to the next. Facing the bleachers, they stand in a semicircle behind Fred, their eyes either downcast or focused on him as he leads. Natalia joins them, then Justina, who knows the dances by heart. Her arms swing gracefully from side to side, synchronized with the others, four generations dancing the same dance. Ages merge. In Justina I see a young girl learning from her elders; in a little girl I see an old woman dancing with her eyes closed.

Every few minutes the drummers reach a deafening crescendo, then abruptly they stop. If they like the dancers, they wait only a moment before drumming again. The length of the song reflects the drummers' pleasure in the dancers. Sometimes the drummers make the young dance for a long time, teaching discipline and endurance.

In this dance, the drummers go easy on the dancers because many are as old as Justina. After two sets the dance ends. Fred steps back to sing with the drummers and the women leave the floor, many of them passing their dancing fans to the girls walking on, high-school students practicing to dance for the governor in Mountain Village next week. Two brothers kneel in the lead positions, the girls standing behind, all of them waiting for the drums. The younger brother watches for a cue. Both wear red shirts, the older boy a Chicago Bulls tank top with the number twenty-three on his chest. Basketball rules in the villages because it can be played indoors all winter.

The drums thunder; the kids flicker to the beat. The girls' feet are stationary, but their knees bend like reeds swaying in the wind. They glance at one another, nervous and giddy. The rhythm grows fast and intense, the singing a high, wailing keen, as if the drummers are trying to pass on a sense of urgency and need. The boys momentarily falter, but recover after a few beats, their confidence unshaken.

This dance continues for a long time. At the end of each set the dancers move immediately toward the bleachers, but before they get away the drums begin again, calling them back. They must dance until the drums stop. Seven times they're called back. The drummers look on, amused. By the last set the kids are slick with sweat, but glowing with pride. To dance is one thing; to be called back is an honor. A crucial part of village life, the dancing defines them just as they define the dance.

I try to imagine students from my high school performing in such a setting, four generations intermingling, kids of all ages playing together without obvious hierarchy. The dancers don't appear self-conscious. I can't imagine myself up there dancing, not because I would be laughed at, but because I am afraid I would be. I sense that for my relatives and other Yup'ik, dancing is selfless, an expression of the whole. When the child in tiny mukluks dances by her mother, she begins to learn her story, where she came from, where she will go. I see this in the smallest children watching, some imitating the dancers' movements. During one dance, Fred holds his two-year-old daughter, Josephine, on his lap while he sings, his hands guiding her hands through the mirrored motions of the old women.

After the high schoolers' dance, all the dances begin to blend together for me, until I feel I'm on a river of sound, gently drifting to the sea. Hypnotized by the rhythm, I sit watching while dancers come and go, the keening voices settling over me like an elixir. I imagine my mother among the dancers, and for a moment I believe that she is there. In the girl, in the old woman, in all of them.

I turn to Brad, next to me on the bleachers. His fingers are stuffed into his ears. He yells that he needs to leave, his ears are hurting. I realize that I can't last much longer, either. We are just getting up to leave when another cousin joins us. He recognizes me from my first visit six years earlier and welcomes us warmly. As he bends too close I smell whiskey, strong on his breath. St. Marys, like many of the villages, is "dry," but as Natalia told us earlier, it is more damp than dry. Again my mother is near; I grow hot with a confusing blend of pity and shame.

I ask this cousin if he is going to dance. He laughs loudly and mutters incoherently. I look at Fred singing to the drums. These two are similar in age and circumstance, both facing the same issues inherent in straddling two incongruous cultures. Yet one responds by learning the old ways, while the other takes to drink. I look around the room at the children playing or dancing or staring or sleeping. Some will not learn this dance. Or they will learn it and soon forget. Or they will remember but not believe. They will hear the drums, but they won't be called by them. When the drumming becomes just noise, the dancing ends.

Later that night I walk home with Fred. We are about the same age, and since my last visit I have come to feel close to him, despite the distance that separates us and the very different lives we lead. The October night is cold. I see Fred's breath rising, sweat still glistening on his brow from four hours of dancing. I never saw him leave the floor. Below us the Andreafsky River shimmers in the moonlight. Fred asks me how I liked the dancing, and I tell him I am learning to like it, that it is very different for me. I joke that the drumming makes my ears ring. He laughs, says that most Eskimos must be half deaf. I compliment him on his dancing, his smoothness and endurance. I tell him I wish I understood the singing so that I would know the stories.

"The stories, you know," Fred answers, "they are important, but maybe not the most important. I don't even understand all of it—some of them are very old. Maybe nobody could tell you the story no more. But the dance it still goes on; I listen to the drum and that's enough. The dance tells a story even if the words are lost."

I listen to Fred's voice, passionate about dancing. I ask him why some people don't dance, such as our other cousin.

"I didn't used to dance either," he says. "For a long time I thought I was too cool, that my friends would laugh at me. But then bad things happened. It was . . ."

He pauses, searching for words. He looks at me, then down to the river.

"Lots of people die here, you know, when they're young. Something is hard, I don't know what, but many of my friends, people I know, they end up killing themselves. Too much drinking, no luck. Things go bad."

We are nearing the fork in the road, where he will go up to his house on the hill, and I will go down to the old Catholic mission, where Brad, my father, and I are staying. We walk in a comfortable silence for a minute, until he continues.

"Dancing saved me, I think. I went one night, came out feeling a little better, a little stronger. I kept going back. The elders, they teach me, help me to see how good it is, how it shows respect to our ancestors, how it gives me pride. Now I know I have to follow more the old way, try to live how we used to, gain strength from my ancestors. Your ancestors. One of these times I will get you to dance. Okay?"

"I will try," I say, not believing it. I have never been able to dance. We laugh comfortably together, shake hands under the moonlight. His hand is thick and warm. We say good night, make a plan to go jogging the next afternoon when he gets off work at the St. Marys airport, where he unloads cargo planes. He turns and heads up the hill to his house.

I go down, past rows of dilapidated houses, the post office, and docks, then up another small rise to the sheet-metal mission, which looks more like an airplane hangar than a Catholic church. Back in the fifties they opened the mission as a boarding school for the Native population, removing children from their families in order to immerse them in a Western education. It didn't work for long; the Yup'ik families simply packed up and moved to St. Marys. That's how St. Marys stumbled its way onto the map: people coming to keep their families intact. The school closed more than a decade ago, replaced by a modern public school. Now they rent dormitory rooms to visitors. The place feels eerie, haunted.

After three days of drizzle, the dirt road leading to the dormitory is thick with mud. I slosh through it, avoiding the deepest bogs. As I near the building I hear rustling in the bushes to my left. I freeze, startled. Staring me straight in the face, less then ten yards away, is a red fox. I'm afraid I'll scare it off, but after a few minutes I realize this fox may not be afraid of me. It regards me with what I take to be curiosity, even longing. Perhaps it has been fed by village children and is only begging for food, but I want to believe it is something more than that. I begin to see, in the fox's eyes, that it somehow knows me, and wants me to know that it knows me. I think of Dora and Charlie Backlund, who died just downriver from here. I feel foolish, but I can't let go of the thought: *This fox knows me.* I shiver.

Writing this, years later, I doubt what I felt then. But I know, in those moments, on that muddy moonlit night, the sound of drums resounding in my ears, I believed that fox was my grandmother. Dora.

A door slams, distracting me. I look around and see the old priest waddling down the dormitory stairs. I turn back to the fox, but it has vanished. "Good evening," says the priest as he walks by me.

"Yes, good evening," I stammer, relieved that it's too late for conversation. I stand a while longer in the deepening silence. I hear the endless movement of river water, and somewhere deep in my ears the echo of drums. I will search for fox tracks in the morning.

WINTER POTLATCH, 1879

Nicuuk was known, at a very young age, for her dancing. When she was two years old she stumbled out onto the dance floor at a winter potlatch and began imitating the movements of her grandmother. Nicuuk loved watching her grandmother dance, loved the way the caribou hair flowed through the air like clouds around her grandmother's calm, focused face. At two Nicuuk was already dreaming of the fans she would someday hold in her hands when she danced. She imagined them with colorful beads sewn into the shape of her doll, Itsaq, whom she held as she bounced up and down, bending at the knees to the steady beat of the drum. Woven from grass, Itsaq was given to Nicuuk on her second birthday. She had black, waist-length hair and a red-and-blue dress painted with berry and charcoal dyes. Nicuuk took Itsaq everywhere. When they were alone she made Itsaq dance as she tapped lightly on her father's drum and swished the fans she had fashioned for Itsaq out of leftover caribou hair. By moving Itsaq through the movements, Nicuuk learned the village's dances and created dances of her own that would one day be absorbed into the village tradition.

During Nicuuk's tenth year a spring potlatch was held twenty miles upriver, to celebrate the end of a long, unusually brutal winter. Many people had died of starvation and the white man's disease, which had caught them by surprise. Confined for months on end, Nicuuk had practiced dancing all winter. When she was called to the floor she felt nervous, but easily settled into the rhythm of the drums. She danced so beautifully that the drummers wouldn't stop. Again and again, with the throb of their drums, they called the dancers back to the center of the *qasgiq*, the communal house. Nicuuk thought she might faint, but she kept dancing as if the din of the drum were the pulsing of her own heart. The people sat mesmerized around the dancers. Even the children watched in dreamy-eyed silence. When Nicuuk waved her fans gracefully through the air, the people saw caribou running across the soft tundra. When she swayed her body from side to side, her feet rooted in the earth, the people saw trees bending in the wind, or grass quivering in waves of summer heat.

The dance was old, so old that nobody knew when it had begun. It told the story of a family that lived alone up in the North Country, where caribou roamed thick as mosquitoes beneath mountains by the sea. They were caribou people, and their lives revolved around caribou. They moved long distances to follow the herd, and sometimes they went hungry when the caribou were scarce or hunting was bad. One winter long ago, no caribou came to the family's home, so they lived on fish until the sea froze and winter closed them in. The children were dying when the father heard a strange scraping outside. He went to see what it was, and rubbing up against the driftwood of their home was a huge caribou with antlers as tall as small trees.

"I am here to bring you life," the caribou said. "We are brothers. You know what you must do." The man gave thanks and cried as he pierced the caribou's heart. He fed his children its meat, and with its bones he fashioned tools for the hunt. With the great antlers he carved a herd of tiny caribou. When his children and grandchildren were grown, he gave each of them one of these caribou, and he told them they were sacred and would bring them good hunting for the rest of their lives. And the people lived and died by caribou.

When Nicuuk waved her fans above her, touching the sky, the drummers' voices rose to meet her. The people thought of sunshine, the months to come, fish in their nets, and caribou sweeping across the land. When they saw Nicuuk dance they forgot, if only for a moment, the loss of winter. They let the dead slide into the next world like salmon slipping back into the sea.

When the dance was finished, people brought Nicuuk gifts. Some wept as they reached out to her. She felt shy, unused to such praise. She wasn't yet old enough to see that the tears she had made were tears of joy, even those shed in farewell to the dead. Potlatches, she knew, were about *catngu*, which meant to be helpful, essential. And she knew that dancing was *catngu*, like blood flowing to the heart. Later in the potlatch, a powerful shaman came to release the spirits of the dead through the hole in the *qasgiq*'s roof. But for years afterward people would say that Nicuuk's dancing had let the spirits go. People said she had strong medicine, though she was never asked to use it in the way the shamans were. Mostly her dancing blunted the vicious teeth of delta winters, brought light where there was none before.

Just after Nicuuk's seventeenth birthday she danced at the spring potlatch in Chaneliak, where she saw Aivrun again for the first time since he had come to visit with her father more than a year before. She had thought about him many times, remembered his yellow eyes and the scar across his face. That winter her father had trapped a lynx and brought it home for her to skin. The lynx reminded her of Aivrun, and it made her sad to see the fire in its eyes faded to smoke, lusterless and gray.

She was dancing when he entered, the only *kass'aq* in the *qasgiq*. Seeing him broke her rhythm, imperceptibly to most people in the room, but she knew that he had noticed. A faint smile crossed his face. She looked at the floor and continued dancing, mesmerizing the audience. Aivrun, too, was caught like a fish in the ebb and flow of her gestures, her tidelike bending of knees. He had heard about her dancing, and he remembered her unflinching stare the first time he met her in the village. He had thought her intriguing, but he was busy with hunting and trapping, and he'd spent the last six months prospecting for gold upriver. He had tried, all of his life, to avoid women because he didn't believe he could settle down long enough to be a decent husband or father.

Nevertheless, he watched Nicuuk, spellbound, until nearly an hour later when the dance ended. Gifts of seal oil, caribou hair, and wolf pelts were laid across the floor. A family from Alakanuk gave a kayak with a whale bone protruding like a spear from its bow. Dancers from other villages took the floor, the drums drummed on. All night into the early morning they boomed through the walls of the *qasgiq*. Dancers came and went, children slept on the floor or in the laps of their mothers, food appeared and disappeared again and again from the long bench, men retired to the nearby bathhouse, a mud and grass hut with a deep fire pit in the middle around which the men sat and sweated, pouring water over red-hot rocks and exchanging endless stories. Everything that happened in the village during the potlatch seemed framed by the sound of the drums, a deep throbbing that shook the ground and echoed off the riverbanks and hills for miles around. The animals knew when it was potlatch, and sometimes they wandered in to the edge of the village and watched from a distance. Ravens perched on the highest homes, or soared above the *qasgiq*. A new energy was born, year after year, no matter how hard the winter. The river was breaking up; life was beginning anew.

Nicuuk danced many dances that night, well into the morning. Aivrun would one day joke that the dancing became a test of wills: who would give up first, the dancer or the dance. Aivrun watched every dance, every move Nicuuk made. She knew he was there, felt his eyes, but never once, since that first fleeting glance, met his gaze. Nicuuk's father, Yugisaq, was aware of the game, and he approved despite the fact that Aivrun was a *kass'aq*. They sat together, watching the dances and talking about Aivrun's journeys upriver. Nicuuk's mother also saw, and she worried. She was distrustful of the Russians, especially when it came to Nicuuk, who was well into a marrying age. Nevertheless she brought Aivrun food. He thanked her, but only nibbled at the dried salmon and whale blubber. He had no appetite.

Soon after midnight a dance began that was like no other dance the people had ever seen. Nicuuk was among the eight female dancers behind Kitluk, the old master known far and wide for his drama and skill. The drums began telling the story of how the world began, how the great Raven, using his talons, carved out the Yukon and Kuskokwim Rivers, the mountains and streams of the delta. The story was familiar, one heard every year again and again with the changing of the seasons. But this time it was different; this time Raven flew endlessly, until it seemed that creation was eternal.

The air was charged. Kitluk arched his back more than anyone had ever seen. His ribs pressed tightly against the skin of his chest, his spine bowed backward, his body convulsed to the drums. His knees sank into the floor, his old but well-muscled arms fanned out like wings, and his face twisted in agony. Ever after people would swear that Kitluk nearly took flight that night, that Raven had tried to break free.

The second time around the drums grew louder, the pace quickened, the room heated until people dripped with sweat. Following Kitluk, Nicuuk closed her eyes and swooped into Raven's world. Her fans sliced at the floor, like giant talons bringing forth the river. As the singing shrilled, her jaws clenched, her lips parted, and her bare feet clawed the dirt floor. Watching, people worried. Aivrun stared, knowing only that he was changed, that he would never leave this place again. He was afraid, watching her, yet more afraid not to.

There was never a longer dance. The drummers endlessly called the dancers, until all but two had fainted to the floor. Many people had gone home to sleep, others dozed around the room, the drums steady but distant in their ears. Nicuuk and Kitluk danced until the sun's first light fell on the raven perched atop the *qasgiq*. When it lifted into the silver dawn the drummers knew the dance was over. Kitluk slumped forward onto the ground, Nicuuk buckled at the knees. The last thing she saw was Aivrun's eyes, staring at her from the shadows of the room.

Excerpt from *The Last Light Breaking*

NICK JANS

☞ NICK JANS is a teacher and writer in Ambler, Alaska, an Inupiat Eskimo village on the edge of the western Brooks Range. Since arriving in Alaska in 1979, he's also managed a trading post, worked for a big-game guide, and traveled over forty thousand wilderness miles. *The Last Light Breaking* is his first book. The son of a career diplomat, Jans grew up in Europe, Asia, and Washington, D.C. In 1979 he visited Alaska in search of adventure and found a home instead. Jan's nonfiction and poetry have appeared in *Alaska* magazine, *National Fisherman, Christian Science Monitor,* and *Rolling Stone.* Recently he was named a contributing editor to *Alaska* magazine. *The Last Light Breaking* and other books by this author can be found at fine bookstores everywhere and at www.gacpc.com. ☞

The Noatak Lynx are playing their archrivals from the coast, the Kivalina Qaaviks (Wolverines). The green-clad Lynx are up by seven points late in the fourth quarter, but the Qaaviks, like their namesake, are going down fighting. The Noatak middle school students, thirty strong, chant and clap in deafening unison with the three cheerleaders:

"*Beat 'em, bust 'em, That's our custom. . . .*"

From the coaches' seat on the Noatak bench I hold up two fingers, and the Lynx set up a half-court offense, passing, feinting, using the clock as we've practiced a dozen times. But Steven Koenig, the Qaavik star forward, anticipates a pass and steps up for the steal. He drives the length of the court and swoops past a defender, flipping in a reverse layup and collecting a foul. A roar of dissent goes up from the partisan crowd, while the thirty Kivalina fans, windburned and frostbitten after their sixty-mile snow machine ride, shout their approval.

"He sure foul!"

"Man, ref, so cheap!"

"Just like you can't see!"

"Don't listen to them, they don't know nothing!"

The two local officials, one a white high school teacher, the other a young village man, a former Lynx, try to ignore the abuse. After he's ridiculed by name, though, the young man turns to the offender and offers his whistle and shirt.

"Want to ref, *kumaq?*" *Kumaq* is Inupiaq for head louse. The older women, bundled in their bright flowered calico parkas even in the gym heat, cackle; others join in the laughter, and the game goes on.

Koenig, whose father captains a traditional whaling crew, sinks the free throw, and the lead is down to five. Rattled, my sophomore point guard dribbles the ball off his foot as he tries to break Kivalina's press. Koenig has his radar switched on now; he sinks an impossible eighteen-foot jumper off the inbound pass, and the Lynx lead by two with thirty seconds on the clock. I call time, and my team gathers in a tight huddle as an earsplitting female voice launches into a singing call and response, a third of the crowd, child and adult alike, joining in. The heating ducts rattle and the walls of the tiny gym boom with a hundred screaming voices:

"Beat the Qaaviks. . . ."

"*Beat the Qaaviks. . . .*"

"Somebody oughta . . ."

"*Somebody oughta . . .*"

"Somebody gonna . . ."

"*Somebody gonna . . .*"

"Beat 'em. . . ."

"*Beat 'em. . . .*"

The Lynx inbound the ball, beat the press, and manage to ice the ball for the win. Kids pile out of the stands, mobbing the home team, high-fiving and joining in a hand-linked jumping mass at center court. Parents beam their satisfaction, and old men hobble up to me, showing the gaps in their teeth.

"We sure win them, ah?"

"Real good our boys this time!"

"Sure glad we never lose to them Kivalinas!"

I shake hands and smile back, equally relieved. The Lynx are in the chase for the regional championship, and everyone expects great things of us. After four years of coaching, I know how much winning means to the village, and how quickly I'll be blamed if we lose.

The crowd disperses slowly. Tomorrow is the second game, and then, weather permitting (Kivalina is notorious for the worst winds in the region), the Qaaviks will fly in chattered Cessna 207s back to their home village; the Noatak girls, who have been playing there, will return on the backhaul. The total cost for transportation is over four hundred dollars, and this is an inexpensive weekend, since the two villages are relatively close to each other and to Kotzebue, the home base of the charter company. When you figure that there are eight small villages in the Northwest Arctic Borough School District with basketball teams, and that each school plays between ten and twenty regular season games, two per trip, you get an idea of the expense—and that's just travel. Not counting the buildings, the yearly cost for the school district's basketball program—coaches, uniforms, equipment, travel—is well over a hundred thousand dollars. The People want basketball that badly. The residents of Ambler, when asked for input on the design of their new school, specified that a gym was first on the list, and they got what they asked for: a basketball floor with cramped classrooms tacked on as an apparent afterthought.

The whole phenomenon is astounding when you consider that fifteen years ago, only three of the ten villages in the NANA (Northwest Arctic Native Association) region had gymnasiums; twenty years ago, only Kotzebue, the hub of the region, had one. Noatak has had its gym for less than ten years. Each village was guaranteed its own high school (and by extension, its own basketball court) by the state supreme court decision known as the Molly Hootch consent decree, which was implemented in the mid-1970s. The suit argued that every child had a right to a complete education in the home village, instead of being sent to large regional schools. The state of Alaska was obliged to build a high school in each village that requested one—close to a hundred buildings, and the teachers to staff them.

Luckily for the state, implementation of the Hootch decree coincided almost exactly with the completion of the oil pipeline. In Noatak, the last village in the region to get their school (completed in fall of 1981), construction costs ran well over a million dollars, and the tab for a new elementary was nearly 2 million.

Apart from education, the state's lavish expenditure altered village life forever. Noatak is a typical case: in just a few years the new gym with its basketball court has become the center for the young of the village, just as the church is for the elders. Many students arrive at school a half hour early so they can shoot baskets, and they'd play ball every day in physical education class if they could hound me into it. After school there is an hour and a half of basketball practice. All but two of fifteen high school boys are on the Lynx team, and the percentage is nearly as high for the girls on the—dare I say it—Lynkettes. After practice the kids walk home, eat supper, do some chores or a little homework, and head back for their scheduled hour in the gym, which they get six nights a week. While they're waiting for the elementary school and junior high students to have their turn (toddlers are out there dribbling rubber play balls, seven-year-olds heaving shots over and over at the hopelessly high rims), they socialize and do homework. At precisely 8:00 P.M. they're on the floor, shooting around and choosing sides. After their time is up, they watch the young men of the village play city league pickup games. There's a ten o'clock weeknight curfew for students; at the constable's siren they head home to watch television or finish their homework. At 7:30 the next morning, a handful of the faithful are out there again, shooting layups.

You won't find many tall players this far north; pure-blooded Inupiat reach six feet only rarely, while the largest half-breeds clear six two. The big man for most teams is around this height, while occasionally a true monster of six four might emerge, forcing coaches to devise defensive strategies to neutralize this Eskimo Abdul-Jabbar. Lack of height prevents most otherwise talented players from ever going on to college ball, where the average guard is taller than most village centers. If the local sport of choice were hockey or baseball, the ranks of college and even professional teams might well be sprinkled with wiry, explosive defensemen and shortstops with names like Ontogook, Foxglove, and Cleveland.

But basketball is one of the few sports that could have caught on in the Alaskan bush. Field sports are out of the question; in the northwest arctic, the first snow flies in September, and is still melting when school lets out. It's too cold outside for hockey most of the year.

Individual sports—cross-country running, skiing, and wrestling—would seem perfect for small schools, since they require little equipment or indoor space, and even schools like Deering, with its nine high school students, could field athletes on an equal basis. A few years back, cross-country skiing was a varsity sport in the northwest arctic; Noatak, in fact, produced some of the finest skiers in the district, until basketball came along. Now skiing is officially dead as an interscholastic sport. Wrestling and cross-country running have yet to gain regional acceptance, though in 1982, Eliot Sampson, a pure-blooded Inupiat from Noorvik, shattered the course record on his way to winning the state cross-country title. Eliot, nicknamed "caribou legs" in his home village, ran away from everybody—the big-school Alaskan urban kids with their high-tech shoes and expert coaches—smiled shyly, and returned home to lead Noorvik to the state finals in basketball.

When you see how the northwest arctic villages have dominated the state in basketball, you can better understand the lack of interest in other sports. The best local teams, some from schools with fewer than thirty students, sometimes beat schools six or eight times larger—Kotzebue, Nome, and Dillingham. Since the 1983–84 season, there has been a new division of the state championships, specifically for schools of under fifty students. Since then, northwest arctic teams have won eight state titles and finished second several times. The statistic is more impressive when you consider the competition. Every year there is at least one team in the finals with Caucasian players five inches taller and twenty-five pounds heavier than their Eskimo opponents. In 1985, for example, my Noatak boys' team, with our tallest player at five feet ten inches, faced Klawock, which had two players at six feet four—and almost won. In other years, Kiana, Ambler, and Noorvik have won the title against far larger opponents.

There are different ways of interpreting the impact of all this time spent at the gym. Even though parents turn out for all the games, many also complain that basketball takes up too much of their children's lives. Few boys are out hunting ptarmigan or rabbits after school, or following their fathers on their traplines. Most girls have never learned the traditional skills of cutting fish or preparing caribou sinew for thread, though their mothers do these things and much more in everyday life. A common complaint among parents is, "*Adii*, just like my kids are never home. Always school."

Much of that schooltime is pure basketball. Parents could certainly stop or slow this trend if they wished, but exerting such control seems a strange notion to most Inupiat; children have always been free to choose. Besides, school is recognized as a good thing, as it has been since the first missionaries established schools around the turn of the century, drawing scattered camps together into villages. From that time on, the Inupiat were moving inexorably toward a future of orange balls and fast breaks, toward a time when the warm, communal atmosphere of the gym would seem a natural extension of their culture.

Clarence Wood takes a darker view. Though his two boys have both played ball for the Ambler Grizzlies, he's never seen a game. Even the year that the boys won a state title, he refused to watch. "I tell you what," he grumbles, pointing at the gym across from his house. "That's a bullshit in there. One big bullshit." Disgusted, he loads his sled to go caribou hunting alone.

Basketball is more than a childish preoccupation. There are no less than six men's city league teams in Noatak, each with a roster of at least eight, plus three women's teams. Nearly everybody between ages eighteen and thirty-five plays on one of these; there are two hours per weeknight allotted to city league, and on weekends when the gym is free of school-sponsored games or activities, the games start at six and go to eleven, sometimes on both Friday and Saturday nights: the Renegades versus the Bullets, the Napaaqtugmiut against the Warriors, the Cousins versus the Women's City League, and so on. No one remembers the scores, and few remember who won from week to week, though some games are hotly contested, sometimes degenerating into shouted obscenities and shoving matches. Players jump from one roster to another, and the style of play is freewheeling, more reminiscent of in-your-face street ball than the organized play of the high school teams.

Perhaps the saddest vision in village basketball is that of a former high school hero, a former regional all-star, who now lives to play city league. Maybe he was a great high school athlete, but he was also only five feet seven inches, and had no desire to leave the village for college in the first place. He stayed in school mostly for basketball, kept up his grades so he could travel with the team. Now, five years after graduation, he is still living at home, sleeping most of the day, waiting for the gym to open at 10:00 P.M. so he can relive a time when people cheered him and the games mattered. There are more of these city league heroes than you'd wish. Some actually consider themselves professionals because local sponsors buy them uniforms and fly them to tournaments. One former player of mine smiled as he described city league as his "career." Some go away to college or technical school and come back six months later; a few enlist in the Army. I can't help wondering what their lives would have become without basketball—better, worse, or the same?

You could consider all this basketball a travesty: outside influence run amok, all these thousands of man-hours wasted. True, many of the young have become much less active in traditional ways, but others do run traplines and hunt caribou and keep their extended families in firewood in addition to playing ball; food does get cooked, new mukluks are sewn, and babies are raised. Many villagers will say there is less drinking because of the gym, and certainly most of the young men in town and many of the women are in fine shape from their nights of running up and down the floor. Serious violence—fights and gunplay—seems to be on a decline regionwide, and maybe this decrease is partly due to a healthy release of aggression on the court.

Also, basketball, especially at the high school level, is a tremendous source of village pride. When Kiana swept to both the boys' and girls' state titles in 1984, the village and the region exploded in a frenzy of Eskimo patriotism. In a time when the Inupiat find themselves increasingly dominated by outside forces, basketball is, paradoxically, a source of assurance and identity.

Basketball also provides a community focus, taking over the function of traditional Eskimo games. In the past, a community would divide into teams or a neighboring village would visit for the purpose of friendly competition, and there would be an evening or even days of games, resembling a modern track and field meet in organization and aspect. The individual events were, for the most part, ones that could be held in the more limited space afforded by a community building or even a large home during the long, dark winter. Feasting, exchanging of gifts, trading, wooing, and simple socializing were as important as the actual competition. Some games focused on brute strength. Consider the head pull, a woman's game where two competitors faced off in push-up position with a wide strap or belt hooked over their necks. The idea was to pull the opponent over a line or yank the belt free of her arched neck. Other games, like the one-foot-high kick, were a test of both agility and explosive power; here, a small hide ball was suspended on a string, and the competitor had to take off from one foot, strike the ball with the other foot, and then land balanced on the striking foot. The event was held like a modern high jump, with competitors eliminated as they missed, the mark growing higher until only one remained.

Some events, like the seal hop and the ear pull, were simple tests of pain and endurance. In the seal hop, contestants were in a lowered push-up position on toes and knuckles; the idea was to hop the longest distance without allowing any other part of the body to touch the ground. The hopping surface was often hard or irregular, and skin, even flesh, was abraded from the knuckles as the contestants hopped along the floor, muscles straining.

There were other games: the two-footed high kick, leg wrestling, finger pull, and stick jump. People still play these games, but less and less frequently at the village level.

It's basketball they want. On winter nights the cry echoes across the expanse of bush Alaska:

Beat 'em, bust 'em . . .

In just a few years, it's become their custom.

COPYRIGHT ACKNOWLEDGMENTS

ABOUT THE EDITORS

LARRY KANIUT is one of the great state of Alaska's finest adventure writers. Though he has spent the vast majority of his adult life in Alaska, he's not an Alaskan native. After attending college and marrying the love of his life, Pam, in the lower forty-eight states, Larry received an offer from A. J. Dimond High School in Anchorage, Alaska, to join the staff at the brand-new school and teach English and reading. After he accepted, he and Pam prepared for the journey north.

In his effort to entice publishers to edit a book of Alaskan adventures about the prospectors, pioneers, and pilots so that he'd have a textbook for his Literature of the North classes, Larry was asked instead to write a book of Alaskan bear stories. He began compiling stories in January 1975, continued teaching, being a husband and father, working with young people at church, and starting a 2,400-square-foot addition to the home he and Pam had built in 1970. That book, *Alaska Bear Tales*, was completed in 1980 and sent to the publisher, reaching the public in May 1983. To date, the book is in its sixteenth printing.

During their thirty-eight years in Alaska, Pam and Larry continued to harvest the waters and hills of Alaska, providing fish and game for their family, mastering some great recipes such as salmon pâté and smoked salmon.

In 1993, Larry began ground school in hopes of earning his private pilot's license. He passed the written exam in the spring of 1993 and began flying with Heidi Ruess and her son Rick of Arctic Flyers on May 18, 1994, passing his check ride with her April 9, 1995.

Norm Bolotin of Laing Communications asked Larry if he'd consider doing a second bear book, resulting in *More Alaska Bear Tales* in 1989. Within a few years another publisher, Kent Sturgis of Epicenter Press, asked Larry to produce an adventure book which resulted in *Cheating Death* in 1994. While Larry was in Los Angeles with Kent promoting that book, another publisher, Ludo Wurfbain of Safari Press, asked Larry to compile yet another bear book; and *Some Bears Kill* was released in 1997. During the winter of 1996–97 Larry wrote an Alaska adventure romance called *Trapped!*, which Cliff Cernick edited, a gracious act that motivated Larry to pursue publication.

In September 1998 Stephany Evans agreed to be Larry's literary agent, and she sold *Danger Stalks the Land* to St. Martin's Press two months later. It was released in November 1999.

Several summers Larry worked construction, carpentered, worked as a commercial fisherman, or served as an assistant guide.

Larry continues to gather stories about man's indomitable spirit and is completing a book of Alaska flying adventures with co-author Jack Gwaltney. Larry's other activities include moving hay into the barn for Pam's horse, gardening, shopping for Pam, remodeling their home, encouraging others to write, signing books, teaching classes, and sharing in the writing process through classes and workshops. He also works on half a dozen novels and other adventure books when he's not involved in trying to find a Piper Cub to purchase and fly.

DENISE LITTLE worked for Barnes & Noble/B. Dalton Bookseller for ten years as a bookstore manager, then for four more years as their national book buyer for science fiction, fantasy, and romance. She was selected as Bookseller of the Year by *Romantic Times* and by the Virginia and the New Jersey chapters of

Romance Writers of America. She launched the company's genre magazine, *Heart to Heart*, and wrote it for its first two years of existence. She also was closely involved in launching its fantastic fiction magazine, *Sense of Wonder*.

She then joined Kensington Publishing, where she ran her own imprint, Denise Little Presents, as well as editing fiction and nonfiction projects throughout the list, including books by a number of bestselling authors. Several of the romances she edited and published under her imprint were nominated for RITA Awards by the Romance Writers of America.

Since 1997 she's been executive editor at Tekno Books, working for Dr. Martin H. Greenberg. Her books, published and forthcoming, include *Perchance to Dream*, *Twice upon a Time* (winner of the New York Public Library's 100 Best Books of the Year Award), *Constellation of Cats*, *The Quotable Cat*, *Murder Most Romantic*, *Alaska: Tales of Adventure from the Last Frontier* (with Spike Walker), *Creature Fantastic*, and *The Nora Roberts Companion*. Her short fiction is included in *Civil War Fantastic* and *Alternate Gettysburgs*.

She lives in Green Bay, Wisconsin.